OIL SHEIKHS

One summer in the early '70s, a chauffeur spent two months driving a Saudi Arabian prince around in his brand new £12,000 Rolls Royce Corniche. On the day His Highness left, that chauffeur drove him to the airport. He checked him in and asked what he was to do with the car. 'Keep it,' came the answer.

To the prince it was a gesture in keeping with his culture; largesse to those who serve well. To the chauffeurs of London it was something to dream about. To the gaping airline staff, it merely confirmed the image of Arabs as idiots with too much money.

D0995778

Oil Sheikhs

Linda Blandford

A STAR BOOK
published by
the Paperback Division of
W. H. ALLEN & Co. Ltd

A Star Book
Published in 1977
by the Paperback Division of
W. H. Allen & Co. Ltd
A Howard and Wyndham Company
44 Hill Street, London W1X 8LB

First published in Great Britain by
Weidenfeld and Nicolson, 1976

Printed in Great Britain by
Hazell Watson & Viney Ltd, Aylesbury, Bucks

ISBN 0 352 30139 2

To Stephen and April

Contents

Illustrations   vii
Exchange Rates   viii
Chronology   ix
Acknowledgements   xi
Prologue   1
History: 571 and all that   3

London   9

London for sale · Great sheikhs · Arab fever · The
name of the game · A taste for it · The black sheikhs
of the family · They also serve · The Arabs are
coming

Saudi Arabia   43

A town called Alice in Wonderland · The gilt complex
The factory · All the king's men · A pride of princes
A real geezer · Climbing on the Bandar waggon
Pity the poor princesses · The rise of the meritocrats
Falling in with the set · 'You know what I mean?'
Banking on a war-horse · Race against prejudice · The
closed book · Ahmad and the nurse · A modern
Babel · One long party · Intelligence at work
Dinner with the head of intelligence · The film strip
Bin Ladin's lamp · Goodbye to all that?

Bahrain   145

Playing happy families · Emerald isle browned off
The blonde in the desert · 'We're not rich, you know'
But can you bank on it? · Jaded pieces I · Jaded
pieces II

Kuwait 179

The men who came in from the cold · Singing the
blues · The Sellers market · The odd couples · Ways
and means · No exit · Crows and peacocks · The
thoroughly modern Sabah · A day in Cairo · The
thoroughly exceptional Sabah · Nights and knights
Gatherings at the country club · The loner

Qatar, Abu Dhabi, Dubai and Sharjah 239

Nutty present, dotty past · Boredom by the sea
Down toward the pirate coast · Home with the wives
Royal flush · The day disaster struck · From bad to
worse · Something old, something new · Something
borrowed, something blue

Epilogue 275
Index 281

Illustrations

1 King Khalid of Saudi Arabia (Camera Press Ltd)
2 Crown Prince Fahd of Saudi Arabia
3 Sheikh Yamani, Minister of Petroleum and Mineral Resources
4 Sheikh Hisham Nazir, Director of the Central Planning Institute of Saudi Arabia (Camera Press Ltd)
5 Sheikh Abdullah Alireza, Deputy Minister of Foreign Affairs
6 Jiddah (by courtesy of William Halcrow & Partners)
7 Prince Saud Ibn Faisal (Camera Press Ltd)
8 Adnan Khashoggi (Camera Press Ltd)
9 Sheikh Isa bin Salman al-Khalifah, Ruler of Bahrain (Camera Press Ltd)
10 Sheikh Sabah al-Salim al-Sabah, Ruler of Kuwait (Camera Press Ltd)
11 Sheikh Saud Nasir al-Sabah, Kuwaiti Ambassador to Great Britain (Camera Press Ltd)
12 Sheikh Nasser Sabah al-Nasser, Governor of the City of Kuwait
13 Sheikh Rashid of Dubai
14 Feast given by the ruler of Dubai, Sheikh Rashid (Keystone Press Agency Ltd)
15 Sheikh Zayid's palace in Abu Dhabi (John Hillelson Agency Ltd; photo Marc Riboud)
16 Sheikh Zayid's Rolls-Royce and accompanying guards (John Hillelson Agency Ltd; photo R. Dipardon)
17 Sheikh Khalifa Bin Hamad al-Thani, Ruler of Qatar (Camera Press Ltd)
18 Sheikh Khalid Bin Muhammad al-Qasimi, Ruler of Sharjah (Camera Press Ltd)
19 & 20 Modern development in Sharjah (by courtesy of William Halcrow & Partners)

Exchange Rates

For the sake of continuity (inflation etc.), I have found the available rates of exchange in the middle of buying and selling prices for the time I was in Arabia (i.e. 17 November 1975).

£1 sterling is equal to:

Saudi Arabian riyal 7.25
Bahraini dinar 0.809
Kuwaiti dinar 0.601
Qatari riyal 8.09
United Arab Emirate dirham 8.09

Chronology

[AD]

c. 571 birth of Muhammed

622 flight of Muhammed from Mecca to Medina (the Hegira) – commencement of Arab calendar

632 death of Muhammed, beginning of Caliphate

c. 638–643 Arab (Muslim) conquest of Syria, Iraq, Iran, Egypt

c. 661–715 conquest of Spain, North Africa and Central Asia

1099 fall of Jerusalem to Crusaders

c. 1498 Vasco da Gama sails round Cape of Good Hope – European fleets first appear in Red Sea

1516 Ottoman victory over whole of Caliphate

1744 alliance between Muhammed bin Saud, petty chief in Najd, and al-Wahhab, puritanical Muslim revivalist

1766 al-Sabah family arrives in Kuwait

1789 al-Khalifa family arrives in Bahrain

1798–1839 British treaties of protection with Gulf sheikhdoms

1803–05 Wahhabis capture Mecca and Medina from Ottomans – al-Saud family power begins

1901 Ibn Saud captures Riyadh

1917 King Husein and Lawrence of Arabia lead Arab revolt against Ottomans

1917 Balfour Declaration

1919–30 battles for control of Saudi Arabia between King Husein of the Hijaz and Ibn Saud and Wahhabis

1922 Oil struck in Saudi Arabia

1927 Ibn Saud king of Saudi Arabia

1930–38 Oil struck in Bahrain, Kuwait, Qatar

1933 American oil company concession agreement with Saudi Arabia

1948 state of Israel recognised by UN

1949 Sheikh Rashid becomes ruler of Dubai

1953 death of Ibn Saud

1960 OPEC formed

1961 Kuwait becomes independent sheikhdom

1964 King Saud deposed – brother Faisal becomes king

1966 Sheikh Zayyid becomes ruler of Abu Dhabi

1967 Aden becomes communist People's Democratic Republic of Yemen

1970–1 British withdraw from the Gulf

1971 Bahrain and Qatar become independent sheikhdoms

1971 United Arab Emirates formed by federation of Abu Dhabi, Dubai, Sharjah, Ajman, Umm al-Qaiwain and Fujairah

1971 Sheikh Sultan becomes ruler of Sharjah

1972 Ras al-Khaimah joins UAE

1972 Sheikh Khalifa becomes ruler of Qatar

1975 Assassination of King Faisal – brother Khaled succeeds

Acknowledgements

I have no difficulty in deciding how to start this page of acknowledgements. Susan Mary Richards worked with me on the project
almost from the start. There were many people she met in Arabia
and her meticulous reporting contributed to many of my chapters.
I have valued her support all along the way. Without her there
would have been a book, but it would not have been the same
book.

I doubt that I would have finished it without the encouragement
of Christopher Falkus (in particular), Susan Loden, George
Seddon, Pearson Phillips, Tony Smith, Lynn Harrell and Mrs E.
Pendlebury. I would also like to thank Andrew Barrow who
helped me with research in London.

That I started it at all is due to Larry Hughes of William
Morrow, whose idea it was, to Giles Gordon, who persuaded me
to do it and to the *Observer* newspaper, who gave me leave of
absence at short notice.

Many people helped me in London, New York and the Arab
countries I visited. They are too numerous for me to name them
and I know that most of them would rather I did not. I am grateful
to them all.

I am especially grateful to my parents. I understood their concern and appreciated their interest.

L.B.

Prologue

The task of the poet, in Arab tradition, is to eat at the great man's table and after dinner to compose a eulogy. He honours his host's beauty and heroism and makes no mention of warts or deficiencies.

I lost no opportunity while I was researching this book to explain that I am no traditional poet, merely a curious journalist.

I scattered letters of intent across Arabia like confetti. They contained a variation on the statement, and I quote, 'there is a need to explain, in personal and human terms, a world that is concealed from us by ignorance, self-interest and even fear.'

The ignorance is largely of the Arabs' making. They don't encourage independent Western journalists, except by express invitation. The Herculean task of squeezing a visa out of Saudi Arabia nearly put an end to the whole enterprise. The self-interest is ours. In the West (I say after browsing through ten years' of press coverage of the area), we look to the oil-rich Arab nations only for what they can best do to serve our purposes. The fear really got going after the Middle-East war in October 1973, oil embargoes and price rises. Western industrialised societies discovered that they were vulnerable. Oil sheikhs have been accorded the blame for practically everything bad that has happened to us since and were hated as our new overlords.

Bemused by political causes, pros and cons and prognoses of oil reserves, some of us wanted to know who these people were. I had the chance to go and find out. Horrendous tales of corporation presidents having nowhere to sleep prepared me for a life of physical misery; I was also acutely aware that I couldn't afford to pay for hotel accommodation if I found it. I asked some governments to bale me out of this predicament. 'If you could help . . .' I said, not specifying, but hinting hard. By the way of an insurance policy, I had stand-by sofas belonging to acquaintances' acquaintances and a conviction that 'something would turn up'.

This conviction is shared by every journalist who has spent enough years travelling. I've landed in too many countries without a suitcase or a contact (one newspaper expected me to bring my passport to work every morning as a matter of course). Naturally I assumed that 'something will turn up'. It always has. Arabia was no different only more generous. In the desert in the old days they offered the traveller coffee, food, a bed and wouldn't murder him for three days. After that he was on his own. For weeks I was given hotel rooms, cars and hospitality such as I have met nowhere else in the world. The trip cost Saudi Arabia, Bahrain, Kuwait, Qatar, Abu Dhabi, Dubai and Sharjah (the seven oil autocracies most of us mean when we say 'Arab oil states') a considerable amount of money. Gulf Air gave me free tickets. I'm not playing poet when I say that I, for one, found travelling with them almost trouble free (Saudia is another story) despite the ominous warning from their London office: 'You're seeing us at our best here.'

Someone has asked me how I met the people you'll meet in this book. I can't explain. It's that optimism again. For sanity's sake, every journalist has to believe that there are people all over the world wanting to be friendly enough to make an assignment possible. (Sanity? There are only two clichés known to good news editors: 'Don't complain, don't explain' and 'There's no such word as can't.')

Two problems haunted the trip. Firstly, I expected regimented programmes of desalination plants and experimental farms and had no intention of going along with them. There were no such programmes: I was allowed a freedom that I'm told is unique.

The other problem never went away. In order to get there at all one fact had to be concealed. My being Jewish turned out to be something of a strain. But it was what made the journey personally important. I felt that it mattered for me, and others like me, to accept and understand the Arabs, not as 'Arabs' with all the emotive connotation of the word, but as human beings.

Human beings don't lend themselves to eulogies, even in the countries that this book is about. These countries are the ones that give rise to the stereotype of the oil-rich Arab getting down from the camel and into the Cadillac, off-loading his wealth around the world. They're the ones with almost feudal autocratic rulers, plus so much oil and so few people that they have large petro-dollar surpluses.

Of the other oil giants, Iran is Muslim but not Arab; Iraq is socialist. They both have nearly forty million people apiece. The significance of these differences became more apparent as I went along.

I didn't set out to complete a definite analytical survey. Each person and each group of people in this book represents one aspect of their country's rich society. All I've tried to do is to work out what those Arab sheikhs are doing in London, their new gathering centre: I wanted to clamber into the walled gardens of Arabia and find out what life feels like to the men, and particularly the women, who are trying to get by on those oil millions.

I've done what I wanted, but I fear that despite all my attempts to explain this book as I went along, Arabs still regard a journalist as a modern poet and therefore a eulogist. That's one responsibility I can't accept. One responsibility I did accept, however, was the confidence of certain individuals who talked to me. In some cases I have had to change names and camouflage identities. I hope the words speak for themselves.

History: 571 and all that

What the average Westerner could dredge up from memory of Arab history can be summed up as: crusades, caravanserai, camels and corsairs.

For centuries, the Arab world never meant much more to Europe than a wave of foreigners (invaders or pirates) splashing on its shores. Otherwise it was just a land block between the old world and the fabled wares of China and India. It was always on the way to somewhere else. It only got its name, for Westerners, in 1902 when an American historian invented the term 'Middle East'. It has such a strange, elusive past – you can't digest it in terms of kings, countries and borders as we in the West have been schooled to digest our own history.

From an Arab perspective, their history got going properly in the seventh century (our Gregorian one; they have their own calendar). A man whom legend describes as a former camel driver, born around AD 571 was living in comfortable circumstances married to an older but rich merchant's widow in Mecca. It was a prosperous town, a centre for pre-Islamic pilgrimages, and on the trade routes for the caravans that came across the unruly tribal desert lands to the Christian Byzantine Empire in the north.

The man's name was Muhammad. His business success gave him the leisure to develop his mystic qualities. A voice told him that he was the messenger of the one God, Allah. The holy book, the Koran, was divinely revealed to him. Scorned by the merchants in Mecca, he was welcomed in the rival city of Medina where his preaching inspired a military-minded evangelism.

From that sprang a revolutionary religion that within a hundred years of Muhammad's death had established an empire that stretched in the west to Spain (where its rule was far more civilised than the bloodthirsty orgy pictured in trashy novels). In the east the empire ran to the borders of India.

In one form or another, that empire survived until World War I. It had its ups and downs. A desert-spawned Arab empire, lean, ascetic, religiously motivated, went the way of most empires and fell victim to petty intrigues and internecine squabbling. It grew soft on sybaritic pleasures. While it was having a soft down in 1099 the first Crusade sailed from Europe to redeem the Holy Places around Jerusalem for the Christians (infidels to the Muslims) from the Muslims (infidels to the Christians).

The Crusading mercenaries, carpet-baggers and idealists did well; they even regained Jerusalem. But the balance of power was shifting in the Muslim world. In 1171 the nephew of one of the empire's more remarkable Turkish commanders emerged from

he dust of the fray: Saladin. In ten years Saladin established a
ew, strong power base in Cairo, took back Jerusalem and even
utfought Richard the Lionheart of England.

After that, the Crusaders were a minor inconvenience com-
ared with Genghis Khan and his mighty Mongols. They
ressed in from the cold steppes of Asia and one way and another
t was a bad few hundred years in the empire. A semblance of
rder finally manifested itself in the mid-1400s. The Turks had
earned soldiering well: early on under the Arabs, later under the
aore sophisticated Persians. They had learned it so well that
having craftily brought firearms and cannon from Europe) they
verwhelmed the Arab forces (no firearms), occupied Cairo,
lucked the puppet Caliph (in theory the religious and secular
eader of the whole Islamic world) and set him up in Constan-
inople. Non-Arab Turkey became the new power centre of
Muhammad's legacy. The Ottoman Empire was run by a batch of
ocal governors, taxes and nominal (firm when required) control.

They left the Arabian heartland pretty much to itself. Who'd
vant all that empty desert and useless land where tribal chiefs
ought and raided? No one very much until the sixteenth century
vhen the European powers learned to sail round the Cape of
Africa. The Persian Gulf became vital to the passage to India.
The Portuguese, then the Dutch and French jockeyed for position
here. The Gulf Sheikhs (mere nothings compared to the strong
Persians on the other side of the water) found themselves the
ubject of unwelcome interference. It was left to Great Britain,
nostly in the shape of the East India Company, to establish her
presence by means of treaties. From 1820 onwards she negotiated
vith sheikhs who ruled countries with no borders but who could
ecognise the protection (and menace) of British men-o'-war.

The pirate coast was made to give up its profitable corsair and
laving careers and all was quiet on the eastern front apart from a
ew snarls from Persia.

Then came World War I. The Turks joined the Kaiser. The
3ritish thought it expedient to encourage Arabia to revolt
gainst Turkey. The famous Lawrence attached himself to the
Iashimite leader in Mecca, went in for daring exploits like

blowing up trains and they all ended up in Damascus. The Hashimites had hoped to administer a new independent Arab world.
All they got (eventually) were poor consolation prizes – the
thrones of Iraq and Jordan. The French and British in 1917, in
one of the last of the old-style 'sphere of influence' treaties,
carved up the left-overs of the Ottoman Empire. France got
Syria and Lebanon; she had already acquired Algeria and Morocco. Britain took Iraq and Palestine (with Transjordan). Egypt
had been declared a British protectorate and the British government controlled almost the whole of southern and eastern Arabia.

Saudi Arabia was left out of this general carve-up but the
Hashimites met their end there too. They were defeated by a
young tribal sheikh, an al-Saud (whose ancestor had joined up
with an Islamic reformist, al-Wahhab, in the 1750s and imprinted
Wahhabi zeal on central Arabia). This new style al-Saud won a
kingdom for himself by marrying guns with Wahhabism and in
1926 he took Mecca. The Hashimites left; at 36 the sheikh became
King Ibn Saud and ruled for 21 years.

Arab history since then has been the result of four influences:
oil, Israel, socialism and European ad-hocery. Oil gave the area a
new meaning for the West, particularly America. The establishment of Israel in 1948 gave a new meaning to Arab identity.
Four wars were to follow: Arab nationalism, reborn at the end of
the nineteenth century and forged by the struggles against
European domination, was tempered in those fires. Then came
Arab socialism. King Farouk went first in 1952. Nasser's rallying
call was about to be launched and Syria was the first to answer.
King Faisal of Iraq bit the dust and the country went socialist.
After eight bitter years of fighting, Algeria became independent
and socialist. The British lost Aden and South Yemen went
communist. Tunisia became a republic. King Hussain in Jordan
has hung on by his teeth, so too has Morocco's King Hassan.
But in 1969, King Idris lost Libya to the most extreme nationalist
of all – 28-year-old Muammar al-Qadhafi, a lieutenant in the
Signals Corps, xenophobic, right-wing but a Nasser Mark II.

The pre-war snatch and grab saga of oil development is well
known by now. After the post-war production of oil started,

the little sheikhdoms down the eastern side of the peninsula got richer and more insecure. The British, having lost India, were ready to pull out. They had, at least, had the foresight to draw some very peculiar frontiers for the people who had happened on to some of the world's most valuable real estate. In 1922 the British Political Resident in the Gulf had taken a pencil and decided what Kuwait should have (more literally what bits of Kuwaiti sand Iraq and Saudi Arabia should have). Kuwait was granted 'independence' in 1961; its frontiers still cause trouble. Qatar was simpler; it stuck out of Saudi Arabia and was left there. In 1971 the British pulled out of the Gulf altogether, leaving behind an even greater tangle of borders in the United Arab Emirates.

Absorbing Arab history is as unwieldy for a newcomer as eating spaghetti with a knife and fork. Absorbing the present can sometimes drive you crazy. Don't expect simple patterns to emerge when travelling through Arabia and across the Western world with the oil sheikhs – sheikh as in 'shake down' (well, nearly) not as in 'chic' by the way. There aren't any. Excitement, certainly, but you can't iron out and put into tidy, logical piles countries as crazily 'disordered' (to us) as these.

The names themselves are a barrier. I've made them as easy as possible, only there are so few first names to go round that nearly everyone's called the same. I can offer only one or two rules. A man has his own first name, the name of his father and his family name: so King Faisal was Faisal, the son of (bin) Abdul Aziz, of the family of (al) Saud. And in case you've missed the point of how there is no point: King Faisal called his father King Abdul Aziz (it was the man's name after all); the Saudis called him King Abdul Aziz (there's even a street named after him in Jiddah. It's the main one: King Abdul Aziz street). The whole world knew him as King Ibn Saud.

In the summer of 75 anyone who came from an oil-producing country in the Middle East was automatically dubbed a sheikh. That at least was one word we could latch on to. I certainly did (ergo the title of this book). Strictly speaking, wrong again. Few Arabs are sheikhs. In Saudi Arabia sheikh is a special title (it means 'old man' which doesn't sound like much of a compliment to the youth-crazed West). It's given to honour distinguished men or the head of a large family – and many of these 'old men' are young (you may be catching on by now). In Saudi Arabia sheikh is nothing much; anyone royal is a prince. The other countries aren't quite so pretentious: all royals and only royals are sheikhs. But let's face it: we're not talking about the Hapsburgs, Romanoffs or even Windsors. We're talking about members of a 'royal' family that happen to rule a few thousand people on some valuable real estate. A few years ago, they were only one family who happened to be a bit stronger than the others. Ruling nothing very much doesn't make you very much. All that's changed. Now they have oil and to the West all oil Arabs are oil sheikhs. They're the new breed of Arabs that seem to be over-running our world. Are they really the corsairs of today?

London

The Arabs Arrive

Popular London joke circa 1975: The prime minister's private secretary comes into his boss's office. 'Excuse me, sir, but the pope and an oil sheikh are waiting to see you.'

'Oh dear.' The PM frowns. 'Who should I see first?'

'May I suggest the pope first, sir, you only have to kiss his ring.'

London for sale

If one had to pinpoint a moment in time when London realised that it had become the Arabs' new home-from-home, it was the day in August 1975 when airing mattresses appeared over the window-sills of a £300,000 mansion at 10 The Boltons.

The family of Sheikh Zayid of Abu Dhabi had just moved into this fashionable patch, opposite Douglas Fairbanks Jnr. and next door to an outraged Conservative MP who telephoned to ask his new neighbours to tidy up the offending window-sills.

Long limousines kept twenty-four-hour vigil outside the gate. Occasionally they swept off and returned to disgorge heavily-veiled and masked figures in black. Chauffeurs struggled behind up the stairs under familiar sludge green plastic bags from Harrods. The rare man, white sheeted, appeared to dispense instructions. More unexpectedly, the normally deserted church in the middle of this dignified garden square acquired two regular fixtures. Sheikh Zayid's teenage daughters, who adopted the church as their recreation ground and were to be seen trotting around after the vicar like two shy lambs.

This was the moment when a new game spread in some of the more supercilious dining rooms of upper-crust Kensington. It was called 'spot the shepherd', the object being to see who had the most white-robed Arabs moving into their neighbourhood.

Knight Frank and Rutley, international estate agents of the kind dealing mainly in top-drawer, high-value properties featured in costly colour brochures, sold flats and houses to Arab clients for over £2 million in a few months. Hamptons, the most exclusive agents of all, flew prize Arabs up to distant Scotland to expose them to the available delights of draughty stone piles and attendant sporting lands. It didn't work at once; agents like Hamptons plan long term. It was only another year before news broke that 'an unknown Arab' forked out £2 million for a prime cut of beef-rearing Scotland – Sheikh Zayid's men again.

Where Arabs did establish themselves in rural communities they became legendary. A Sussex farmer, John Thorold, was astonished to find a rare Snow Goose scratching around among his barnyard hens and ducks. It had strayed from the wild-life park up the road belonging to – Sheikh Zayid. When he took over Buxted Park Health Farm, one-time haunt of recovering statesmen and starlets, the traffic through the local railway station dropped off. All the white-haired station master had ever seen of Zayid were those newspaper photographs in which the sheikh looks like a sinister Hollywood gangster. 'He makes no difference to us 'cos we never see him. He comes in by helicopter for a few days a year, that's all. He's never been seen in the town though they say that at least the place buys its meat from the local butcher.'

English country folk don't like to feel ignored by the big house. If the new squire is an Arab, resentment starts to fester. At first it takes the form of local grumbles. At Buxted they were already moaning at Zayid's plans for a game reserve. 'What if one of them tigers gets out?' Later it bubbles into dislike of Arabs in general.

But mostly the Arabs' horizon didn't extend beyond London and the surrounding green belt. Newly-impoverished stockbrokers were only too happy to off-load their oil-fired, centrally-heated, mock-Tudor liabilities. With Beirut gone, London became the new summer centre for reasons more functional than the availability of gaming tables and the £1 million credit extended to chosen Arabs at certain clubs. The British capital offered instant communication with Swiss banks, offices back home (the New York eight-hour time difference was pronounced 'a nuisance') and a whole host of other resident Arabs.

Americans were quick to latch on to the dollar potential of the new Arab custom for an ailing New York real estate market. It might not be the choice for a second, third or even tenth home for Arabs but they would still have enough left over, after shopping elsewhere, for the odd fourteen-room apartment in Manhattan. On the ball New York agents were fired by some extraordinary news leaked from Olympic Tower on Fifth Avenue: Adnan Khashoggi had bought the apartment below his new multi-million apartment to catch any drips from the glass-sided swimming pool under construction. Meanwhile London property men were only just waking up to the influx on their doorsteps. Some weren't even aware that Khashoggi had bought into Eaton Square, where the cream of the British aristocracy hang out, some years before.

In that summer of 75, he acquired a friendly neighbour. The head of Saudi Arabian intelligence, Kamal Adham, moved into, or at least bought, a nearby flat for £400,000. Why should he move in? Adham already owned desirable properties in London and had been making do with a luscious stretch of dwelling space in Grosvenor Square, opposite the American Embassy. Pity Khashoggi wasn't at home in London much: round the corner in Cadogan Place Sheikh Ahmad Zaki Yamani discreetly snitched a fifth-floor flat for a mere £70,000. They managed to keep in touch; Khashoggi lent Yamani his yacht for a spring cruise around the Caribbean after that particularly hectic summer and winter.

While London gossip columnists were oohing and aahing over the cool half million (before decorators' bills) paid by Dubai's multi-billionaire ambassador extraordinary, bushy-browed Mehdi al-Tajir, for Mereworth Castle, along the motorway in Kent, they slid over his purchase of another dream palace at 26 Rutland Gate for £400,000. In those famous, foolish sixties, this had been a celebrated house in London, belonging to one of those new, short-lived millionaires thrown up by Bernie Cornfeld's IOS organisation.

For that matter, Cornfeld himself wasn't left out. Having made a chunk of his fortune selling 'the people's capitalism' down the Gulf (before he was black-listed), Cornfeld, now somewhat on his uppers, made some pocket money. He let his house (including built-in basement discotheque) at 1 West Halkin Street to a family from Qatar for £500 a week.

It seemed in that long, hot summer as though everyone had suddenly become a property expert and Arabist. Everyone from bona fide estate agents to travel agents and a host of others with loose Arab connections (even down to society women who heard those magical words 'thinking of buying' over dinner) were in on it. London, normally deserted in summer by the smart British in search of Scottish fly-fishing or southern sun-tanning, was a hive of fixers, of middle-men, of go-betweens.

Contrary to public myth and wishful thinking, few Arabs turned up with a suitcase of money to buy any old, over-priced heap. They deliberately paid over the odds for the advantages of a quick, trouble-free deal. Compared to back home, London offered bargain prices. And many's the shark who backed out of a hotel suite rejoicing over his commission, thinking he had put one over on Arabs who agreed a purchase behind dead-pan masks. Only when the door was shut, did the utter, knowing contempt find expression on the faces of his 'victims'.

Even the families with regular hotel suites started to examine property brochures. The clincher came one morning in September. The lobby of the Hilton Hotel was torn apart by a searing explosion; the Irish bombers had started on a new tack. For days afterwards every de luxe London hotel was periodically evacuated after bomb scares. Flat rentals took another boost; £400 a week was the going rate for some rather small staging-posts behind King's Road.

But not everyone cashed in. Arab fever gave rise to misleading tales. In Priory Walk off the Boltons, a couple off on holiday to France put their flat up to rent. Its value to Americans: £120 a week. An emissary arrived from the Kuwaiti embassy. His

English was impeccable, his after-shave a delight. Each room, he said, was more charming than the next and he would rent it for some cousins for £300 a week. But the owners had heard stories from a friend who let his flat to an Arab family. The breakages and mess, he said, were terrible.

Only after the couple had turned down the Kuwaiti offer, did their friend remember to add the rest of the story. After he complained to the embassy about the disarray, the same sweet-smelling Kuwaiti diplomat had come round on the same day with a wad of £20 notes to make more than generous amends.

Great sheikhs

The hotel bomb scare died down and the passing trade of international Arabs resumed its sweep through the lobbies of their favourite hotels. Park Lane has pride of place. The Arabs pack the place like sardines, from Grosvenor House, down past the Dorchester, Hilton, Londonderry House to the Inn on the Park and their newest prime stopping place, the Intercontinental Hotel. It's graced by many because of the manager, veteran hotelier Max Blouet, known to them from his, and their, years at the Georges V in Paris.

Ironically, the one hotel you would expect to find them in comes somewhere in the also-rans, the Park Tower Hotel in Knightsbridge. In 1974 this hotel (complete with Miami-style, candy-coloured coffee shop) passed into the hands of 'Arab interests', none other than Ambassador Tajir of Mereworth and Rutland Gate. Kensington hotels left out in the cold found another way to compete. The Royal Garden Hotel and the Gloucester, for example, offered a hefty discount to visitors booked through certain Arab embassies.

But the Royal Garden had another attraction: Middle Eastern restaurants nearby that were prepared to send men carrying steaming pots, covered with tin foil, on the dangerous dash across one of London's busiest High Streets. When they reached the safety of the basement entrance, they carried their offerings up to the suites where television screens flickered day and night, sometimes with sound, sometimes without.

Even the switchboards had learned how to nurture Arab clients. They like privacy. Asking for someone by name rarely works. 'He's not staying here' is the usual answer. Even knowing the room (or suite) number produces the inevitable question, 'Who are you calling?'

But for outsiders, the hotels with Arab clientele could always be distinguished by the presence of the upper end of the car-hire trade with patient, attendant chauffeurs. The number of limousines on hire in London doubled in three years thanks to the Arabs.

It has been said that no man is a hero to his valet. No Arab is a stranger to his chauffeur. Dick is forty-seven with a soft pinkish skin and an utterly forgettable face. After twenty years in the army, he took to chauffeuring. He likes the uniform and sense of knowing his worth. In August 1975, one of his grateful customers gave him £3,000 to buy a second-hand Daimler limousine. Now he is in business on his own. He's a cheerful cockney chap who tugs on a pipe and complains bitterly about the unskilled young men muscling in on the limousine trade.

'Now you have to understand which Arabs you're talking about. Most of the ones you hear about are just the big nobs' servants. And even they have more money to spend than most of our big nobs. Sex and gambling is what they want from London. Gambling's easy. I belong to most of the large clubs myself and I just slip them in. Wads of money, they've got. When it comes to sex, if they're very low types I take them to one of those sauna joints. Well, it's no more a sauna than you've got in here. The sauna's £4.50, then for £3 the masseuse will go topless and for £5 she'll give light relief – if you see what I mean.'

'If they're a bit higher up, I'll take them to one of those places with hostesses. Then it's a couple of bottles of champagne at £11 each with the girl they pick out and if they want any more, it's negotiable. Some of them don't want to bother with all that, in which case I'll pick up a girl from the streets. To go back with him it's £15, sex in the car is £5 (lucky I've got a big car) and her place is £10.'

'I know them all. After all I've been driving long enough. Now that's the servants and that's what most people think of when they say Arabs. If they're secretaries or something, they'll want a girl from an escort agency and they'll send me to pick a good one and bring her back. Blonde and big boobs goes down well. It's a change, ain't it? That might be £15 an evening to them (and my cut from the agency of course) and the rest is what we call "negotiable". There's broad-minded girls and there's straight ones. I make sure I pick the broad-minded ones. My gentlemen don't like it if they're not co-operative.'

'Then there's the real tops. The sheikhs. They don't use any of that. They want complete secrecy. That's where my little book comes in handy. I know a few good girls, £80 a time for Americans, several hundred for Arabs. Sometimes I'll just be sent to get them. They'll come into the hotel suite, the ADC says "right, in there" and they'll go into a pitch-black room (they like the curtains drawn so she can't recognise him after), get undressed and probably be out ten minutes later. Some of my gentlemen can go through three or four a day like that.'

'I had one who actually got me to take him to this girl's flat. Well, he had to, his wife was in the hotel. He said, "Dick, you'd better make sure you can trust her." It was just me and him, not even the ADC. He was there for three hours; he even sat talking to her, that's unusual. She got thousands out of him that fortnight.'

'Sometimes they take them out to dinner, but that's rare. If they do, they'll tag along behind in another car so it looks as if they're with some of the entourage. They have to be very careful. There's a man with a flat near the Albert Hall who runs some of the best girls in London. One of them gets at least £1,000 and she looks so good she could be royal herself. £1,000 and I'm told she doesn't even screw. She's just there for decoration. One of my gentlemen went out with her. I didn't understand it. Still, it's not my place to ask. You can't with Arabs, you see. With anyone else, if you get him a girl you can say afterwards, "Well, how did it go, sir?" Not with an Arab. You'd never drive him again.'

'I often feel I'm living off immoral earnings myself. Basically I'm getting a cut from the agencies and girls for selling their bodies aren't I?'

Dick is a bachelor. He lives with his mum. Looking after women who aren't his mum is a treat for him.

'My favourite is going out with the women. I've done a lot of them from Qatar. They come down with all their veils and that, carrying these vanity cases. The cases are stuffed with £20 notes, you couldn't squeeze in a matchstick. The bodyguard always comes too. He's usually "carrying" though I don't know if the police turn a blind eye to the guns these blokes have. It's supposed to be illegal isn't it?' It isn't just supposed to be; it is. There was quite a stink at London airport in 1972 when one of the Qatar ruling family, no less, was found to have guns in his suitcase.

'First thing, as soon as we're round the corner from the hotel. Off come the veils, particularly with the young ones. First stop is always Marks & Spencer. They don't speak English and I go in to make sure they don't get had. Well, money's just paper to them. They don't know about change. They'll buy every shape, size and colour they can. They go a lot for bras and frilly panties. We always have a giggle about cup sizes.' He laughs and waves his hands around, cup size C. 'They'll buy one of everything in every colour – never spend less than £200. They're so used to someone else paying that sometimes I have to catch them before they walk out of the shop without handing over the money. Nasty business a little while ago. Some Arab's wife, diplomat he was and all, got done for shop lifting in Marks and their embassy closed for two weeks because they were so bloody furious.'

'Next day we're back at Marks & Spencer and then it's more parcels to go up to the room. And you know what's the funniest sight of all? All the old women sitting around picking out every St Michael label in every damn thing they've bought. Well they have to, don't they? It's owned by that Jewish lot that gave all the money they get from the Arabs to Israel. Funny do I call it.'

Dick reckons he makes £500 a week with a good Arab; £45 a day for the car, plus tip, plus rake-offs. But his limousine hero of that summer was the one who spent two months driving a Saudi

Arabian prince around in his brand new £12,000 Rolls Royce Corniche. On the day His Highness left, that chauffeur drove him to the airport. He checked him in and asked what he was to do with the car. 'Keep it,' came the answer. To the prince it was a gesture in keeping with his culture; largesse to those who serve well. To the chauffeurs of London it was something to dream about as petrol for their ten miles per gallon limousines looked ready for another price rise.

To the gaping airline staff, it merely confirmed the image of Arabs as idiots with too much money.

Arab fever

It's a bad day for chauffeur Dick when one of his Arabs falls ill, or just goes into a hospital. He usually knows which hospital it will be.

A few years ago, there was only one. It was the first to contract Arab fever: the London Clinic, a non-profit making nursing home run by the élite of Harley Street private consultants. It was used to being trendy. It was used to such novelties as Elizabeth Taylor having a world-publicised virus there and Bianca Jagger popping in with flu. But some time during the late sixties, another clientèle nudged out the face lifts and the nose jobs. Notices in the wardrobes were printed in Arabic too.

At the start, the London Clinic wasn't totally equipped to deal with all the problems that arose. One night on the fifth floor is well remembered. After the night nurse had settled the patients with cocoa and sleeping pills, and was tucking in to a good read, a dreadful screaming was to be heard. A woman patient from Qatar flown in that day for an emergency operation had come round suffering from the beginnings of culture shock.

The night nurse, a brisk Australian, didn't get very far in comforting the woman. Her patient didn't understand a word of English. That was only the beginning of the disturbance. The house doctor was called. The woman was as shocked at being examined by a man as she was at finding herself in pain. He didn't get very far either; he didn't understand a word of her squalling. As she got better, she might have found solace outside her room where there were any number of heavily-veiled Arab women drifting around visiting husbands and children. She wouldn't budge. The first time she had peeped out, she suffered embarrassment all over again with the view of a crocodile of Arab men in dressing gowns and slippers out for their constitutional along the lino-covered corridors.

To private clinics' nursing staff in those days one Arab was much like another. They never knew whether they were dealing with the wife of a ruler or the wife of a servant. All rich Gulf states fly problem cases free to the medical services of London. Kuwait even has a special office round the corner from Harley Street to deal with these sick visitors.

It's interesting to note how quickly attitudes changed towards Arab patients. In 1972 it was quite common for some private nurses to complain openly to their English charges recovering from a pampered ski-ing accident or a patch of nervous exhaustion about the strange, uncivilised foreigners in other rooms. By 1975, every private clinic in London kept a warm bed on hand for our Arab friends, and an even warmer bedside manner. The success of a 1974 newcomer, the Wellington Hospital, had a lot to do with it.

Beside that most English of institutions, Lord's cricket ground, is a large concrete block named after one of the nation's greatest warrior heroes – the Duke of Wellington. The Wellington Hospital was founded by an enterprising shipping company (the British and Commonwealth Group) which realised there was money to be made using its experience for caring for people suffering from the rigours of travel, in tending those travellers oppressed by illness. Arab travellers.

They were never muddled in their approach at the Wellington, a medical phenomenon so far unique to London. The whole place is geared for what they call 'Muslim patients', including a special, closed-circuit television channel devoted to Arabic programmes. It's celebrated for its extreme luxury (the well-publicised Château Mouton Rothschild '64 at £27.50 a bottle). But it's the small touches that go down well. There's the miraculous floating X-ray table that allows a radiographer to move a patient by pushing a button rather than by trying to mime the message that they should 'please shove over a bit'.

On Eid (the Muslim present-giving holiday), every Arab patient wakes up to find a basket of fruit with a greetings card by his bed. The full-time staff interpreters know the subtle differences of local Arab dialects. Head porter Lindsay Harris (known as 'the sergeant') delivers the steady stream of £50 wicker gift-hampers from Fortnum & Mason with the panache of a British army-trained Santa Claus.

Bodyguards are accepted. One of the Saudi king's brothers arrived with eight. Children are allowed to scamper around the corridors talking to Mummy through the intercom at the nursing stations. The clinic accepts the free-and-easy family atmosphere without which most Arabs feel estranged.

As a result over £2 million worth of petrodollars a year are recycled through this medical haven (with its waiting list for the £100 a day de-luxe suites), carefully supervised by Medical Director Dr Arthur Levin (Cambridge-qualified, ex-London teaching hospital), oozing bedside confidence.

'What's so strange about us going there if Dr Levin is a Jew?' asked one grateful Arab ex-patient. 'Eight centuries ago when you were dying in ditches and fighting in crusades, and we were the ones with the medical skills, Saladin's personal physician was Maimonides the Jew.' Ouch.

Medical service is an area in London that Arabs still seek out despite competition from America. King Khalid of Saudi Arabia went to Cleveland for his open-heart surgery, but most of his fellow Arabs bring their coughs, slipped discs, gall-stones and tooth decay to that patch of black-jacketed, gold watch-chained London around Harley Street. In the summer of 75, a fashionable London dentist found a busy Kuwaiti needing urgent treatment in his chair. It involved the carving of custom-built, best porcelain-capped teeth.

The Kuwaiti was so pressed for time that he despatched a hired Rolls-Royce with a set of impressions of his teeth across the country to Devon, where the dentist's best mechanic lived. The Rolls waited until the gleaming new dentures were finished then ferried them back to Harley Street.

Over the odd glass of sherry in their clubs, London doctors still marvel at their luck. One sporting fisherman and eye specialist has trained his secretary to offer a tactful hint that a gift token from Hardy's in St James's, the royal tacklemaker's shop, never comes amiss. One less-prepared surgeon is a bit stumped about what to do with his new racehorse. It was an unexpected gift from an Arab patient now minus an appendix.

The name of the game

Victor Lownes, American Anglophile, slow-talking, quick-thinking, veteran of the rich night-scene, sips soda water in the restaurant of the Playboy Club. Brown-louvred shutters block out the green view of Hyde Park by daylight. Lownes is the supremo of Playboy in Britain. Playboy has almost the monopoly on top Arab gambling money. 'The Arabs don't ever learn. They don't care how much they lose. We've had the best quality ever this summer.' The gambling freaks roll in twenty-four hours a day to throw money across his tables.

Gaming clubs that in the 60s flourished on American or Jewish money are licking their wounds. The Americans seem to have run out of money and the big Jewish losers have learned better. Lownes has the contented look of a man who is always one throw ahead. He has been busy. He flies to the States every fortnight helping to reorganise Heffner's troubled organisation. But his London end is so smooth that he even manages to get away to spend weekends at his ample country manor in Hertfordshire.

Where Arabs gamble, security in the clubs is tight. Important Arabs are never addressed by name. Staff know which ones to bankroll for credit. They make sure that no press leaks occur that might frighten the pigeons away. It's one reason Arabs steer clear of

Las Vegas. It frightens them; the pace is too fast, the gaming rooms too crowded. They feel exposed and at the mercy of gossip-column narks. Ever since the story splashed over the Paris press that Crown Prince Fahd of Saudi Arabia had dropped half a million dollars on the Riviera (by no means his first such misfortune), the top Arabs have become even more security conscious. They gamble in the afternoons when chances of being seen are slimmer; it's called 'going to a business meeting' as far as their families are concerned. And London gambling clubs don't forget the price paid by the South of France for that deplorable lapse. In that summer of 75, Monte Carlo was noticeable for the absence of previous regulars from Saudi Arabia.

Perfectionist Lownes scrawls an angry note for the house manager: there are no fresh limes. And then his face breaks into what passes for a smile as his gaming manager, Bernie Mulhurne, comes up. 'Seen the figures then, Victor?' In August 1975, the Playboy Club, according to Bernie, cleared two million dollars profit on its gaming tables. At his other establishment, round the corner in Berkeley Square, the Clermont Club, the regular titled in-crowd who used to sit downstairs are no longer prominent, playing backgammon among themselves. Lownes arranged a fleet of limousines to ferry restless customers from the Playboy round to the Clermont. Now the Arabs eat there. The Arabs gamble.

Berkeley Square is Mayfair's village green. Long slender girls with souped-up tans and souped-up Minis come here at some time of the day to signal to men with long fat bank accounts. They meet for lunch in Mortons, get taken for dinner to Annabels, go gambling at the Clermont. They're not so much the butterflies of London's society as its moths. They flutter around whoever is burning money this year. In the 60s they were to be seen around the men from the movies or the mutual funds, the property millionaires, the asset-strippers. Now they go for Arabs.

Flashback to Cortina in 1968: Sharon and Roman Polanski, current cult figures, are celebrating Christmas with carols on the record player, gifts all round. Annie's there with her movie producer husband. Berkeley Square 1975; Annie slinks out of a limousine with her Lebanese boyfriend noted for his acquaintance with the newest cult figure, the ruler of Abu Dhabi (a place practically no-one had heard of when the Manson murders were hogging the limelight). That's what 1975 is about for those who always seemed to gravitate towards money in the 60s.

But the Arabs don't like the girls on the make. As a rule they dump them fast and brutally. And when the Berkeley Square girls get spiteful they grouse to their traditional enemies, the gossip columnists. More hostility on both sides. Gaming clubs are safer; they only cost the Arabs money. With men like Victor Lownes they feel at ease.

Victor can sip easily on his soda water mulling over the two million dollars. But he has a decision to make. Eighteen months ago, Graff, the Knightsbridge jewellery shop, rented a £1,500 a year showcase in the Playboy. Now they want to open a shop on the premises. The shop will be built into the first floor landing. For this space, 8 feet by 4 feet, Graff are offering apparently £50,000 a year rent for five years.

Victor and Bernie agree on principle that it's worth pursuing the idea. Lownes agree to continue negotiating. Lawrence Graff, 38, fair haired, sharp, friendly, has worked his way up the jewellery trade to Knightsbridge. His shop is a sumptuous setting of Muzak, smoked-glass, potted-plants and suede sofas. Its atmosphere is more akin to a hairdressing parlour than a craftsman's showcase. He is at this moment selling jewellery to a fat, slouchy Arab. Well, to his wife actually. The Arab gets bored and goes out for a walk. No one would look at him twice in Knightsbridge let alone recognise Prince Abdullah, brother of the Saudi king, himself king of the military.

When you talk about jewellery and you talk about Arabs in London, three names crop up: the Hilton, Kutchinsky and, more and more frequently, Graff. Graff, his hair deliciously styled to flop just right, has the warm personality of a cab driver made good. 'Hello,' he greets Prince Abdullah's fat, blank-faced wife. 'How's your heart? It's grown bigger since last week.' The princess's heart-shaped £150,000 diamond drop, last week's bauble, hangs on her heaving bosom. She gives Graff a hearty smile. Only later in Saudi Arabia will I find out why his relaxed attention gets such a response.

Graff doesn't push. He's building slowly for the future. He sends a man regularly to Saudi Arabia and on round the Gulf. He doesn't go himself. He's Jewish. In the shop it seems irrelevant. He, the princess and the prince (who is back, having been bored quickly with his walk) swap the chat of friends. Graff goes downstairs to order tea and talk to me as he rummages through his safe. 'Anyone who tells you the Arabs are stupid have never done business with them. Not in areas that they know, anyway. A fourteen-year-old boy from Bahrain spotted a tiny flaw in a seemingly perfect stone last week quicker than most jewellers could. And if you try to sell the Arabs gaudy, flashy settings, you might as well shut up shop. They look for value. The second they think you're driving too hard a bargain, they don't say a word – they just vanish. I'm more careful to be absolutely straight with an Arab than with the most experienced European dealer.'

Oh yes, the Arabs know about jewellery. They sniff out the men they'll let buy for them with concealed caution. One New York free-lance jeweller confided that after he was asked to start a collection for some Saudis, he was astonished to learn that the Saudi Arabian consulate had been checking him out: 'It was when I got a call from an old customer in California telling me the Saudis had been on to him that I realised how efficient they can be. I'd thought my clients were hanging back because they couldn't get round to making decisions.'

The Arabs are sniffing Graff out right now, and he's grateful. They don't waste money buying good stuff for floosies. For them the jangling gold chains (£150 a piece) will do. The good stuff stays in the family.

Graff bolts upstairs. Prince Abdullah has expressed an interest in some emeralds. The Muzak is piping 'The Impossible Dream'.

A taste for it

The Arabs are in a bit of a cultural fix. When the oil barons of Texas made money, they knew whose taste they wanted to emulate, that of the old money. They wanted to live like the brahmins of the East Coast moving in each others' wood-panelled dining rooms. It took a generation or two to get it just right but at least they had a blueprint for the homes that were the flag-ships of their new-found wealth. When America first grew rich, it had the European civilisation that had spawned it offering a style to copy, heirlooms to import. In the Middle Ages even, success equalled riches. The lord had a baronial hall crammed with works of art. Those robber barons knew all about conspicuous consumption.

But the Arabs have their own culture, their own roots. Their ancestors didn't set up shop in the middle of the desert in a great stone heap. In Arabia, success equalled strength equalled mobility. It meant having allies, courage, influence, strong family groupings. Intangibles that could not be projected by the trappings of wealth.

So the arrival of the oil-rich Arab has led to misunderstandings in the market place of Europe. When today's Arab leader walks in-to a shop to bulk-buy presents for his friends and followers, the story spreads that Arabs have gone spend-crazy. Wily Sheikh Rashid from the pirate coast, now more respectfully labelled the United Arab Emirates, pops into a Bond Street jeweller. He's ruler of Dubai, Vice President of the UAE and he's come to pick up a hundred pairs of gold cuff-links (£700 each) and five Piaget 18-carat white gold, diamond-set watches (£20,000 each). Naturally the rest of Bond Street glares with envy.

But it's when the Arabs come to furnish their London homes that the green-eyed gods of envy have a field day. Arabs didn't have any furniture let alone antique furniture. What they have is money to buy whatever takes their fancy or whatever trusted advisers tell them is the thing to have. But they learn quickly. In 1974 there was a veritable flotilla of fixers in London waving their powers-of-attorney and blank cheques from Arabs while mocking the gullibility of the men who had signed them. By the autumn of 1975, the Arabs were signing fewer chits for casually-met go-betweens.

When the money first poured in, dealers looked east to India. Middle-men made a killing buying up furniture from broken down places in India and peddling it to Arabians. What was good enough for the maharajahs was good enough for the oil raj. In 1974 the Indian government clamped down on the exporting of its 'works of art' (pretentious Victoriana covered in silver, embossed with jewels for the most part). The European dealers started pushing their own heritage.

Whole showrooms did (and do) disappear on jumbo jets and juggernauts en route for the Gulf. Kitchen equipment, antiques, pictures and loads and loads of bathroom fittings. But it's in London that the bathrooms come into their own, treasured far more highly than the antiques. It was predictable really. The bathroom was the one area guaranteed to capture the Arabs' imagination. Water has always been so precious to them and Muslims have a fetish about cleanliness. Bathroom designers have made a fortune out of providing exotic surroundings for the piped water that gushes freely into the London homes of Arabs from countries where having enough for a hot bath is still the greatest luxury.

Prominent among the purveyors of watery dream worlds is a small, stout, stately man of Polish–German origin, Godfrey Bonsack ('chandeliers converted into showers are my speciality') of Mayfair. He's renowned for his 'Bonsack zoo', individually designed bath spouts in the form of frogs, toads, rhinos, turtles, elephants, porcupines and any other creature to order if suitable for spout conversion. Price per spout: £250 to £800.

He gives Arabs bathrooms equipped with TVs, costly hi-fis, coffee tables on hydraulic hoists, monogrammed sunken baths with cushioned head-rests, Versailles-styled washbasins – thousands of pounds' worth of sensuous bathing. Monogrammed towels from the House of Dior add the final flourish.

When they can drag themselves away from the bathroom, Arabs tend to go for shops that 'sound right'. Sometimes Harrods, mostly Asprey of New Bond Street. 'At last,' says John Asprey, young, sandy-looking export director of this temple of costly gewgaws, 'they're buying good quality.' It's been a long battle. Asprey's are in a better position than most London shops to assess changing taste in the Peninsula. They have three mini-Aspreys in Oman, Abu Dhabi and Dubai and are investing heavily to open a maxi version in Kuwait. They would soon hear of any fall off in the 18-carat gold, jade-handled £353 beard comb.

Younger, trendier Arabs in London go more for the sci-fi, satin-chrome and glitter look. Decor kings of the young Arab pads are the Zarach brothers in Sloane Street. Andrew Zarach, usually to be found in open-necked shirt and jeans, specialises in custom-built knick-knacks: a ten foot high brass palm tree incorporating ostrich eggs (£3,500), white leather covered bed with obligatory built-in hi-fi (£2,000), a set of steel-framed, suede-covered chairs (£230 each) and miles of mirrors on walls, doors, ceilings, not to mention the odd shower with multi-jets (as featured by David Hockney in the film *A Bigger Splash*).

When Arab-mania spread through the New York decorating establishment ('Have you got an Arab yet?' became a familiar greeting), the Americans went out and landed hotel and office jobs in the Gulf. Apart from a few well-placed men like the Asprey family and Zarach, the short-sighted London designers thankfully accepted the jobs that fell on their desks and then blew the future by bitching. 'Any interior decorator would just die on the job, dear. My client brought in tea urns, brass tables, lanterns, cushions, the lot. He put a model of the Eiffel Tower next to an exquisite piece of fifth-century BC bronze I found him. He even had his name in Arabic produced as a neon sign to swing over the bar. I ask you? He completely messed up my design concept.'

His client also heard about this dinner-party moan. Arabs' pride is very touchy. The client never came back. But glitter loses its charm. Slowly but surely, the big-time speculators are moving in for the real kill when the Arabs tire of over-priced tinsel. They are waiting for them to acquire the European habit of selective collection rather than indiscriminate massing. 'A few already are,' says one knowingly.

The dealers will be ready for them. Some have been secretly

searching out early copies of the Koran. In that summer of 75 competitors took note when one of the richest bookdealers in the world, H.P. Kraus of New York (included in his list: a million-pound Gutenberg Bible), bought 44 loose, hand-written leaves of a tenth-century Koran at a Sotheby's auction for a mere £1,200. The speculators have found a new seam to mine.

While the vultures were sighting their prey, everyone on the ground just enjoyed the celebration. Well, nearly everyone. The British Museum was preparing a Koranic exhibition for the World of Islam Festival which didn't go unremarked by one of the festival's co-ordinators, Iraqi-born Gida al-Askari. The daughter of a government minister, herself educated genteelly at Miss Ironsides' and Edinburgh University, Miss al-Askari commented bitterly on the new Arab craze: 'In 1967, my first year at Edinburgh, during the Six Days' War, I was ashamed and humiliated. People were unbelievably hostile. And the moment oil prices entered into it, I found people clamouring to be friendly just because I'm an Arab. It doesn't seem to occur to them that I'm not necessarily a rich Arab.'

Is it so surprising? Purdey's, the aristocrats of the gun trade, were cock-a-hoop over the increased sale of their double-barrelled sporting shotguns, gold-inlaid at £20,000 a pair. Noel Mander, an organ builder, had to combine work on a £250,000 contract for St Paul's Cathedral with the construction of a walnut, mahogany and rosewood organ with 700 pipes for a corner of the Sultan of Oman's drawing room. The sultan, a music freak, also found himself a famous organist to take home to play with it. Even the British police weren't missing out on the act. The Metropolitan Police Dog Training Centre at Biggin Hill started training German shepherd dogs in the intricacies of security work – for export to Arabia, naturally.

The black sheikhs of the family

King Saud of Saudi Arabia had forty sons and a bad image. He went in for gold-plated Cadillacs, watches for visitors, concubines and morphine. He died in exile in 1969; the image lives on. King Saud's sons came from many mothers. They came in varying shapes, sizes and colours. They have two things in common: apparently unlimited access to funds and no government power today.

A favourite habit of young King Saud bloods has long been crashing expensive motor cars. Residents of Kensington Court, a quiet square in London opposite the royal park, are at any moment likely to be startled by any one of three Lamborghinis frequently bearing wounds imposed by their royal owner – Prince Turqi, 23, son of Saud.

One day at London airport last summer, a tall skinny youth delicately arrayed in white by Yves St Laurent, hung around with gold chains, slim black briefcase in one hand, slimmer black handbag in another, emerges among the tourists off the flight from Spain. Waiting by the plane is the British Airports Authority's top people's greeter. 'Your car is waiting downstairs, Your Highness' (a long black limousine with a disgruntled driver called Harry. 'The trouble with Arabs is that they always keep you waiting, they never let you know whether you're wanted.').

'Your Highness had a good journey I hope.' His Highness Prince Turqi is whisked off to the De Havilland VIP lounge where his passport is taken away for stamping and airport lackeys produce his plastic, string-bound suitcase. There are some gaps in His Highness's kit of status symbols. His Highness complains. He isn't at all well. He's in great pain. After three weeks in the Marbella Club (he went for a weekend) he has returned with a bad back and a temperature. He talks vaguely about water-ski-ing accidents and the bumping of a high-powered speedboat.

He does, however, perk up a little when he opens his briefcase on the way into London. It's full of photographs. He's had a party. 'It cost me £6,000 but it was the party of the season. Everyone said so. Everyone was there. People keep telling me that I have to get to know the right people, and I have. Look at her' (he points to an over-ripe, well-covered blonde) 'She's a princess.' Which princess? 'I don't remember – a princess. That's a contessa.' Which contessa? 'A contessa,' he says impatiently, hurrying on to show a baron from Austria. No, he can't remember his name either.

The car pulls up in front of his new flat. It's an alleged property coup. A friend found it, he explains. Asking price £96,000. His friend went to see the agent and came back advising him to offer £84,000 in ready cash. He went to the bank, drew out the notes, waved it in front of the agent's nose – and bingo, the flat was his within three days. Turqi doesn't like waiting. The long mansion block corridor of his first-floor flat is covered in plush red velvet wallpaper (of a style familiar from Indian restaurants). It's a modern decorator's delight. Zarach's men have left their mark of chrome and glass furniture, squishy sofas, electronic toys – and a pile of bills.

It's time for Turqi to summon a few friends. He doesn't like being lonely and his Afghan hound is boarded out. First to arrive is his 'very best friend', David Fu Tong, big, burly son of a Liverpool-Chinese restaurant owner from around the corner.

While Turqi's off tending his ailing back, David holds forth on all he's done to bring the royal up to the mark. 'When I first met him he was down in this real dive of a disco all the time. I didn't know he was a prince, did I? I just thought he was an ordinary bloke like me. Anyway, I got to know him and as soon as I found out what he was I said, "Turqi, you listen, you can't go around with scrubbers like these. Not you. Rich and royal and everything." I said, "You have to get to know the right people." He needed a real friend like me to tell him straight.'

'Anyway, I got Turqi going to better discos. But I still say, he's got to get to know the right girls. He could know anyone. But he just won't bother. I've said to him time and again, "If you want to take out a really classy bird you have to have patience. They don't go out with you just like that." But Turqi if he wants something he has to have it right away.'

Next to arrive: Michel, an Iranian friend who was in Marbella with Turqi. He has in tow an Austrian model he's brought back from the club. On goes the soul-music at maximum volume. Out come the photographs. 'You've really made it this time, Turqi, they really liked you.' Alfred, the chauffeur, is bringing more photographs back in the Lamborghini which he's driving home overland. The model isn't happy. Michel's put her in a cheap hotel off Cromwell Road and she hasn't got enough to do and Turqi promised to come home earlier.

The doorbell buzzes somehow over the deafening rock. It's David's wife, Marion ('I've been working the clubs since I was sixteen and now I'm a croupier in the Victoria Sporting Club. Oh, we've had a wonderful season'). Marion is a sample-offer sized blonde with dark glasses. She's very concerned about Turqi's poor back and his temperature and her small son, apparently, has missed him a lot. 'He thinks the world of you, Turqi, he's always asking when you'll be back.'

The evening jives on. It's eleven o'clock. Turqi makes another call. Half an hour later the buzzer goes. 'You're going to meet my wife now. She's a really educated lady. And my children, they're the best.'

She appears. Princess Khalthoum is twenty-four; she's wearing a red nylon top and black, washable long skirt. Khalthoum. In this crazy, noise-infested room (particularly now that Sara, three, and Saud, eighteen months, are racing around screaming), Her Highness is a monument of calm dignity. Every now and again, the couple exchange quiet words in Arabic. For a moment all the acting and pretence drops away and Turqi seems real. Then he's distracted and the show goes on. Khalthoum smiles now and again. She examines the photographs of That Party and nods approval. It's as if it's the most natural thing in the world for her to be summoned halfway through the night (from where isn't yet clear) and then dismissed half an hour later (to where still isn't clear) when their children begin to demand too much of the available limelight.

David is despatched to get food. Turqi is in a predicament. He doesn't like eating out in restaurants much; although he'll sit for hours in Tramp, the dolly-spotting discotheque. ('You'll never see him actually dancing,' contributes Michel, 'or even talking. He just sits there and the girls just kind of nab him. After all, with all that gold and jewellery hanging around him, he's obviously something special isn't he?') Turqi doesn't want a living-in servant. His daily maid, Connie, who turns up with her grumbles and her small son, manages all right. But he does like to eat at home. Not, of course, in the dining room with its vast, oval table covered with curtain-matching fabric that looks like a cottage garden. He likes to eat at home around the kitchen table without anyone going to the bother of cooking.

So David goes off to the Persian restaurant nearby and returns with an army's ration of third-rate food. David busies himself getting it ready while wife Marion sits glued to the round, plastic-domed television and the model sighs heavily listening to the heavy rock. At two o'clock in the morning, the party sits down for a supper, involving much tomato ketchup spilled over His Highness's spotless white attire.

At three o'clock in the morning, the music still rocks on and I stagger home to sleep.

At three o'clock the next afternoon, Khalthoum is just waking up. It's the religious month of Ramadan. She fasts (unlike her husband) and rises late to kill the hungry daylight hours. Her Highness is staying in a flaking, formerly grand, rooming house in Queen's Gate Terrace where the balcony is a noted landmark at present for local shopkeepers, impressed by the size of her bra cups hanging out to dry on the line.

Khalthoum lives in Riyadh. She's used to not seeing much of Turqi now that they are married. They married four years ago; he left for Texas two weeks later for a three-year air force pilot's course that he never quite completed. He left her pregnant. She saw him again for a while, hence young Saud, and she has been summoned to London to be with her husband. She arrived two months ago and spent the first month in a suite in the Inter-continental Hotel. Turqi rented this humble, two-bedroomed, sparsely furnished flat for her when she found the constrictions of hotel life impossible to bear with two young children. Turqi doesn't know how shabby it is. He hasn't seen it himself.

The television set is on permanently. Cheap plastic toys litter the floor. Saud is sitting on a potty demolishing a plate of chips. He and his sister display all the spontaneous warmth of children brought up in a protected environment. The Ethiopian servant girl glides around noiselessly picking up the debris of two children confined to the flat all day. Behind Khalthoum's passive acceptance is a perpetual sadness. 'Of course I mind that I'm not with Turqi. I'm sad all the time. But what can I do? I'll say one thing. He,' she points to Saud, 'won't grow up like that. Turqi and I grew up together as children in the same house. My sister married his father. We were like Saud and Sara and now . . .' Her face shuts again. The moment of confiding is over.

While her husband bucks up his energy in his so far unrealised ambition to be an international businessman (credit cards, chicken farms, jeans factory and the like), Princess Khalthoum lives in Riyadh and goes to the university. She is studying psychology.

Meanwhile, a few streets away, in the splendour of his new, multi-bedroom-studded London home, Turqi has taken to his bed. This is unfortunate. The model, fed up with Michel and her cheap hotel room off the Cromwell Road, has moved in. Turqi has relegated her to the smallest guest room. She is still sighing. David has discovered a few puzzles in the Marbella Club bill. He's planning to fly out to Malaga with Turqi to help his friend to sort the matter out. Only right now, Turqi is unable to move.

After talk of strained muscles and speedboats, His Highness's trouble is revealed. He has a boil on his royal bottom.

They also serve

You know what it's like when you go to a theatre that has no curtain between you and the stage. The house-lights dim, the stage lights slowly come up and figures take shape. At first, they're mere shadows. In the end, they're bright and real. I'm beginning to feel that – I'm in the audience of such a theatre – slowly the stage is lighting up.

A telex bolts into my office from Riyadh. Sheikh Yamani's chef-de-cabinet and right-hand man, Ibrahim Obaid, is coming to London. He wishes to see me. Obaid, thirty-seven, is a grave, slightly vain man (in contrast to his boss who's very vain). He has dark hair, a dark beard, which he strokes often, and we spend long almost silent hours together in his Carlton Tower Hotel suite-cum-office while he tries to figure me out and I give up trying to figure him out. I still don't know that in his country you're not an individual, you're a type: to be put in a clearly labelled jam-jar. There are two types – men jam and women jam. In my innocence, I'm still trying to talk to him like one person with a job to do to another.

Our silent conversation obviously wins him round because he invites me to lunch with his wife, Souad. Then one evening, a large jump up the ladder of approval, he invites me to their flat. Their flat. Why the hotel suite? It's an office bolt-hole, but his wife would never ask him about it. That's something else I'll understand in Saudi, but try this in the meantime. She and I are in the Carlton Tower lobby one afternoon after lunch waiting for her husband to join us (he's buzzed off for half an hour). Souad's nine-month-old son is uninhibitedly screaming his head off with fury at being stuck in his push-chair. I suggest that Souad collects the key to Ibrahim's suite and we go upstairs where baby Ahmad can get out of his chair and make some noise in peace. Souad's sophistication drops away. She blushes and I realise that she wouldn't take her husband's key under any circumstances without his permission. She'd rather endure that frosty look from Carlton Tower guests and staff.

So I'm interested to see what life's like in the flat. I'm even more interested to see if he'll get round to talking about Yamani. In all those hours together neither of us have so much as mentioned the oil minister's name. Come to think of it, it's very odd that Obaid's here at all. Normally, every appointment with Yamani is arranged through Obaid: he's never away from the boss's side. And at this very moment, there's a vital OPEC conference going on in Vienna where the oil producing nations are deciding whether to put up the price by ten per cent (the Saudis' figure), or thirty-five per cent (favoured by the Iranians). There isn't a major Western newspaper that doesn't have an overkill of reporters covering the conference.

I pitch up at the Obaids' flat in Curzon Street (one of those softly-carpeted service blocks much frequented by Arabs). It so happens that some hours ago Yamani stormed out of the Vienna conference room and flew to London for the night. All over London, journalists are trying to find Obaid because the rumour's spread that he's here too. What's Obaid doing? He's having a good laugh at the discussions I'm having with Souad about what clothes I should take to Riyadh. His mother's chipping in too. She's a natural scene-stealer; it's the first time she's ever left Saudi Arabia and she doesn't speak a word of English (she's here for a month about her rheumatism, and goes for physiotherapy every day). We may not share a language of words, but I get on with her from the start. She notices that my cup of tea is empty. She reproaches her son in Arabic who reproaches his wife in Arabic who apologises to me in English and refills it. Ibrahim's Carlton Tower suite isn't big; the flat wasn't designed for giants. But there's always room for tea-kettles and coffee-pots – the Arab symbols of hospitality.

Mrs Obaid Senior asks where I'll stay in Riyadh (Souad translates). She's shocked to hear that I plan to make do with acquaintances' sofas. Ibrahim promises her that a hotel room will be taken care of (Souad translates again). I'm ready to jump in with a question or two of my own when Ahmad pinches the moment with some more screaming. The storms of OPEC don't invade the flat. The Obaids are all far more concerned about Ahmad. They're waiting for him finally to get drowsy enough for bed. They're also waiting for a baby-sitter and, after that, for a merchant banker and his wife to arrive. They're off to Annabel's nightclub for a bite of supper.

Miss Ward, a silvery haired, trained nurse turned doctor's receptionist, enters timidly. She's here to mind Ahmad. Miss Ward is diverted by Ibrahim from her discreet path towards the nursery to stay out of sight.

'Come, join us; sit down, may we offer you a drink?'

'Oh, no, really. Well, perhaps a cup of tea.'

'Please may I ask your first name?' Obaid.

'Christine,' Miss Ward's rather embarrassed answer.

From that moment Christine is one of the family. ('Oh dear, I wish I could find somewhere to hide. I've never been treated like this before and I feel so conspicuous.')

Souad is delighted at discovering Christine. She laughs and jokes with her, trying to persuade her to become the Obaid family fixture in London. The summer has sent a never-ending stream of well-vetted baby-sitters out of the specialist employment agencies into Arab-rented homes. It's not only the doctors, dentists and physiotherapists who are finding a call on their services – other more humble servants are much in demand. The Brompton Bureau (one of London's choicest) has supplied twenty butlers, forty housekeepers, fifty daily cleaning women and ten chefs to Arab homes in and around London during the summer ('they'll never accept Spanish or Portuguese staff as Americans used to when they had money. Only English will do.')

'I'm so glad you're English, Christine,' said Ibrahim, 'I wouldn't like to trust Ahmad to a foreigner.'

There follows a long discussion about the merits of screaming versus nursing on demand and then, Christine too is drawn into the problem of what I should wear in Riyadh. What I should wear? I still don't have a visa and here's Yamani's number two who won't even discuss the subject.

In the middle of all this, the merchant banker and wife arrive hot-foot from their Eaton Mews South pied à terre. The milk-and-roses' frightfully English wife doesn't appear to be the least thrown at being outshone by Souad's evening get-up and if she's slightly flummoxed at being introduced to the baby-sitter as 'our very good friend Christine', she doesn't let that show either.

Somehow we all find places to perch while Ibrahim distributes photographs taken at a beach party in Saudi Arabia thrown for Senator Edward Kennedy. Miss Ward is now completely over-come. Mrs Obaid Senior, who's obviously seen these photographs before, still can't remember what a Kennedy is and has to have it explained again.

When Miss Ward is nervous, she has a habit of gently patting her neat hair. By now it's received a veritable battering. She'd give anything to wrest baby Ahmad from his father's arms (Ibrahim won't put him down; this is the first but not the last time I notice how physically affectionate Saudi men are with their children). Obaid doesn't notice Miss Ward's concern but the banker notices the time. They have a table booked at Annabel's and it's time to move on.

Miss Ward's final wide-eyed look is reserved for Obaid's elderly mother. With Ahmad more or less settled, Mrs Obaid Junior wrapped up exotically for a night among the rich or famous, Mrs Obaid Senior ties a head scarf on and dons her coat. She's firmly escorted out by Yamani's number two to join his friends at Annabel's for a spot of dinner dancing.

Miss Ward's stunned. 'I don't know any of my English employers who'd actually take their mother out to a place like Annabel's unless she was used to that sort of thing. I don't understand them, I simply don't.'

She doesn't understand. Here am I, having been summoned by telex, having spent hours now, quite pleasantly, with Yamani's man, surely sent to sniff me out, and he hasn't said a word about the small matter of a visa. I'm late for a dinner party elsewhere; Ibrahim finds a taxi for me. Just as I get in, he says quietly, 'I'll look forward to seeing you in Riyadh, Linda. So will the minister. We'll arrange whatever is necessary.' That's brinkmanship.

The Arabs are coming

In a secret world known to its inmates as 'the Palazzo', behind blackened walls reached through a great square Italianate courtyard other servants are beavering away. In a dingy, high-ceilinged room, its walls covered with tatty maps and esoteric family trees, the servants of Her Majesty's Government at the Middle East desk are in the nearest they get to a flap.

Crown Prince Fahd of Saudi Arabia has let it be known that he might just consider making his first 'official visit' to Britain. With the intricacies of an army HQ planning a major offensive, diplomats in shirt sleeves hang over their paper-laden desks plotting success. Robin Kealey, a fresh-faced Arabist, is blocking out huge charts trying to juggle government ministers' time for mini-Cabinet meetings with their honoured guest. If he agrees to come, that is.

There's a hitch. The Duke of Gloucester had been provisionally booked to greet HRH at the airport ('it's hard getting royals at such short notice') and escort him to his government-booked-and-paid floor of Claridge's Hotel. But word has come from our man in Saudi Arabia that there will be no crown prince alighting on the tarmac at Heathrow unless Harold Wilson is there to say 'hello' in person.

Impasse. Wilson sends word via his man at Number 10 Downing Street that he doesn't drive to airports for lesser fish than heads of state. Kealey plugs in the electric kettle, makes a stiffening cup of coffee and decides against sending alarming messages off to the ambassador. Maybe Wilson will come round. He does, but not until a few, hair-raising days before the visit. Snap. Crown Prince Fahd doesn't confirm that he will show up until a few days before either.

The prime minister is going to have HRH to an intimate dinner at Number 10 on Monday – the first day of his visit. There will just be a cosy gathering of about ten or twenty senior ministers with a few bankers from the City. The point of the exercise is becoming abundantly clear. It's Treasury stuff.

Sure enough, on Tuesday morning, he is to be ushered into the Chancellor of the Exchequer's second-floor Treasury Office with its impressive paintings (borrowed from the National Gallery) and two marble fireplaces. In this hushed sanctum, the chancellor hopes for 'useful exchanges' with the Saudis' new strong man over the long rosewood topped conference table. On the agenda for the meeting some stripling had typed 'reduction of sterling investments'. A wiser, more experienced senior had tactfully inked out 'reduction' and written in 'retention'.

Afterwards there will be a trip, hardly a sight-seeing tour, to the

Bank of England to chat with Sir Gordon Richardson, the Bank's currently very anxious Chairman. He'll stay for lunch, of course. Nothing too heavy because there's another dinner party at Downing Street in the evening. This time at Number 11, the chancellor's official residence.

So far, the desk has made up three different guest lists. They have thought of going upstairs to ask the computer's advice. 'You ask the computer who is interested in what, who has just come back from where and it produces a list of people who might do. Of course it doesn't always tell you whether they've died or not. We've decided not to bother the computer for a small dinner party.'

It's called 'a cultivating Prince Fahd visit' or, as the confidential memo puts it 'taking a leaf out of the Americans' book'. There won't be any floodlit football matches or opera galas ('he's known to enjoy gambling slightly but that's not the thing you can include in an official programme'). But Her Majesty's servants are sparing no effort to make His Highness feel sufficiently well cultivated.

Even the Queen is going to do her bit. She's having Crown Prince Fahd to lunch at the palace before he leaves (not that that will impress him much, the guest palace in Riyadh is a mighty impressive place efficiently run by an English manager, graduate of Trust-House Forte five star hotels). The whole campaign is geared to the hope that before he departs Crown Prince Fahd will sign an Anglo-Saudi memorandum on Economic Co-operation. It certainly isn't to give him a chance to get to know London. He only left the place a few weeks ago after a long private holiday at his house behind Knightsbridge (a stone portal affair, rather like an expensive prison).

When the men from the Foreign Office do a job, they spare no effort. Messages fly back and forth from Saudi Arabia. Yes, Sheikh Yamani is coming. No, he isn't. By the time that fateful Monday arrives and Wilson presents himself at the airport where he actually kisses the royal hand, the desk has been through a harrowing time.

By then I am in Riyadh. I scan the television set for news of this momentous visit. It warrants a few seconds at the bottom of the programme. If the British have had trouble getting their tongues round their Arab guests' names, the impact of such world famous ministers as Anthony Wedgwood Benn, Roy Mason, Denis Healey, Eric Varley and of course James Callaghan on the Saudis is not obvious. The Saudi Press Agency puts out a digest of the day's events in London. It features such mythical heroes as Antoni Wedgodobil, Royai Masoon, Denis Haley, Arick Faarli and James Kalahan. But when the princes, ministers and diplomats pour home to Riyadh they bring good news. Crown Prince Fahd was so well pleased that he's made off to Venice for a few days to recuperate at the Gritti Palace.

Saudi Arabia

Behind the Looking Glass

A town called Alice in Wonderland

It's an average day in the lobby of the Al Yamama hotel. Walter Faulds, an old Africa hand and architect, is doing the *Daily Telegraph* crossword over a cup of practically undrinkable tea. He has been in Riyadh for three weeks. Fortunately, he does not yet know that he is doomed to be here for another three weeks. Mr Faulds is waiting.

His British firm is just about to sign a design deal for part of Saudi Arabia's new Olympic stadium. Not that Riyadh could house the Olympics. Communist countries wouldn't be allowed in. Nor could women compete. But the Saudis want the best Olympic stadium in the world, so they will have it. All of this leaves Mr Faulds, with his rapidly greying hair and suede shoes, waiting with resignation for Prince Faisal bin Fahd. The prince, as director of youth welfare, possesses the crucial signature for Mr Faulds's contract.

The whereabouts of Prince Faisal are a mystery. His office says he isn't there now. He might be there tomorrow. But Bukra Insha'llah (tomorrow, God willing) is a well-known catch phrase. God might not be willing tomorrow. He very often isn't. And meanwhile Prince Faisal's office staff have been saying that for three weeks.

The lobby captives are the concubines of the seventies, shut away in purdah at the pleasure of their Arabian masters. Everyone fears quitting the lobby in case That Call comes. Outside is Riyadh, capital city of the richest oil kingdom on earth. Beyond is desert; orange, barren, frightening. There's nothing romantic about the desert if you get stuck in it. In winter it burns the brains, scorches the temper and soaks the skin in seconds. Now imagine the summer.

Riyadh is in the middle of Arabia and it's hot madness. It is tension charcoaled daily under the desert sun. Has some unseen Dr Strangelove run wild here? Nothing is predictable. Tempers flare like dry tinder. Something intangible and inexplicable sends goose pimples across one's spirit. The place only looks like a modern city, more correctly a modern building site.

But there are millions of dollars' worth of contracts up for grabs. The hotel lobbies (such few as exist) throng with businessmen, nerves and expense accounts stretched to breaking point, baffled by an entirely alien culture.

Around one table near Mr Faulds huddles a group hawking bullet-proof Cadillacs. At another sits an Egyptian psychiatrist playing with his worry beads. He's here to set up a psychiatric unit at the £100 million plus hospital King Faisal Medical City up the road. ('A psychiatric unit in Riyadh? Nonsense, it doesn't exist,' says a government official. 'We don't need psychiatry. We have Islam.') But the Egyptian is real all right. He's waiting too. He's waiting on the hospital's Executive Director, Jack F. Frayer, an ex-football player from Makin, Georgia ('where ah have the prettiest Herefords you all ever saw'). And in case that doesn't work, Maharishi Mahesh Yogi (who shot out of obscurity by the Ganges when the Beatles embraced him) has a rep in town trying to sell the Education Ministry on transcendental meditation. Bill Lear has flown in to find finance for his newest jet. But that morsel is lost on the group of engineers whispering in one corner. They're worried silly that their foundations for the new university site haven't allowed for sand erosion. This is the desert. It's merely decorated with high-rise buildings.

Another multi-disciplined architect is nonchalantly covering his attempts to eavesdrop on their worries. He's designing a flashy villa for the cousin of a minor prince whose brother is a minister. Perhaps the villa will lead to an office and shopping complex? Everyone in the world chasing money is here.

At odd moments, dead-pan Saudis drop in to watch the performers. Western visitors can't distinguish a local taxi driver from a tribal chief. National dress is a great equaliser. For the hustlers, operating is about as easy as watching a film backwards and upside down. Everyone has his contact. Every businessman waiting for That Call is about to make millions. Some do. More never find out whether their contact has a contact with the right contact or not. Better-informed lobby watchers extract sadistic delight seeing a newcomer oozing charm at a Saudi known to have no more power to arrange anything than the doorman (probably less).

The doorman can at least arrange women. Many is the black bundle that has tapped late at night on the bedroom door of a man who has made a point of befriending the doorman. There are a few diversions in the waiting game. The hotel manager, Mike, is one. Mike was raised in the United States. He has just arrived. This back-slapping teeth-flasher is having to learn how to wear his thobe. He's not a delicate man so the lobby knows of his difficulties in peeing without spotting his long white frock as he holds it above his waist in the loo.

The lobby also knows that he has a friendly supply of illegal scotch that he shares, except on days when the hotel's owner, a tall, dignified Saudi, puts in an appearance. For a while Mike has been moonlighting. At eleven o'clock every evening, the lobby gathers round the television set to watch Mike stutter his way through the news in English, trying hard to keep his unaccustomed head-dress in place. It's the one guaranteed comedy show of the day. As an encore he rushes back to the Al Yamama to ask how he did. Lousy.

Usually at about this time, the patient Mr Faulds has a last cup of cocoa, folds his *Daily Telegraph*, collects his key and retires to re-gather his strength for another day of waiting. But tonight his boss, Ian Fraser, is flying in from London. Fraser, a big, cheerful man, arrives sporting a naval blazer and white moccasins – just the thing for the South of France. This lynch pin of the international jet set brings news at last of Prince Faisal. He has finally been run to earth. He's comfortably ensconced in a suite in the Dorchester Hotel in London where he's officially ill. Not too ill, however, to have been seen dining in Annabel's. It's hard for the men playing the waiting game in Riyadh.

By comparison, life for a visiting Western woman is much simpler. The rules are clear. You have to be completely untouchable that's all. Before the journey began one British Arabist offered some advice: 'The only way you'll get round that part of the world, my dear, is on your back.' It's the one way not to travel; too limited a view.

The first clue was laid in Dhahran, centre of the oil-producing eastern region. It's the window through which foreigners swarm en route for Riyadh. It's limp hot in the airport. I feel damn silly standing around in a long nightdress (where else can you buy a long-sleeved, high-necked demure cotton dress in autumn except in a lingerie department?). I feel even sillier when I find out that an OK on an airline route on Saudia, the national airline, doesn't necessarily mean a seat on the plane. It's the OK to fight for one. Arab men in thobes and brief-case-toting Westerners are attacking the check-in counter. The only other woman in sight is bundled inside what looks like a black laundry bag guarding the ladies' lavatory.

A Saudi, impeccably attired in a Western suit (made in Taiwan two days ago), glides over. The sight of his crocodile overnight case and heavy gold watch gives rise to hope as he disappears into the scrum leaving behind the promise of a seat. A nearby Brit drawls knowingly: 'There'll be a high price for that favour.' The Saudi re-emerges in triumph and shepherds his flock on to the plane, across the desert to Riyadh. At the brand new airport ('this is only temporary, we're building a new one in five years') he relinquishes responsibility for me to the Head of Passenger Relations, giving orders for a supply of Pepsi and cake. He still refuses to give his name but offers instead a small, stiff nod: 'You are a guest in our country. I hope you have a pleasant stay with us.'

Saudis in Riyadh aren't used to having unescorted women flapping about. Until they are, the few they allow in are privileged and protected, providing they observe the rules. These include such clauses as: shut off any signals that can be misread as an invitation. Remember at all times to be as sexless as Snow White. Sit in the back of a car automatically unless invited up front. Don't smoke in public places or before anyone unknown (that nearly all Saudi men and women smoke like chimneys in private is part of the contradiction). Don't allow Mike the Manager through the bedroom door at two in the morning when he arrives to offer advice on how to deal with men. Pay no attention if trouble-makers suggest he's spreading word that you're a slut. No one in the lobby would believe that any woman in her right mind would have a man in her room here. The hotel corridors are patrolled constantly by sharp-sighted staff and everyone works on the assumption that rooms and telephones are bugged. Paranoia is a disease that goes with Riyadh's claustrophobia as malaria goes with swamps.

A Western woman here is safe – suffocatingly, frustratingly safe. I am no longer a person. I'm playing the part of being a guest. The Saudis' obsession with form, ritual, outward appearances and what other people think, creates raging, inner tensions. I find eventual release in a flood of tears over the bedroom sink – then the concerned room-service man, good Arab that he is, knocks at my door to see why I am unhappy in this country.

There can, of course, still be misunderstandings. It's eleven at night. The telephone rings. A high court official has just finished work and he's prepared to drop by to talk. In the lobby, the piped rock-and-roll blares across a conversation centred around royal matters while contract hunters stare curiously. 'I think,' says the official, his face inscrutably blank, 'that if you don't mind, we'll go round to the house of some friends to talk.'

Nothing unusual in that. Once inside the cemented circle of power in Riyadh, you're led around all manner of strangers' homes at all hours to find tea, coffee and unquestioning hospitality. This time, the house is in a dark, unlit back-street. The friend opens the door, greets the courtier and closes the door behind us. Through the hall, into the living room. By now accustomed to the Saudi habit of giving away as much as a Chinese poker-player, I register no surprise at the illegal Playboy magazines stacked in the bookshelves and nude centrefolds adorning the walls. They add an almost homey look to the slinky room with its discotheque-style lighting, low sofas and stash of Akai stereo equipment and bottles of scotch.

My predicament: to walk out would be embarrassing. I can't

be found running around the streets of Riyadh at night alone. To ask immediately to be driven back to the hotel will lead to a confrontation. What if he refuses? The friend has disappeared and the court official is oiling himself with whisky. He tells me the villa's rented by a group of married men as the communal bachelor pad (prostitutes, mainly Egyptian, and a river of co-operative air hostesses keep it well supplied, it seems). But I'm in the capital of a people whose tribal, desert traditions haven't all been cashed in for petrodollars. There's a way out if I keep calm.

'Do you mind being here with me?' leers my host meaningfully. Mind? I'm scared stiff. But I say pleasantly, 'Not at all. I'm a guest in your country and so I know you will not harm me. I'm under your protection.'

I now have him in a complete moral dilemma. As a Saudi, challenged with this age-old appeal of the desert, he's incapable of infringing his sense of honour. As a man, he's dying to jump on me. He blusters away for a time because he's about to lose face and that's one of the worst disasters an Arab man can suffer. He even begs me to stay the night, locking myself in one room while he sleeps in another – he doesn't want his friend to know what's happened. I turn down this invitation. 'The hotel will worry about me.'

In the end, the Saudi in him wins through and he weaves his way towards the door, out to the car and drives me back to the hotel. I totter into the lobby, shaking with relief. 'Did you have a productive time?' asks the cosy Mr Faulds as we share our late night cup of cocoa. 'It's been boring here as usual. How I wish something, anything, unexpected would happen.'

The gilt complex

A leading Saudi government official drops me off at the hotel after a more conventional business meeting followed by lunch at his home. It's not my first visit to his family and I'm interested to hear an American's comment as the car roars away: 'That man has everything. He's educated, bright, rich and successful. It has all dropped into his lap.'

But has it? Follow that man home, out of the public eye, and you find another Riyadh. The black oil spurting from underground is not as simple a blessing as the biblical manna arriving from heaven. Behind the high walls of Saudi homes there are casualties. That man's wife is one. How could it be otherwise? I know how hard I find it living up to the Saúdi view of women – treasure or tramp. There's nothing between. I'm not helpless by nature but here I am not allowed to walk out of the hotel alone, treated like a china doll.

This wife can't take it. She sits in her living room hooked on cigarettes and tranquillisers. She's in her late twenties, shrinking, wasting away, her face pale and pasty. Her long slender legs hang listlessly below her short Paris couture skirt and skinny T-shirt. In some ways life was easier for her mother. There were slaves then but a wife still had work. No Californian-style kitchens a generation ago, no air-conditioning, no schooling abroad or glimpses of an alternative life to the prison of the women's quarters.

The daughter has lost and gained from progress. Several times a week she covers her face with a mask of make-up, slides into long gowns, mechanically arranges the jewels that label her the possession of a multi-millionaire and they go out together; that's avant garde for Riyadh. They go out to sit within the four walls of other friends. Walls can be a haven; they can feel like a coffin.

'My father arranged our marriage when I was sixteen. I remember our honeymoon, sitting on the plane with this stranger, and I didn't know how to begin talking to him. I didn't know the first thing about contraception so I had four children in four years. How could I take care of a child? I was a child myself.

'Now I've grown up. I'm not a child any longer, but he won't see that. You think I don't know that my husband suffers too? I've stretched out and longed for him to see that I'm not the stupid child he married, that he can trust me, confide in me, let me share some of his worries. He doesn't want to. He doesn't want me to grow up.

'I went to a European boarding school with normal girls. Do

you know how hard it has been for me to adjust? Women can't drive here so I can't leave the house without a driver for the car. When I do go out I have to put on a long black cloak and cover my face. I suffocate. I know other women say it'll disappear one day. But what about now? It's now that the veil suffocates me, now that I'm humiliated.'

I understand only too well. One weekend I'm invited away by another family. With great embarrassment they ask if I'd mind covering my face. If I was fair, everyone would recognise me as a European. Because I'm dark, they fear people who know their family will take me for an Arab – an unveiled Arab woman would dishonour them in the eyes of others. It's an eerie experience. I do suffocate, but what's worse is the way that I, I don't exist to the people around me, who see a black anonymity of a person who isn't there because she can't be seen. It is humiliating.

How can this woman's husband begin to understand that? Or see that he lets her out of the country to a freedom she can't handle and then brings her back to a constriction she can't bear?

'Of course, I rule my house. I decide what food must be cooked when he telephones at twelve from the office to say he's bringing ten men home for lunch. I arrange for the meal to be served while I disappear so that no men can see me. Has time really brought more freedom? It's brought the freedom of tickets to Europe. If I want to go away I only have to ask. And what do I do there? I go shopping, sit in a hotel room and daren't go out because there's always someone from Riyadh who might see me and tell his family.

'He's unfaithful. There isn't a husband in Saudi Arabia who isn't unfaithful. Not here of course; here they're angels, and hypocrites. I mind, but what can I do about it? We don't discuss it because we don't discuss anything that matters. Every now and again I scream and scream at him. He wouldn't hit me. He couldn't. To do that would be to admit that I'm another human being, not a doll, not a child.'

This woman isn't unusual, but I can't name her. To make her unhappiness public, or that of other women who talk openly to me, would dishonour the family. That's the real crime; a family's honour is its life-raft in this society. So this depressed woman sits at home and everyone around her pays the price for her confusion. Her husband is, as she says herself, a good man.

'I love that woman. She can hurt me more than anyone. But what do you want me to do? I give her jewels. She shrugs. I give her thousands of pounds to buy clothes from Europe. She complains because she can't wear them in Riyadh except at home. "Then why buy short skirts?" I ask. Why must she remind herself every day of what she can't do?

'I work all day. Must I fight every night? She says I don't talk to her. When am I supposed to talk to her? It's part of our way of life to have an open house with friends walking in at any time. I can't lock our door to make time to talk to her. And I don't want to – what else is there that matters in life but your friends and your family?

'I don't believe in her covering her face but I wouldn't bring shame on my family by letting her be seen unveiled in daylight. But at night, if we're going by car to friends, I don't even ask that of her. I just ask her to put on her cloak and a thin chiffon scarf. Don't women wear headscarves in Europe? Is that a terrible sacrifice? Ten years ago I couldn't have driven with her sitting beside me in the car, let alone without a veil. I couldn't have let her go to Europe for the summer to get away from the heat. Why won't she see how things have changed for the better?

'Work? Of course she can't work. Why should she need to? We don't need the money and my family wouldn't like it. Sometimes I think the old days were better. Life is getting too complicated. I'm afraid of what's happening to all of us.'

One of his friends is standing on the site of the three-million-dollar villa he's building. It will have soft beige terrazza floors, many courtyards, a swimming pool, a 'bachelor' room downstairs for his male friends, a boudoir to take morning coffee with his wife. There are hidden gardens and waterfalls glimpsed through the windows. This will be his first home of his own. He and his wife started in a large family compound. Now they share a house with his brother's family. The next step is the house on the hill – one man, one wife and three children.

He grew up in an old mansion teeming with people and the protective warmth of a traditional Saudi extended family. This empty marble house will seem like a mausoleum to him. Every Saudi multiplying his millions asks himself at some time—is the change worth it? In those lonely moments of doubt that foreigners don't witness, few answer 'yes'.

The factory

Once upon a time it did indeed seem very simple. When King Ibn Saud agreed the first oil concession with the Americans for 35,000 gold sovereigns in 1935, the sale was his to make. He had conquered a kingdom and, to make sure nobody forgot it, he named it after his own family. He left behind a few other souvenirs.

Opposite the small shops selling plastic toys and women's panties in Riyadh's equivalent to Regent Street, there's an old mud fortress. On one side stuck into the wall is a remnant of a sword. It was left there at dawn one day in 1901 when Ibn Saud took the fortress and town from his enemies of another tribe. It was his first victory – he was twenty-one years old and had ridden with a band of only forty men across the wasteland of the Empty Quarter to do it.

The battles had only begun. But Ibn Saud's policy towards his enemies (neatly summed up by one diplomat as 'kick 'em in the teeth, then marry into the family') has left behind some more troublesome souvenirs. Rather a lot of al-Saud. When Ibn Saud's son Faisal came to the throne there were 375 riyals in the state coffer (so they say) and about 3,000 al-Saud princes. Faisal's brother, King Khalid, inherited a country whose state revenues for 1975–6 come to 110,935,000,000 riyals and he's also inherited about twice as many al-Saud princes as there were before. It's no wonder that the local nickname for the al-Saud is 'The Factory' – they turn out new models like Detroit on a good day.

Not for nothing is the country the al-Saud 'company store' and every royal a shareholder. Oh yes, they hand it around to lesser citizens but there aren't too many common-or-garden Saudis to cut in on the kitty. Officially there are supposed to be seven million (or is it eight) Saudis. More likely there are under four; population figures around here are always a secret and politically sensitive issue. But no matter how the king's government hands out the wealth, Saudi royals get first shot at it. There's enough for everyone; the place is choking on its money.

I can't find out exactly how the al-Saud make money, how much they have or where they keep it (trying to do so might be a rather unhealthy occupation), but they have it all right. Just how rich the princes get depends on what they decide to do with their lives. Some are only stinking rich; they drop out, draw their pocket money and do nothing.

They're a bit more careful how they do nothing these days. The Factory's come a long way since the days of King Saud's twenty-five-million-pound al-Nasiriyyah Palace complex with separate palaces for his four wives, thirty-two mansions for concubines and thirty-seven palaces for select princes. His successor, King Faisal, was an austere man, not given to flashy living. His habits caught on. One of them was thrift: he lived poor but he died rich.

In a sentence: there's no such thing as a poor Saudi prince. Some princes do nothing but they own land and have the sense to find business managers to capitalise on it for them. Some princes go into business secretly; others go into it openly. Others go into government and some go into the lot at once. It's hard to work out who's making how much, let alone for whom and from whom.

Less ambitious princes hire out their names to foreign business-men to help them win contracts; such hiring fees come heavy round here. Other more go-ahead types actively use their names to go see some powerful relative themselves and do the winning in person. That's how you get the unconventional situation (to Western eyes) of one of the king's brothers threatening to sue a British company – he's after his half-million-pound unpaid commission on an arms deal made with his government. Except when you boil it down, the deal was made with his brother, the minister of defence.

The arms business in Saudi Arabia, as everyone knows, is something else. It's worth a fortune to anyone who gets into it. And the princes got into it first. They've been helped by all that mutually-suspicious, inter-family strife. There's a key saying in Arabia (the most important to remember along with that more hopeful thought about God being willing tomorrow). It goes: 'I against my brother, my brother and I against my cousins, my cousins and I against the world.'

There are many important princes whom even prominent Saudis have never met. There are many they've never even heard of. Some years ago, one such prince, Musad, was better known in Cairo (for certain costly personal eccentricities) than in Riyadh. He made the French newspapers when he was found dancing naked in a Paris fountain brandishing a sword. King Ibn Saud didn't appreciate the joke at all so he brought him home to comfortable house arrest. Faisal gave Musad money later to buy a house in Beirut and shove off. But in 1975 Musad's name became notorious. It was his son who shot Faisal and mislaid his head in a public square.

They took their time to set an execution date (doubtless they had a few questions to ask the assassin first) but that was a very bad period in Riyadh when everyone wondered whether the brothers and cousins would go against each other – or hold firm against the world. After that momentary al-Saud aberration, the Factory stood together and everything settled down under a new king. A few itchy-fingered princes left out by Faisal were given some new slices of government cake and everyone went back to business as usual.

It's very neat; until you know what 'business as usual' means. Khalid is the king; his half-brother, Fahd, is crown prince, now emerging as strong man and a reformed character (to the regret of casinos everywhere). The crown prince's full brother is minister of defence in charge of the regular armed forces of well-paid volunteers. But the king's full brother runs the National Guard, a crack force drawn from tribesmen whose fierce desert loyalties run thick in their veins (and whose tribal chiefs appreciate the gold bars they get for volunteering their followers' services).

The regular forces and the National Guard are kept so separate that neither knows what arms the other's getting from where or when. The government watches its outside enemies. The army watches the country. The National Guard watches the army. The middle-men commoners make a bomb out of broking arms to both, the princes don't do too badly and even the generals don't get forgotten.

The Saudis get very sore at the West's attitude to the big commissions and pay-offs involved in selling arms here (although they've felt much better since it's come out that various European countries have been up to the same lark). The West calls the Saudi arms deals corrupt. The Saudis don't like that; they see commissions as 'fees for services rendered' and pay-offs as a traditional part of patronage. Noblesse oblige, after all. Here noblesse always feels obliged to give out to others and sometimes to take a rake-off for itself.

Whatever statements His Majesty's government makes in public, in reality no one makes money (well, hardly anyone) without the consent of some royal faction. Every powerful businessman in Riyadh, the centre of government, has been drawn into the royal web or he wouldn't be successful. That's how the company store operates.

Being in business, even the company store business, simply doesn't mean the same thing to the Saudis as it does to us. Prophet Muhammad was a business man, after all. He gave it a very good name. 'Trade' doesn't have a pejorative ring at all about it, as it does in Britain. It's everything to many Arabs: their lover, their joy, their inspiration, their game, their way of being with people and of talking to them. It's not simply an obsession with making money. Business is an 'honourable profession' to the Saudis, so why should the royals be exempt? It's a little unfortunate, however, if sometimes their private and public interests overlap. Arms is a question of security, yes. It's also just another form of business, the national sport that's about the only area where Saudis can legitimately scheme and plot.

Anyone still drawing breath over recent American congressional hearings into the Saudi arms trade should bear in mind a tale told of King Ibn Saud. A man needed a contractor to deliver a consignment of a hundred cooling fans. He invited bids for the job and was delighted to find one fifty per cent lower than the rest. He accepted it, and in due course a donkey and cart arrived carrying one hundred ladies' fans. The fuming businessman took news of this swindle to King Ibn Saud to get justice done. The king said the deal was fine; fans he'd said and fans he'd got. It wasn't sharp practice, merely ingenious. It doesn't matter if it's only another Saudi tale; the point is, *they* tell it. And of course the resourceful fan-seller wasn't a Westerner, he was Saudi.

All the king's men

Adnan Khashoggi (whose Northrop and Lockheed commissions alone came to several hundred million dollars) couldn't have functioned without the knowledge of Prince Sultan, minister of defence, and Khashoggi has been a great buddy of his full brother, Crown Prince Fahd; Régine's in Paris was a favourite haunt of the stout twosome before Faisal's death.

But Adnan Khashoggi, known as AK to all and sundry, is just one of a myriad of middle men. There are many others whose interests are as intriguing as Khashoggi's but more discreetly pursued. By now most people have caught word of AK, with his private Boeing 727 jet with its six TV sets and gold-plated bathroom, his close links to certain European party-givers with their coteries of available women. They might even recognise his much-publicised South of France based yacht, Mahomedia. He's not exactly the Garbo of the arms world.

Few people would look twice at Ghassan Shakir driving his Mini (very occasionally his Rolls) around London where he has a Grosvenor Square apartment but stays at the Dorchester for convenience. No one would notice him arriving in Geneva to see his three children at their Swiss boarding school or going into the Olympic Tower building in New York where he has an unlisted office on the ninth floor. When he toured Disneyland with his kids, he was simply another proud father – the trip to Los Angeles was their reward for passing their exams.

Ghassan Shakir arranged one of the most controversial military deals of 75, recruitment of former members of the US Special Forces and other Vietnam war veterans by a private contractor, Vinnell Corporation of Los Angeles. Their brief: to train Saudi National Guard troops to protect the oil fields. It was a deal that set off alarm bells. Was this a straight mercenary outfit or a 'spooks' set up? And if so, who was spying on whom? Who were the Saudis protecting the oil fields from – America, Iran, Israel, internal sabotage? Ghassan Shakir's name cropped up almost unnoticed in American Congressional hearings; there's been no newspaper publicity about him since. That's no coincidence. If Arabs like Shakir start hitting the headlines, you know they might be on the way out, and he certainly isn't.

Shakir, thirty-nine, grandson of an officer in the Ottoman army, is a graduate of St John's College, Cambridge, where he read law and English literature, won blues for cricket, soccer and tennis and stuffed a potato up the exhaust of Princess Margaret's car. He's something of a sport, enormously smooth with a husky velvet voice that, should he run short of other things to do, would make soap powder advertisements sound like exercises in erotica.

I get to like Ghassan in Riyadh. Without saying a word he somehow lets me know that he sympathises with the ridiculous spectacle of a Western woman covering her head with black chiffon (by now I've been reduced to that to make life easier; it saves hostile stares). More important, he neither flaunts nor hides the fact that he drops in on some of the most powerful princes in Riyadh whenever he feels like it, and he neither bluffs nor hedges when asked about delicate matters. This is the man who arranged Vinnell's contract for a commission that an American congressman, already inured to Saudi customs, called 'suspiciously large' and he sits in his black cushioned office offering endless cups of sweetened tea and bitter cardomum coffee and I suspect that he genuinely doesn't understand what the fuss was all about.

'Why can't you understand that this isn't the West, it's Arabia?

There's nothing evil or wrong in taking a commission for your services on deals like this. Ultimately all arms arrangements are made between governments. I've fixed dozens of much bigger contracts before and as far as Vinnell are concerned I've spent eight years helping to establish them here. This contract could have come up anywhere in the Middle East. It's not my fault that it came up in Saudi Arabia and the American press has such a phobia about our country that there was a ridiculous fuss. God has bestowed on this country fantastic wealth and I like to think I'm serving my country and my God.'

His business mind works like a computer; his soul is troubled. 'Technology doesn't have all the answers; human beings count more. You can build 45,000 prefabricated schools in a year and they're worthless without the teachers who feel for children. You can look at the buildings and think you know it all. But you will never know on what soil you will die. You will never know what sex the embryo is in consummation. Suddenly you don't see the sun and then the sun rises. Our religion is perfection but only God is perfect. In business, in politics, human beings can't be perfect. We don't judge them harshly for that; only for forgetting the perfection of God.'

To listen to the Saudis, who bring Him into the conversation rather a lot, Allah must have a very keen nose for business. But they're not having me on – don't confuse the beliefs of a man like Shakir with Richard Nixon having Billy Graham home publicly to pray at the White House and then going on with life and Watergate. Most Saudis don't see a contradiction between what they believe in and what they do. Islam cuts so deeply into their being that they haven't grasped that if they're not careful they'll soon be serving two gods – Allah and Mammon. It often sounds outrageous to me to hear Allah join us as we chat about deals; many Saudis truly don't understand why I react as I do. This country is founded on a religion, a demanding, exacting religion. Apparently there couldn't be an arms business if Allah hadn't had it in mind.

Shakir's divorced from his first wife; he hasn't remarried. He travels the world with his Italian girl friend but he wouldn't dream of bringing her here to Riyadh. It's not out of fear of offending his patrons and princes. It's out of respect. For Shakir has very powerful patrons and he's far more influential than he appears, in many ways now more significant than Khashoggi. Shakir's the only Saudi allowed to hold an official position in a foreign government (he's adviser to the Sultan of Oman) and his more regular businesses are an empire in themselves – among the many companies under his aegis in Saudi (Reynolds Tobacco, Middle East Airlines, Air France etc) is Rover. Now Rover, as part of the British Leyland group, was on the blacklist when he took the agency but military needs and spare parts supersede idealism.

The son of a self-made millionaire, Shakir is a self-made multi-millionaire: 'I started from zilch really. My father lent me his surname and that was my only capital.' You have to be well in with the al-Saud to handle Shakir's business deals, and he is – he'll tell you openly that he's off to see the foreign minister, Prince Saud, at home and the foreign minister's staff talk warmly of Shakir.

Shakir doesn't talk so warmly of foreigners: 'Believe me, I feel shame as an Arab when I see the way some of us behave in London. But I have no respect whatsoever for some Westerners when they come here and don't bother to learn the first ways of the country. For instance, in the Arab world you never cross your legs and put the sole of your shoe in a man's face – it's an insult. If anyone older comes into the room you get up. You'd be astonished how these small things have a bearing. Westerners come here with no respect for our customs so they have no right to point fingers at Arabs who go to their countries and behave like wild animals.' I'm not surprised the foreign minister's staff go for Shakir as they do. As an independent middle-man, he's able to say quietly what most of them would probably love to shout if only they weren't diplomats.

But there are some middle-men whose names you don't even mention in the offices of the princes they know or serve. The only way to show you how mysterious some other businesses are in Riyadh, how exceptional Shakir's directness is, is to tell the curious tale of a prince, a luncheon party and how I gaffed by mentioning the luncheon in the prince's office.

The prince holds one of the biggest jobs in Riyadh and he's promised to see me – this is a real promise, after a while you do get to know the difference. Unfortunately, he's forever off to the airport to greet some foreign head of state, but to pass the time another Saudi fixer I've met takes me to lunch with the prince's business manager.

The Saudi fixer I'll have to call Muhammad. He might suffer a certain discomfort if I name him and the Saudis aren't going to like my telling this story anyway. Muhammad started life guarding his village's flock of sheep. He now owns a flock of limousines and an intricate web of companies. I couldn't even begin to guess how he evolved from shepherd to one of Riyadh's big-time wheeler-dealers.

Our host I'll call Abdullah. He's an unprepossessing man with an unprepossessing home. It's a strange party; some American executives are here because they're trying to lean on Muhammad to lean on Abdullah to lean on the prince to okay a huge programme they have in mind.

The twinkly-eyed Muhammad takes barely concealed delight in the awkward way that the overweight American executives sit on the floor trying to enjoy the traditional Arab feast of a sheep whose teeth grin macabrely on its platter. The grim-faced host utters no word in English. The Americans shower unctuous compliments on him through Muhammad. Not a business word crosses the sheep's teeth, but the spectre of money hangs over us all. Host Abdullah unexpectedly turns his glittering eyes towards me (one of the first-ever female guests at his table). 'What did you expect before you arrived in our country?'

The American jaws tightened. Since I don't want anything out of Abdullah and have long since decided that Saudis prefer honesty (in small doses) I reply: 'Grim-faced, frightening men with no sense of humour. Have you ever seen a photograph in a Western newspaper of a smiling Saudi?' The American jaws freeze. Abdullah tears apart another bit of sheep flesh. Then he asks if I would like to see his wife. A singular honour; an old-fashioned Saudi like Abdullah never mentions his wife in front of foreign men.

She's crouched in the outhouse over huge cooking pots. She's young and exquisitely beautiful. Her husband calls out for his troop of children and without a word leads the way upstairs. He points to a vicious-looking wooden truncheon hanging on his bedroom door. Through an English-speaking daughter he communicates the fact that it's for beating his children. It's feasible. He has an unflinching, brutal face and a bark for a voice. A moment of Dr Spock-conditioned horror. Then his children can't keep up the charade. There are peals of laughter. Abdullah guffaws. 'How could I ever hit a child of mine? Look at them. What do you think I am – a monster?' Yes.

But this monster has abruptly been transformed into a human being. The man with his guard down will never be seen by his other guests downstairs, now beside themselves with worry. I understand their worry – later. Abdullah handles millions of dollars' worth of investments and businesses for the prince he works for. These businesses operate in areas in which the prince has absolute power over the granting of contracts. Of course a few of the contracts come Abdullah's way; it's some Saudi princes' way of lining their own pockets without being too crass about it. As a result, Abdullah in his unprepossessing home is no pauper himself.

I gaffe by not realising just how unofficial a channel Abdullah is for the prince's own money-making interests until after I try to leave a 'thank you' letter for him in the prince's official government office. There's a ghastly silence. His chef de cabinet in clipped tones professes never to have heard of him. I'm not astonished that I never do meet this particular prince.

I do have a bad time trying to keep away from the American fellow-guests. They're convinced that one way or another I've sunk their hopes. That's how important princes can be in Riyadh. In the land where great riches are created by the loosing of the fertility demons from the West, the royals are Gods.

A pride of princes

This is the tale of three princes. All they have in common is what all Saudi princes have in common. From the moment they were old enough to understand anything, they understood that they were very special beings.

It is part of Bedu tradition that any man has access to his ruler and members of the rulers' family, to moan. No one could imagine a Welsh tramp marching in to Number 10 Downing Street to have a grumble at the prime minister, or an Appalachian family going along to the White House to complain to the president about the state of his fences. But this is Saudi and I didn't understand how fundamental a change it will be when fewer and fewer poor Saudis will be allowed in to the offices of the great at will (once government becomes more formal) until I went to lunch with Prince Abdullah bin Faisal al-Saud.

Prince Abdullah, eldest of Faisal's sons, is one of the few important old-style princes left. By the time he was born his father, then aged sixteen, had fought in desert wars, travelled to London to beard the British Foreign Secretary and seen the grave-scarred battlefields of Flanders. Abdullah was raised in desert ways and brought up in Riyadh when it was a walled-in mud city.

Today he lives in a small villa in Jiddah. There are no armed guards; any ragged Saudi can walk in. Abdullah used to have a palace until he separated from his wife. He gave it to her fully-furnished and she sold it to King Khalid for sixty million riyals.

No one has warned me that Abdullah is the only one of Faisal's sons to bear his image. It's uncanny and I can't conceal my shock. He understands at once. 'It's my curse,' he says with moving sadness, 'I see this face that was his every day that I look in the mirror. When he died the beating of my heart ceased. Did you ever hear of a man living with an unbeating heart?'

His room is full of men. Some have come to greet him. Some to seek his advice: they want to marry a daughter, need money, a job, they don't know what to do with a grant of land. He listens to each gravely; of course he'll help. A servant enters with a letter and tries to kiss his hand. Prince Abdullah snatches it away angrily but allows him to kiss his forehead instead. He's not that kind of prince.

When he smiles he displays a perfect set of dentures. As a young man a quack took out all his own teeth as a cure for some illness. His generation was too busy to send boys abroad when they were ill, too isolated to send them abroad to study (as all his own sons have done).

He has inherited his grandfather's love of practical jokes (no, I never thought of Ibn Saud as a jokester either). He soon launches into a few of his favourites. There was the time he was so fed up with some friends who were always pestering him to take them to the King's place for lunch that he arranged a picnic sixty miles out into the desert for them. 'We'll meet you there,' he promised. The friends tortured their Maserati over the sands to the rendez-vous. No one and nothing. They got back to town at midnight and never asked Abdullah for an invitation again. Then there was the one played against him in a hotel suite in Cairo – a friend got a woman with a sexy, alluring voice to telephone Abdullah and arrange to meet him. She described herself to make certain that she suited the royal taste – the bust of Jane Russell, the eyes of Marilyn Monroe, the walk of Lana Turner. He dressed himself up like a peacock, rushed over to meet this peach – to find a hag of about fifty-five who took hours to shake off.

Prince Abdullah's affability is deceptive. King Ibn Saud thought so much of him that he nicknamed him 'half the world' and his grandfather made him the country's first minister of health in 1952 to prove it. He was an outstanding administrator but left government under King Saud and never went back. He prefers business: he has the Saudi agencies for Sony and BMW, owns a pipe factory that actually exports in this country where every port and airport is clogged with imports. He's building Saudi's first motor assembly plant – for General Motors. He's got a feel for business and being the king's son helped to get him off the ground.

In the middle of his majlis is displayed his greatest treasure. It's a gold-trimmed model of his oil tanker, *Mecca*, just launched in Japan. It's the first truly Saudi tanker. But why, in the middle of a world recession, with nearly 400 supertankers laid up idle in waters all over the place, go to the expense of building a new one? The Saudi pride rides majestically across the bows of business sense. 'I want it Saudi. I want it good. I don't want something second-hand.'

We go into lunch as a bunch of T-shirted soccer players pitch up. Abdullah was converted to the game after the 48 Olympics in London and helped to sponsor the country's national team, now training under the Spanish ex-player, Puskas.

He writes poetry on the side and the legendary Egyptian singer, Umm Khalthoum, recorded three of his songs. In Arab terms that compares to Leonard Bernstein recording a symphony by President Ford.

Abdullah eats only boiled meats and yoghurt (they look disgusting but he isn't too offended when I pass in favour of the more usual spicy Middle Eastern fare). He usually eats in about ten minutes flat but as a sign of appreciation for unaccustomed female company, he lingers for over an hour talking, telling stories mostly against himself.

His heavy wrist watch (he calls it 'my handcuff') prompts the most moving. It cost a hundred riyals. It was a first anniversary present from his new second wife. His tale of his new marriage starts with his explanation that he'd been alone for many years after he parted from his first wife. 'I asked two young girls for their hands. Both said "no". Very wise. After all, look at me. I'm fifty-five years old and people call me uncle now.' He hates that. 'One of my cousins at teachers' training college told me of a classmate, a beautiful Bedu called Safwa. This girl had already rejected many handsome young men because she said that young men play around and she wanted an old one she could trust.

'I didn't do this thing through other people. I went straight to the girl's house and said "I'm old; you can trust me, and I want to marry you." She told me that she didn't love me but that she would. Very honest. I asked her father and we had the religious ceremony that day. After all for Prince Abdullah to visit her house without marriage would spoil her reputation.

'I took her out for a drive every day for three months. She lived at her father's house and I promised her that if, at the end of those months, she didn't want me, I would divorce her immediately. Not once in that time did I touch her, you understand? At the end of it, I asked her again and she said "yes" and came to be my wife.'

That was two years ago and now Safwa has given birth to Abdullah's only daughter. He had seven sons by his first wife (one of whom was killed in a shooting accident) and this daughter gives him unconcealed delight.

He shyly takes a picture of his wife out of a brown pocket-book to show; male guests aren't even allowed to peek. 'Every time I go out of the house I say to my wife "you are the stupidest girl in the world. You must be – you married me." '

The afternoon sun is calling Prince Abdullah to the unseen Bedu princess and to the black nothing of siesta time. 'I hate to waste time eating anything more than I need and even more I hate to sleep. I love the night when I can read and listen to music until dawn. I think there will be a long time ahead to be bored.'

In the long time ahead, men will only remember that there were once Arab princes like Abdullah bin Faisal.

A real geezer

In the summer of 1975, a former British professional footballer turned coach, George Smith, was twiddling his thumbs at home in the north of England when the telephone rang. A foreign voice claiming to be Prince Abdul Aziz bin Nasir told Smith that he was telephoning from Riyadh and that his older brother Abdullah would like to hear from him at the Carlton Tower Hotel in London. 'I just thought it was one of me mates taking the piss, so I told him to bugger off.' The patient prince phoned again (no mean feat from Riyadh).

This time, out of sheer curiosity, George rang the Carlton

Tower. He landed a contract worth £10,000 a year (plus heaps of extras, all tax free) to manage Abdullah's football team, Hilal, an amateur Riyadh affair. (Anyone wondering whether it would not have been easier, let alone cheaper, for Abdullah to telephone himself from London has not yet absorbed the illogicality of things Saudi.)

Smith found the players spoiled when he arrived in Riyadh. They didn't like being coached. They preferred banging the ball in the net. Smith yelled and cursed at them (soccer is an international four-letter language), ran them up and down the ground and wouldn't let them back into their air-conditioned dressing rooms until they had some order going. Hilal won their first match of the season.

'He's a heck of a guy my prince,' says Smith dangling his toes in a swimming pool, toasting his balding head. 'He's a real soccer man.' Prince Abdullah bin Nasir is the son of King Ibn Saud's twentieth son, Nasir, some time governor of Riyadh, now semi-retired and spending an unfortunate amount of time in hospital. His son Abdullah pursues a healthier outdoor life. He's patron of Hilal for a start. The 'amateur' players live in expensive houses and drive expensive cars, but it's Prince Abdullah's very own team and he's a generous man.

He's also one of the country's toughest, most experienced falconers. He's to be found every autumn afternoon taking the air in the back yard of his Riyadh palace sitting under his Bedu tent, sipping tea, reclining in a plastic deck-chair. For company he has his cronies and sixteen hooded fierce falcons (average cost: 3,000 dollars). It takes time to get pass his gate guards. They answer any stranger with a friendly 'no, he no in'. Being courteous, they don't like to challenge my right to visit.

Prince Abdullah, the hardy desert falconer and football fanatic, is a skinny, pale thirty-four-year-old who looks as though the first puff of wind would send him blowing away in his fine cotton thobe. His handshake is as firm as an old banana skin. The prince has a bad time at Hilal games. His royal awareness forbids him to cheer his team (although there was one never-to-be-forgotten occasion when his self-control broke and he actually waved an arm after a goal). But at the end of each game he's so tense with excitement that he runs with sweat and his knees shake.

His falcons are trained as hard as his footballers. He's training his newest himself – Habdan, a prize from Pakistan. 'Do you know that Sheikh Rashid of Dubai and his sons have spent a million dollars on falcons this season?' asks Prince Abdullah with the sniff that noble Saudis reserve for all mention of Gulf Arabs. 'But Habdan is the most beautiful bird of all. Look at its colouring; look at its eyes.' Unhooded, Habdan is as beautiful as Frankenstein. It's busy scratching His Highness's long, delicate, ungloved hand to ribbons. His Highness doesn't deign to notice. 'This is a bird of strength and of courage. It could fly 200 kilometres a day and still down another bird.' Abdullah's other favourite, Najla, has been sent to the seaside for a holiday. It's good for his nerves. He was temperamental last season and tended to pick and choose his hunting. His feathers were getting a bit tatty too and Riyadh makes him tense. The sea air might induce him to trade in the old for a new, faster plumage.

It's tea-time, so Magaad, the falcons' groom who's been with the prince for twenty years, brings on the raw meat. One by one, sixteen birds tear the flesh apart.

When this spectacle is over, Prince Abdullah goes along to the concrete hut next to the garage to see how his wife is enjoying her afternoon in there. Through the door of the tiny room stares a creature, flowing in traditional silken robes. She's Abdullah's only wife. 'I have the best; I don't need others.' His palace, built eight years ago for sundry million dollars, stands empty. It has the bare, temporary look of a place whose owners prefer to be elsewhere. Abdullah's off elsewhere right now; to one of those enigmatic business meetings royals go in for.

'My prince,' says George Smith, the burly English coach. 'I knew when I met him that I was going to go a bomb on him. He walked downstairs in the Carlton Tower Hotel wearing a sky-blue suit with that gorgeous wife of his in her skin-tight black and red trouser suit and I said to myself straight away: "Whhhoooaaa. That's one hell of a geezer." '

Climbing on the Bandar waggon

Some princes, like Abdullah bin Nasir, make no visible contribution to their country. They're part of the scenery. Others do. All of King Faisal's eight sons, for example. Captain Bandar (Prince Bandar bin Faisal) of the Saudi Arabian Royal Air Force, according to his superiors, is a brilliant officer – when he turns up for duty. He may or may not, depending on what else takes him when he wakes up. But, periodically, he makes an impressive contribution. Periodically, he also makes a contribution to the night-life of London that is impressive enough to make Warren Beatty seem like a stand-in. I had been warned against Bandar in London. 'Trouble,' they said.

Prince Bandar has arranged to carry me off to the desert. Naturally, learning fast about Saudi imprecision, I don't expect the outing to materialise. This is the first surprise: a driver turns up. I feel so safe in this city that I follow without so much as asking who sent him. Not for nothing do the Saudis boast that they have the lowest crime rate in the world. (At a price, but nothing is for free: I do not take up one thoughtful Saudi's invitation to a public execution.) About an hour down the road, shooting along the highway, I have a few misgivings. The driver is one of those silent types. The car turns off, bumping across the undulating dunes. We're in the middle of nowhere. Hello, I think, trouble. Wrong again.

Suddenly: four tents. No one around. In the distance a tall figure strides across the sand. The effect of the total silence (after the raucous abuse of Riyadh's traffic), the shimmering heat haze and the lone man with flowing robes and lofty bearing is straight out of Omar Sharif's arrival in *Lawrence of Arabia*. Prince Bandar's language on arrival is not. His silver-spangled dune buggy broke down some miles away.

The irritated princeling disappears into a tent where a servant has laid out a change of clothes. He reappears in a white Western trouser suit. He's stunningly handsome with an impressive body that snakes on to the soothing Persian rug on the tent floor, propped carelessly against cushions. Whatever he does the rest of the time, today Bandar has decided to play the perfect gentleman: serious, considerate, aware of being his father's son ('My father never told us what to do. We were always given a choice but we knew what he expected of us.')

He talks for hours, easily, sincerely, in English perfected by a private tutor in Princeton and in air-force messes in Britain. More servants pad round silently offering a banquet – rather better, he points out, than Queen Elizabeth's kitchens could manage when she had him to lunch at Buckingham Palace. He talks of his brothers with such respect and affection that it takes some time to realise that they're not all full brothers. Say 'queen' in Saudia Arabia, and everyone assumes you mean Bandar's mother Queen Iffat, Faisal's wife and companion for forty years. Few know the name of King Khalid's only wife and no one remembers that Faisal had another long-standing spouse, Hayya, at the same time as Iffat. Two of the Faisal sons are hers. It's hard for a Western woman to understand how Iffat and Hayya worked together for thirty years to make their children into one solid clump. (After Faisal divorced Hayya in 1940 he refused to see her again. Iffat did and still does.)

'I look at some of my father's brothers,' says Bandar, 'and I don't understand the way they fight among themselves. We were brought up to be close.' As tied as he is to his indulgent mother's apron strings, Bandar has tried marriage, to a first cousin. 'We were also brought up to have only one wife. It was different in the old days, marrying several was a way of uniting tribes and offering protection to women who would otherwise have no home but their father's. It's still better than casting them off and leaving them divorced and stranded as they do in America.'

Bandar's now divorced from his first cousin.

Western toys such as Maseratis, Lamborghinis, Ferraris may pass through Bandar's hands like grains of sand but women slip through much more swiftly. Under all his sophistication, Bandar bin Faisal is just another conservative Arab. We're sitting on a rug on top of a sand dune watching the sunset, discussing a girl who went out with a Saudi in London. She woke up the morning after she finally went to bed with him to find no Saudi but £500 under her pillow. Bandar thinks it serves her right for sleeping with a man who isn't her husband. He means it, at that moment, anyway.

He's had his minor humiliations too. There was the time he was driving his mother along the Riviera. He parked his Maserati while she went shopping and a passer-by gave him the nod: 'You Italian gigolos have a good time.' Even now he can't see the funny side of the story. 'You think that's amusing? Are you stupid?' I manage not to laugh at his fury about the episode in the Carlton in Cannes. 'An American woman came up to me in reception and propositioned me straight out. I explained that I was with five women already.' (His mother and sisters.) ' "You can manage another," she said. Do you wonder that I hate the idea of introducing European ways into my country?' No comment.

At midnight, another feast. 'Would you like a shower to freshen up?' asks Bandar. 'How do you get water for a shower in the desert?' 'Turn on the taps.' But of course, how silly. Bandar's hangers-on join us, two Lebanese brothers. One's a car mechanic, the other a sycophant. 'Bandar's my friend,' starts the sycophant. 'He has taken me in and I love him as a brother. Believe me I'm not getting any money out of it.' Bandar raises an eyebrow. It stops that conversation dead.

At three in the morning the rug is rolled up, the pump is turned off in the desert encampment bathroom (yes, it exists: fully equipped with shower, loo, basin and bidet) and we set off.

'Most of what you've heard about me in London isn't true.' He skids across the dunes, punishing yet another car. 'Do you know how many Prince Bandars there are? Last time I was there, I found a bill for a statue in solid gold that some Prince Bandar had sent to an actress. You English are so carried away by your own fantasies about us that some shops hand over goods worth a fortune to any Arab who calls himself a prince.'

London has one image of Bandar. Another sticks in my mind. It isn't the way we end up at the Lebanese brothers' home to find the woman Bandar calls 'his secret love' – their mother, a cross, blonde, middle-aged lady, covered in blankets and poodles with bows in their hair. She berates him for not showing up for dinner when he promises but while she's laying into him, the phone rings. It's a girl who knows that the Lebanese know Bandar. Could they fix her a date? Bandar nods meaning 'right now' and it's arranged.

It isn't that. It's the way, as the night hugged the desert before we rode back into Riyadh, he talked of his Lightning fighter pilot days during the Yemeni war. 'Do you know what they made me do after the raids, after it was all over? The commanding officer made us go down into the countryside and see what we had done. There were Yemenis who had been holed up in caves with no chance. The stench sickened me. You can't do that to a human being and then expect him to be a soldier. I'm a professional air force man but I don't believe in the military. I don't believe in wasting millions on weapons and keeping the best men in our country under arms. What a waste, what a world.'

Pity the poor princesses

Saudi Arabia's princesses are almost the last fairy-tale creatures left on earth. Sad, pathetic beings for the most part. They're shut away in palaces, soaked in luxury and loneliness. Officially it's as if they don't exist. 'King Saud', says the British Foreign Office's royal family tree, 'was the second king of Saudi Arabia; more than forty sons (and many daughters) survive him.'

Most princesses are doomed to a lifetime in parentheses. They wake in their gilded cages around noon, perhaps later, go for tea with other princesses and then wait for their royal husbands – who probably eat with the men anyway.

Princesses exist to marry cousins and produce princes (and more unlisted princesses). Slaves and wet-nurses looked after their mother's children. Nannies take care of theirs. That's progress. If Saudi folk talk of princes in hallowed terms, they don't talk at all of princesses. Just now and again a mention of one will flicker across a conversation. But slowly, very slowly, these sleeping beauties are stirring.

The house isn't big. By commuters' standards it's unimpressive. Inside a mixture of old and modern furniture stands awkwardly on deep-piled white carpet. None of it matches very well but it's homely. Family snapshots help. One in particular stands out: a moving colour photograph, more of an ikon, of an old man praying. It's King Faisal.

This is the home of his daughter, Princess Latifa. Her name means 'gentle' in Arabic. It suits her. She's gentle and plump, with the look of one who's been told for as long as she can remember that she isn't pretty. Not like her younger sister Lulua. You can see in an instant the generation gap that Saudi's rapid development has compressed to a few years. Latifa was once sent to school in London. Conservatives in her family objected to this experiment. She was brought back after a month and reared at home. Tonight she's wearing an ageing, black lace evening frock and a diamond and ruby pendant more suitable for a mayor's chain of office.

Lulua was a few vital years younger. She was allowed to go to a Swiss boarding school and on to a French finishing outfit. Her English is superb, her French fluent. She's elegantly arranged in Yves St Laurent decorated only with a languid air of boredom. She doesn't see much of her husband and hasn't much patience with her children. To look at Lulua is caviare, Latifa mere fish paste.

There are no flunkies around, no footmen, no guards. There are only four of us for dinner. Lulua, myself, Latifa and her husband – another al-Saud, Abdul Aziz al-Thaunayan, Mayor of Riyadh. He's another good-looker, thirty-six, with a BA from Cairo and a PhD from the London School of Economics. Faisal brought him up as his own son after his parents died. He and Latifa have been close for as long as they can remember. Unusually, they still are.

Latifa has a genuine warmth that starts to show the moment her only son, ten, a small replica of his father, creeps into the dining room to say goodnight. Later we tiptoe into his bedroom to make sure all is well and then Latifa shows me round her home: the one guest room, the serenely plain master bedroom with rare silk screens hanging above the double bed.

Over dinner and afterwards, on the terrace overlooking the swimming pool, Latifa opens up even more. Not that she says much while her sophisticated sister and high-powered husband discuss the intricacies of urban living. But every now and again a smile lights her whole face, and when she opens her mouth it's because she has something to say.

Lulua gets on to the thorny question of the image foreigners harbour of Saudi Arabia. 'The first question they always ask me is, "do you live in a tent?" I ask you. Do I look as though I live in a tent?' Hardly.

'Perhaps,' contributes Latifa timidly, 'it's because they don't know much about us.'

Lulua complains at length about the way Western newspapers emphasise the fact that thieves lose their right hands here. 'They never bother to mention that it needs two witnesses to catch the thief in the act, or that the hand is severed only after the third conviction.' It's Latifa who asks me how many one-handed men I've seen and then asks her husband how many choppings there have been recently. 'Two in three years in Riyadh,' he answers. (As mayor he should know; I suppose he doesn't lie.)

And this gentle princess has in her own way made a contribution to the status of her cousins in Riyadh. With her mother, Queen Iffat, and older sister, Sara, she founded the capital's first women's club: 'The Saudi Progress Society'. She's now actively involved in it and its main patron. A charitable institution in which princesses change orphans' nappies, make and sell embroidered doilies and run a hairdressing service might not sound much of an earth-shattering advance. But in Riyadh, where there are no cinemas, theatres, clubs, where women never enter restaurants or hotels, it was a huge step forward for Faisal's daughter to become something of a public figure.

Princess Latifa looks after her son herself. She would love to be able to have more. Most other, more fertile princesses don't see their numerous offspring from one day to the next—Vickie Caldwell sees more of some of them than their mothers. Along a bumpy, unmade road outside Riyadh, there's an arena with a racing camel tethered by the entrance and forty-seven stunning Arab horses stabled inside around two riding rings. This is Miss Vickie's back-yard, where chauffeurs and nannies deliver royal children each day to train under the long, leggy blonde horsewoman from Texas.

Officially, Vickie Caldwell doesn't exist. She came here on an aid teaching programme thirteen years ago, stayed and the stable sort of happened. She can't run a riding school; co-education? You're joking. She can't run a business – that's not on either. A lawyer (now in the cabinet) presented her with the typically Saudi way out: 'Vickie, you live in a house, you have a back-yard, you keep horses as pets and some of your friends' children stop by to ride them.'

She has very royal 'friends'. These small children demand a lot of themselves, have no fear and absolutely no feeling for the horses they ride. And these aren't docile, hack ponies; they're temperamental Arabs. Princess Bandri sits astride a beast of 15½ hands. At three years old, she already never considers that some living creature won't obey her will. Nearby, Princess Haifa, a few years older, is in trouble. Her stallion is determined to throw her. 'Keep calm, Haifa! It's your own fault; you weren't concentrating,' yells Vickie through her megaphone. 'Just show him you mean business.' Slowly the groom edges towards the animal and seizes the reins. Haifa pushes the groom away.

By the time she can be bullied off her horse, her brother, Khalid, is bubbling with excitement. These are the children of the foreign minister, Prince Saud bin Faisal. Their uncle Khalid has sent his young namesake a staggering black racehorse as a present, 'Queen of the Wind'. Vickie, who spent the summer working out Prince Khalid's horses down in Abha (the Switzerland of Saudi Arabia, trees, mountains and all) handpicked him. Haifa runs round scrounging sugar lumps. Only Khalid hands them over. Wouldn't Haifa like a present too? She looks surprised: 'Boys have racehorses, not girls.' Conditioning starts earlier thàn riding lessons.

Sitting on the side-lines, chattering among themselves, are a group of well-dressed European women. They're nannies. Fiona is a no-nonsense import from England who tries to run her nursery with old-fashioned strictness. Annette, an Australian, is a more affectionate, brassy type. While the children study in the mornings, the nannies meet by one of their palace swimming pools. They travel with their charges; it means de luxe holidays around Europe. But they're still paid semi-servants, a fact not lost on these imperious royal children.

'Does their mother ever play with them?' I ask one nanny. 'Play with them? We haven't seen her for three days. She's either sleeping or off to someone else's palace. Still at least my princess is better than some. She doesn't spend the day on drugs like others we know. They have a miserable life for all their money. I wouldn't be a princess if you paid me.'

Princess Fawzia wouldn't not be one for anything. She's wanted to be a princess since she was a middle-class Egyptian kid playing make-believe with dolls. Fawzia made it to princess when she married one of the king's brothers, Prince Fawaz, governor of the district of Mecca.

A dinner party is underway at a beach house in Jiddah. The host, one of Jiddah's richest merchants, has provided a buffet table loaded with delicacies and an equally generous supply of alcohol. There's a hush over the sea next to the floodlit swimming pool. This is an Occasion. All of top-drawer Jiddah will be here, but that's nothing. Prince Fawaz and Princess Fawzia are coming and they very, very rarely go to commoners' parties. The excuse for this outing is a farewell for the new ambassador to Washington. What could be an idyllic evening turns out to be appalling. The mere presence of royalty injects it with stiff formality.

Prince Fawaz with his drooping eyes, drooping moustache, drooping shoulders, clutches his whisky tumbler for dear life. He's as limp as a stale stick of celery. It's hard to see where he once got the backbone to go over to Nasser's socialist Egypt for two years during the height of the Cairo-Riyadh feud. Still, that's in the past. Fawaz is an example of how the Factory re-absorbs its black sheep. Egypt was a lapse, that's all. Fawaz clings for support tonight to his whisky (which as governor he's ultimately responsible for confiscating and destroying) and to the only left-over from his Egyptian lapse – his forceful wife.

Princess Fawzia is royal enough for them both. Living her part to the hilt, she sweeps into the room, rustling in white chiffon, wearing a crown of rich black hair, offering a large white hand with one emerald rock on her little finger. Her carriage is superb; her smile demolishingly gracious. She's nearly six foot tall, an unnerving phenomenon owing more to Madame de Pompadour than the image of passive Saudi princesses. When the couple finally go at two in the morning (no one can leave before them), she bequeaths the memory of great powerful shoulders supporting a pair of magnificently royal breasts.

Princess Fawzia never allows her breasts to pass unnoticed. It's afternoon; she's receiving a few women at home, another singular honour. There's a long wait in her Louis Quinze drawing room (what else?). It's a stage set for a star. For once the antiques aren't repro but real. The bric-a-brac is spot on for this Versailles-style sailing ship of a woman. There are eighteenth-century enamel boxes on the tables, silver goblets for the guests' orange juice. It's as if someone master-minded the background for how a royal should live. The mistakes are small, but significant. The slightly shiny wallpaper would better suit an enchanting bathroom. The silver vases bloom with red roses – plastic roses.

Princess Fawzia makes another of her stupendous entrances. She's really good at them. Conversation revolves around her ample bosom. Most princesses have an obsession with things medical. Fawzia carries it a stage further. She has the confidence of the very grand who never so much as doubt that intimate details about her breasts will fascinate the drawing room. They have been felt and kneaded by some of the finest consultants.

It needs money to coat this exotic royal life style. But Fawaz is not just prince but governor of Mecca. This is boom-time. He's having to work five hours a day when not so long ago two would suffice.

But the petty cash and affairs of state seem far away from the drawing room of Princess Fawzia and the monologue about her breasts. For once she doesn't have a sister-in-waiting for company.

Fawzia can't have children (she can't have everything) and her adopted son is staying with his mother (one of her many sisters) in Cairo. Not one of her visitors would dare suggest to this Junoesque statue with her marble white skin and royal bearing that she come over for a meal if she's lonely. She's graciousness itself, but loneliness is the price she must pay (occasionally) for drawing an absolute line between royalty and commoners.

I'm never to see the like of Fawzia again during the journey. It's a mixed blessing. Nowhere else is unreal in quite the same way as Saudi Arabia. That's what makes it so intense and so compelling. All these versions of princesses are like figures from Hollywood in the 30s. Like Hollywood then, Saudi Arabia has nothing to do with whatever else is going on outside.

The rise of the meritocrats

If you had had nothing better to do on 9 Shawal 1396 (14 October 1975, Gregorian calendar), and had taken a look at the new and largest cabinet in the history of the Saudi kingdom, you might have assumed that royalty was being over-run by the hoi-polloi.

Out of twenty-five ministers there are now only seven high-nesses. But the others, those with the even more unfamiliar names, they all have links somewhere to the al-Saud. Two, for instance, are of the al-Sheikh family.

That doesn't sound like anything much except more confusion to me at first. But to the Saudis being an al-Sheikh is streets ahead of an English nobleman being able to trace his lineage back to the sixteenth century. It's not just like being admitted to the Royal Enclosure at Ascot in the days when that still counted for something; it's like having an irrevocable season ticket to the place. No amount of divorces, bad marriages or whatever could wipe an al-Sheikh off the Top Snobs' list of Saudi Arabia.

This family is directly descended from al-Wahhab, the austere, puritanical preacher and wandering scholar of the eighteenth century who didn't have much luck until he ran into a minor tribal leader with control of an oasis and access to guns. What a combination – water, shot and religion. The two men got together and between them they over-ran most of the peninsula. Al-Wahhab gave his name to Wahhabism, the Saudis' own Islamic sect and the minor tribal leader was an al-Saud. That's where it all started.

So here we are, a couple of centuries later, and there they are with two al-Sheikhs in the cabinet. They fill two of the most important jobs: Higher Education, for one, Agriculture and Water, the other. Bearing in mind the fortune the Saudis spend importing food and skilled labour and on producing, finding, even buying water, the al-Sheikh are sitting on two major ministries.

And those other ministers? They nearly all come from merchant families made rich by swimming within the tentacles of the al-Saud octopus. No outsiders here. Slowly, though, middle class (by Saudi standards) lads are being hand-picked by the al-Saud and groomed for stardom.

The first to be put under contract, of course, was Ahmad Zaki Yamani, that global piece of oil property. For a while he was the only Saudi most people had ever heard of – thousands of column inches reported his every statement; foreign affairs men pored over his every word with the dedication of code-breakers. Does he mean that the West should have all the oil it wants? Does he want to push the prices up, bring them down or keep them steady? Will he this, will he that? And the irony is that Zaki Yamani has never been able to move an inch (well, two inches) on his own initiative without the king or crown prince's go-ahead. Yamani's a commoner, so back in history (the sixties) he could be dandled before the Western media in a way that was then considered undignified for royalty. He was a puppet, not the string puller. But every now and again he will pull the odd string of his own behind the scenes.

I suspect Yamani has a lot to do with my being here at all. He was one of my main targets for those letters of intent I sent aeons ago when I was still knocking hard on that invisible door they have in those invisible walls. There was one sentence in my letter that would sting Yamani in particular: it was that one about 'in the West, there is an urgent need to overcome the simple, even caricatured images of the Arab world'.

He still hasn't forgotten the time during his globe-trotting, oil crisis days when an American paper reported that he travels with his own army of bellydancers, gourmet chefs and servants. Zaki Yamani travels with his kids (sometimes), his new wife (less often) but in the hectic early seventies the only man he travelled with was his right hand man, my friend from the Carlton Tower and Curzon Street – Ibrahim Obaid.

That was September in London. This is Shawal in Riyadh. Ibrahim comes to pick me up at the hotel. He looks quite different in his national dress. In a Western suit, he's impressive. In his thobe he looks rather scruffy. But he's still the same grave, slightly vain Obaid. By now, I'm so confused that anyone, anything, familiar is reassuring. That's not the only reason I'm relieved to see him.

I've been calling Yamani's office every day, and every day they say Obaid isn't in Riyadh. But I know he is. I've already seen him for lunch; Souad's still in London and he's taken me to his brother's home (who's also abroad) for lunch. There's nowhere else for us to go. Ibrahim wouldn't dare compromise himself (let alone me) by eating with me in public so we have to steal illicitly into his brother's house to be able to sit and talk. We talk about everything – except Yamani.

This evening, he senses that I'm feeling the need to touch or feel something I can recognise from that former life back in Europe. He doesn't say anything; he drives me to his brother's home and without a word puts on a video of the Boston Symphony Orchestra playing Mahler. I can't say whether he likes it or he's bored stiff; he wouldn't show me either way. That's the measure of the courtesy and the silences of the Saudis. Slowly, I'm learning that you can't be with these people by any standards I understand – but that's not all bad, far from it. In the hours I spend 'illicitly' with Ibrahim, he doesn't so much as touch me, except to shake my hand goodbye. There's no physical contact and only unspoken mental contact.

That's only half of his consideration. Obaid has an important

official banquet tonight. I'd never guess from his calm exterior.
He allows the familiar music to work on me; offers a cold drink
and when he senses, correctly as usual, that I feel better he drives
me back to the hotel.

I ask him why I can't get hold of him at Yamani's office. He
doesn't answer. I needn't have wasted my breath. Direct questions
rarely get direct answers if they get any at all. As I'm getting out
of the car at the hotel, Ibrahim says quietly, so quietly that I
almost miss it, 'Call the Ministry tomorrow. Ask for Sheikh
Zaki's office. His Excellency is waiting to see you.'

His Excellency Sheikh Ahmad Zaki Yamani works on the
ground floor of his Ministry. It's marble and white and would be
very tidy except for the armed soldiers littering the corridors. His
ante-room is crowded with some of the top people of Saudi who've
been waiting to see him – the head of the Western section of the
Foreign Office and I have the most interesting chat about labour
unions in Britain (he knows far more about Jack Jones than I do).
It passes the evening hours.

At nine o'clock I'm shown into the largest office I see anywhere
in Riyadh. Behind the desk is a grey-faced, ashen man, almost
dropping with fatigue – on top of that he's got flu. I look at him.
He looks at me. Those famous eyes aren't exaggerated by the
newspaper reports. He's attractive all right.

His voice is like one of those records they sell to put you to
sleep – if I'm not careful I'll drop off and I don't trust him not
to then put me through a third-degree interrogation. He takes his
time to see that I'm not going to relax that far and that I'm not
remotely interested in talking oil. He smiles even more broadly.
'I think I'm going to take you to my home and later my wife and I
will take you to a party. You'll feel easy there; it won't be your
first.' It's the first time we've talked. It's about the fourth time
we've seen one another.

Yamani's one of 'The Set'. It's the substitute for the tribal
and family security blankets he had to leave behind in his native
Hijaz (the coastal strip, another world away from this desert-
locked government capital) when King Faisal picked him out and
made him oil minister at thirty-one.

We drive to his home; or rather he drives me home. He lives in a suite in the side of my hotel. It's his permanent and only place in Riyadh. It has its own entrance, a side-door in a completely dark alleyway surrounded by trees. I'm surprised. 'Aren't you worried about security? Any nut could easily take a shot at you here.' Yes, it's tactless; Yamani was by Faisal's side when he was killed. The man shrugs: 'Allah decides our fate. It's not for me to worry. I hate the soldiers at the Ministry. I will not live with them here.'

How things change. A few weeks later Yamani's one of the ten oil ministers kidnapped at another of those Vienna OPEC dos. Three people are killed and he's held prisoner on board a plane for days afterwards. When he next goes to America (for top level negotiations to, hopefully, conclude Saudi's hundred per cent take over of Aramco) he point blank refuses to arrive until he's assured that 1,100 acres of the Panama City Bay Point Yacht and Country Club in Florida will be criss-crossed by plain and uniformed police with shotguns and walkie-talkies. Now he's security-conscious abroad, less fatalistic.

But there's still no armed guard outside his Riyadh home. Allah's more reliable in Saudi Arabia. Yamani feels safe here, physically. Emotionally, he's not doing so well. He's never been terribly close to the half-brother of his hero and father-figure, King Faisal. Now the atmosphere between Yamani and Crown Prince Fahd is common gossip in Riyadh.

Yamani opens his front door and calls out to his wife. His new wife. Meritocrats spiralling upwards here run into the same problem as their Western counterparts; they outgrow their first wives. Yamani married his old one when he was a lonely law student in New York; they've been separated for nine years. They're not divorced (she'd lose out financially) but he spent a long time alone before he married again. He's been lonely. Cooking (he has aspirations to Cordon Bleu), writing poetry, studying the Koran fills the time, but cuddling his disgustingly snuffly black Pomeranians hardly amounts to a relationship.

That's in Riyadh. In the West, his life is different. This veteran of a thousand press conferences, famed as a playboy with flatteringly cut suits and hairstyling is best known for such personal touches as That Night in Harrods. The Queen's favoured department store stayed open specially; long enough for him to spend some £35,000 working through a (for him) trifling shopping list. Shortly afterwards Yamani glided out smoothly to London airport in his chauffeur-driven limousine with a coal delivery lorry (that had been stopped in the streets and persuaded to oblige) following behind bearing his booty.

That's the Yamani image abroad so it doesn't stagger me in Riyadh to learn from one of his close friends that this celebrity is totally mixed up as an individual. He feels safe only in Saudi but his experiences in the West are fast turning him into an outsider even with The Set.

Yamani's friends were and are very fond of his first wife. As often happens, they take exception to the fact that at forty-five she's alone and he's with a much newer model. A young girl of twenty-four, formerly a biology student he picked out in Beirut – Tammam. The new Mrs Yamani is quite something.

I don't learn much about her at our first encounter. She's dressed to kill, smothered with make-up but hangs back simpering rather shyly. After Zaki's had a short rest, Tammam gathers her black cloak (managing not to put it on as ostentatiously as a woman putting on her first mink coat), winds a suspicion of black chiffon round her hair and her husband drives us away. The Set is waiting.

Falling in with The Set

To explain the shock of any gathering of The Set, it's worth a short diversion. The Ministry of Information has sponsored a glossy, coffee-table spectacular, *The Kingdom of Saudi Arabia*. Pictures of women were ripped out of the unfortunate author's dummy until there was only one left – a woman heavily veiled à la laundry bag. In this tense, religious capital, you rarely glimpse women on the streets. Somehow I still assume that under the black ugliness lurks more ugliness. Perhaps the few unveiled women I've seen so far are exceptional?

I walk into the living room of a small home. It glitters with beautiful women. It hurts my eyes to see them all at once. They're decked out in the brightest evening robes Europe can invent. There's hardly a woman who isn't ravishingly layered with make-up. Were it not for the men's thobes and head-dresses I could be anywhere in the world where rich, over-dressed women gather. That's until the atmosphere gets through to me.

Mixed gatherings are new to Riyadh. It's like being with teenagers at dancing class. There's the same shyness, the edginess of not knowing how to act with the opposite sex. It's so infectious that after a few of these parties, I find it almost impossible to talk to men myself. When one man comes over to where I'm sitting, I feel ashamed somehow – almost as if I'm doing something dirty in the act of conversation. The undercurrent of sex permeates such gatherings by the very absence of its acknowledgement.

With maybe forty people here, the place gets hot despite air-conditioning. But this is Riyadh; necks are high, sleeves are long. A woman wearing a woollen three-piece from Paris won't take off her long-sleeved cardigan; her tank top below is sleeveless. It's like Victorian England all over again where the mere sight of an ankle bred fantasies of desire.

Every arriving couple goes round shaking hands stiffly. Both men and women get up to go through their greetings. The bobbing up and down gets a bit much: when I say stiffly, I mean it. A woman who's just returned from three years in Beirut, from a nightmare of bloodshed, is greeted by the other women she grew up with as if they'd never met.

There are great bowls of cigarette packets – every brand imaginable. It's offensive to smoke your own. In the West you're offered peanuts; here you're offered nicotine poisoning. By this time I'm on five packets a day myself (from one at home) so I'm not complaining. Women sit, talk and chain smoke together. A four for bridge is made up in another room; mental relaxation for some, a way of avoiding desegregated chit chat for others.

A peaceful-looking man sits on a couch puffing away at his pipe.

He's General Zuhair, the air force brass who, with another general now retired, were known to Northrop's headquarters as 'Trumpet and Geranium' in coded messages sent between Riyadh and Century City concerning some £250,000 private arrangements over fighter plane contracts. He's such a friendly, unaffected man. Dr Hasham Abdul Ghaffar joins us; he ran a lucrative dental clinic until he became deputy minister for health. Then his partner ran it and they split the profit fifty-fifty. But he hasn't been made minister in the new shuffle; his nose is out of joint so he's going back to drill richly in his dental retreat.

Hasham's married to Sharifa (a title) Fatma Mandili. Women, incidentally, don't change their names when they get married here. 'Of course not,' says one, 'your name is your identity, your personality. Why should you lose it?'

Fatma's a stunning Jackie Onassis type, the first woman university teacher in Riyadh, the first woman radio broadcaster and a Hashimite (Hijaz's ruling family kicked out by Ibn Saud). She's studying for a master's degree in Beirut and produces a red leather-bound volume of her thesis: 'The Arab element in Tennyson.' It sums up everything: this woman bedecked for a ball while having a few friends in for supper, poring in private over this most Victorian of poets.

It's interesting to note what people mention first when they talk of Sharifa Fatma; some say 'she's a Hashimite' in tones of awe, family names counting for so much. Others dig at the way she hogged Teddy Kennedy's attention when he was in town. Men will often say, 'she's the man of the family', thereby explaining away her 'unfeminine', unconcealed intelligence.

While dutifully reading Fatma's thesis, I keep a careful eye on Zaki and Tammam Yamani. He's sitting on the floor, as usual, with his head-dress off, his short greying hair swaying in time to the sinuous music. He's playing belote (a card game favoured by old ladies in faded novels) with Tammam. No wonder she's not one of The Set's favourites – she's about as self-effacing as Bianca Jagger.

Almira Nazer is one of their favourites – even though she's another of the new wives brought in by an older meritocrat made good. She's twenty-five, has long chestnut hair, a fifteen-year-old's face and there's nothing swanky about her at all.

Her husband's putting up some competition for Yamani. The oil minister's no longer the only teacher's pet: His Excellency Hisham Nazer is juggling for top billing with the al-Saud. Nazer is the confident (his enemies say conceited) resourceful minister of planning who produced the 663-page script for the next five-year, multi-billion-dollar Saudi epic – 'The Development Plan 1395–1400', subtitled 'In the name of God the merciful and compassionate'.

God was jolly merciful last time. The five-year plan before this didn't get more than eighteen per cent of its future shock into existence. If Nazer achieves that it'll still radically change the country. It means importing foreigners wholesale to work this jolting change. How can you do that and at the same time realise the plan's stated number one development goal: 'To maintain the religious and moral values of Islam?'

To look at Nazer leaning back in a chair, watching Almira with pride and talking easily to friends, you wouldn't think he had a care on his mind. But I've seen Nazer in his office too; I can appreciate the contrast of his working and private life.

His Excellency Hisham Nazer works in another pristine ministry, a prototype of tomorrow's Riyadh. No Bedu would wander in here to gossip or moan. Nazer's so businesslike, he's even abolished the serving of tea and coffee. After Riyadh's other hangouts where every office is as matey and liquid as a lorry drivers' pull-up, Nazer's ministry comes as a douse of cold water. On top of that, his conversation is as speedy as a dum-dum bullet.

Few visiting Westerners, their contracts at the mercy of his five-year plan, have the faintest clue how it came into being. The monumental ambition of it is staggering. The minister in charge doesn't lack assurance in his task. He bears the mark of the form swot who rose to be head boy of Victoria College, Cairo. The British boarding school in Egypt that raised future ministers, kings and presidents on a life of cold showers at 6.30 a.m., team spirit and canings for wearing brown shoes with the grey school uniform (Nazer still remembers the day he got whacked).

He knew as a small boy that he was going to make it to this rosewood desk at the top: 'I just had a hunch that it would be this way.' He should be content; his face, the receding part above the jutting chin, is creased with worry. So it should be.

Don't think a great deal of thought hasn't gone into chiselling Nazer's weighty tome (the '1984' of Arabia). For months before it was written he organised dinner parties in the secrecy of Riyadh homes. Various young men from ministries, business, thinkers, idealists, cynics, working royals got together over the rice and lamb to chew over their country's future. At first they met weekly. Towards the end almost daily. The Hampstead set of Riyadh were trying to work out where they wanted the country to go. Outsiders were flown in – mainly from America but from Europe, Egypt, anywhere where someone had twopence worth of planning to contribute.

At the end of all this, Hisham Nazer offered the Cabinet four possible plans: 'Naturally they rejected the first three and accepted the most difficult, the most complicated and the most challenging' says Nazer with resignation, 'but even if it's only a dream, isn't it worth having dreams?' They also chose the most frightening to Saudis. More of a nightmare than a dream. How much change can you absorb overnight? It even frightens Nazer. Fortunately for everyone, after all that effort the Saudi government suggested in March 76 that it was unofficially abandoning the plan – not for lack of cash, for sensible lack of nerve. Even so, huge portions of it had already been signed and were underway.

'Don't you think I don't know that we're in danger of losing a tremendous heritage,' says Nazer. 'Our family unity is our heritage and the strength of our religion. People ask me why an important ministry like this stops for prayer time. I say coffee's out but if it will take us a few more years to make progress if we pray, that's fine.'

He's on thin ice when he talks about family unity – what with that discarded first wife and his second young one, Almira. He picked her himself when she was a medical student at Cairo University. She stayed on in Cairo for two years to qualify with Nazer's approval. He's one of the rare Saudi men that feminists might approve of – no question of her quitting her career for his sake. Now she has a small son and their house is one of the few in Riyadh that could make *House and Garden*.

With his polished, delightful wife and his own lovely, husky voice and American-style vitality, Nazer's destined for a starring role in his country's attempt to make itself liked abroad. Hisham does his duty with goodwill trips but he's discouraged: 'I've studied in the States, I know how hard it is for our people to understand your culture in the West. But some time I don't think anyone in the West wants to bother to try to understand ours.' His attitude hardens every time he goes off and comes back to his office to find letters from people he met abroad. They're not thanking him or expressing interest in seeing him again; they're offering to sell him real estate in Switzerland or the family heirlooms.

It's no wonder that Nazer needs the relaxation of evenings with The Set. It's not much relaxation for me; it's the nearest he'll get to it in Riyadh.

'You know what I mean?'

The Set eats late. Midnight is normal. I've never seen so much food as I do at these little suppers. It makes most people's idea of a Sunday lunch look like aid for the starving. Here's a whole sheep, chicken, vegetables, meat balls – enough for a few hundred.

Almira Nazer, wafting pale chiffon, her gentle voice chatting over the buffet plates, looks tired. That's not surprising. She's the only working woman in the room. Every morning at seven she reports to a local hospital where she's employed as a paediatrician. It may be traditional 'women's work' but at least it's work and Hisham's very proud of his trendy spouse. The Nazers exchange a quick glance; he nods to the door. He makes a point of saying: 'Sorry, we'll have to go. I have a working wife, you know.'

The Yamanis are back on the floor playing belote. They don't look up; they won't leave until much later. By now Yamani doesn't look drawn with fatigue; he's half dead – but he doesn't have a working wife.

We have arranged for me to spend the day with Tammam. The day doesn't start early. It doesn't start until the afternoon when Tammam finally wakes up. The public Zaki, the world's apparent oil sorcerer, is everyone's property. The clue to the private Zaki is the black-eyed, smug puss, Tammam.

At home she's the queen of her court. She always has some companion at her beck and call. It may be her older sister, Johara, a psychology student, who she's bossing around. It may be an intriguing French woman of a certain age who's come to stay. To say Tammam's like Anne Boleyn at Henry VIII's court would be an exaggeration. To say she's like a pop star who's had a number one hit and is big in Hamburg would not.

Tammam can't make up her mind how to fill her time today (what's left of it). The bookshelves offer astrology, history, explicit picture books on sex techniques, philosophy, Gayelord Hauser. Tammam doesn't feel like reading. The video shelves offer everything from Mohammed Ali's latest fight to *There's a girl in my soup*. Tammam doesn't feel like a movie. She wouldn't think of going shopping, not in Riyadh. Tammam's very sniffy about where she shops and the city's provincial stores aren't her mark. No, Tammam feels like giving me the benefit of her advice.

'I'm quite modern, I want you to know that. I think a girl should get to know a boy, have coffee with him or something. But no more than that, you know what I mean?' It's one of her favourite expressions. Tammam knows exactly what she means. 'Every man, however educated he is, wants a virgin for a wife. And it's not difficult to hold a man – for an Arab woman that is. I think you Western women have forgotten how to do it.

'I have a friend who is very pretty but she went to school in America and stopped using make-up. Her husband came to see me one day and asked me to show her how to do it. She doesn't look like a woman without it really. You know what I mean? And I see you don't use make-up either for that matter.'

The day passes under Tammam's tutelage. At nine she goes to

make herself ready for her master. It takes an hour; her dressing-room table is an arsenal of scent bottles and beauty products (nearly as big as the arsenal of vitamin pill bottles on Zaki's). The make-up, the canary-coloured evening dress, the hair carefully curled down to her waist seems to me overdone for a quiet supper at home with her husband. But, as Tammam has pointed out, 'an Arab woman knows instinctively how to do the right thing'.

The minister of petroleum and mineral resources finally staggers in – he's beat. Tammam now switches roles; she's Lolita. She robs Zaki of his head-dress, sits him on the floor and plays belote. The young temptress goes through an ABC of seduction with this forty-five-year-old man with his soft eyes and soft paunch. She reduces him to a woolly lamb; she's even seduced his pomeranians, who adore her and yap at everyone else bar Zaki. She flirts outrageously with her husband, giggles, cheats with much smacking of cards and lips to trap his attention. It's almost a pity to have to interrupt the performance for supper – another feast.

While Zaki is offering to read my horoscope (he's Cancer and an expert on the subject), I'm working out how to ask him what the hell's happened to his chef-de-cabinet, Ibrahim Obaid, the one who led me to him in the first place. This time Ibrahim really does seem to have disappeared. Zaki gives me an opening. 'Who do you think arranged your visa?' he asks in such a way as to suggest it might have been Zaki himself. 'Ibrahim Obaid,' I answer innocently.

He withdraws and doesn't say a word to me until we're nearly finished eating. (It takes weeks for me to find out that Obaid resigned, because he didn't get a ministry of his own, it's said, and was no longer working for Zaki all the time his office said I should ring back tomorrow when he might be in. That's Saudi Arabia.)

'How would you feel if you suddenly found you had to live here?' Zaki starts again.

'As an expatriate? I don't think I'd like to be a stranger in a strange land anywhere.' Zaki shrugs impatiently at my evasion. I enjoy the man too much to dodge after all. So few people ever ask anything straight out, I feel I've insulted him.

'I would suffocate.'

Zaki smiles. He's content. Tammam jumps in, saying that I'm not very good at explaining myself and then rushes him off for more belote. Early in the morning, when they're still playing Mary and her little lamb, I leave them to their double bed in the shabby hotel suite.

Tammam has one philosophy about life. It's a woman's job to please her man. 'Now listen to me. You're older than I am and I don't mean to be unkind but you evidently haven't been able to hold a man so far. Just remember that every man, no matter how big he is in the world, he's a child. You know what I mean? Not a child to cry or anything but he needs warmth, love, affection and that means that when he comes home from the office he must find you cheerful and beautiful. That's how you make sure that he will always come back.' And the last devastating thrust. 'Then you'll be able to get anything you want from him.'

Banking on a war-horse

There were other commoners once with great power. They helped Ibn Saud to found and then run his domain. They came from abroad bringing the education the desert Arabs lacked. Some of them stayed. One is today's eminence grise, King Khalid's only official adviser, Dr Rashad Faraun, once Syrian, now Saudi.

In a green villa in Riyadh, two old fox-hole buddies reminisce about the last forty years. Once they went to war with Ibn Saud (somewhere safe in the back lines); now they both have white hair and statesmen's bearing. There comes a point in some men's lives when they've become so important that they stop moving their heads – they merely incline an ear. Both Dr Rashad Faraun and his pal, Dr Medhat al-Ared, Saudi Ambassador to the UN in Geneva, reached that point many years ago.

Faraun, mandarin and medicine man (retired), sees more of King Khalid than any commoner and most princes. I'm here alone with Faraun and his crony by accident. He invited me to dinner on the phone the other day and I make a point of turning up on the dot of eight as arranged. When I knock on his door he looks happy to see me, but puzzled. After a while he explains why; he was waiting dinner for me last night. But he isn't the least put out. 'Would you like to join us; we're only talking.'

Only talking? Better still. But he's looking puzzled again. Finally he confesses that he can't believe I'd want to waste an evening with two old men. I must want something; a favour, an introduction. Why don't I tell him straight away and he'll see to it? It takes me a while to believe he means it; Saudi men aren't normally given to humility. Faraun can't see that he's interesting in himself.

He's far more interesting than the king's young interpreter who'd been obliviously boring me for hours before I came on to Faraun's. This spoiled brat of thirty plus, who looks vaguely like Laurence Harvey (if you call that handsome), was told by Joan Kennedy when she was here that he should be in movies. Now he's even more full of himself.

Poor dear, as royal interpreter he had to travel back across the desert on His Majesty's caravan from the court's summer quarters in Taif, a green hillside resort on the west coast. The experience has almost destroyed him; he doesn't see how he'll recover. His aristocratic features curl with distaste as he describes the journey: 'I'm worn out. We had to wake up at dawn and wash in a tub of cold water. Ugh, that cold water. Then I couldn't get out of the tub for the scorpions. At night I was so scared I couldn't sleep a wink. Ten days in the desert is awful. Nothing but heat, flies and boredom. And what do you think they did all day? Nothing, absolutely nothing. They just sat around and talked about the old days.'

Now I'm listening to Faraun describe the same journey to al-Ared. Travelling across the desert with the king and his brothers is Faraun's idea of a good time. It needs stamina; even in October the sun beats mercilessly. Only six months ago this adviser was in a Cleveland hospital having open-heart surgery and here he is, beard trembling with pleasure, telling al-Ared of his trip with the court.

'It was splendid. There's nothing like the peace and the stillness of the desert. Word passed round that the king was coming and the tribesmen came from miles around to see him. We sat up all night remembering how it used to be. Nothing like now of course. Now we travel with about 300 cars, what with all the court officials, the princes' servants, telephone operators, cooks and those generators humming all day.'

Ambassador Al-Ared nods understandingly, his eyes moistening with nostalgia behind his thick spectacles. These two men have stitched, patched and advised three generations of al-Saud kings (excluding Saud whom neither would serve). When al-Ared came here it wasn't even a country. Ten years later he was joined by an old comrade from Damascus University – Faraun, who had escaped from Syria after being condemned to death for resistance work by the French (who were in charge of the place then).

In 1948 King Ibn Saud appointed Faraun as Ambassador to France. The French refused to accept him as he was still officially under sentence of execution. Ibn Saud threatened to break diplomatic relations. Faraun went to Paris; he gets a kick still out of that twist of fate.

The personal physician turned royal adviser and, along the way, grew rich. But passing an evening in this empty house, puffing on his cigar with al-Ared, is the real treat for him. For me too, but for one problem. I'm not hungry (it's a relief to miss out on one of those gigantic meals for a change) but I'm dying for a cigarette. Out of respect I, as a woman, can't smoke in front of Faraun. Thank heavens he doesn't notice how his cigar smoke is getting to me.

The two men smile at each other and remember the days when Faraun delivered royal babies and slept at the bottom of their beds when they were ill. Al-Ared recalls his first operation; on the floor. 'When I operated on a table, I thought that was progress.' After going round the King Faisal Medical City with all its electronic wonders, meeting these two is like coming across a record shelf where there are old 78s in bare brown covers. And yet, Faraun's name opens all the Riyadh doors that matter.

We're waiting for Madame Faraun, who's flying home from Taif via Paris; intercontinental travel at this level of wealth counts for as much as a taxi ride. The Farauns have been married for thirty-seven years. Rashad sent home for a wife soon after his escape from Syria. The family shipped out a sixteen-year-old cousin, Jamida, born in Syria but raised and educated in Jerusalem, then under British mandate with at least some facilities. She came to a town with no schools, electricity, telephones or aeroplanes and not much water.

Faraun keeps looking at his watch. To divert him, al-Ared reminds him of the time he shared a tent with H. St John Philby – the ex British politico, explorer, Arabist and father of double agent Kim (now a retired KGB officer in Moscow). St John Philby had converted to Islam and was entitled to some more wives; pretty useful since his English one, Dora, didn't go much on hanging around the desert with her husband's hero-king, Ibn Saud.

The king ordered al-Ared to find Philby a new Saudi wife: 'You chose well,' recalls Faraun, 'she was a fine girl and she gave him a good son. He teaches at Riyadh University you know.'

Before I can get my mind round the oddity of finding out that the half-brother of the British diplomat who betrayed us and America to the Russians is alive and well and living in Riyadh, the door bursts open. A black figure enters; the indomitable Madame Faraun is back. She throws off her veil; what an astounding sight. A young-looking blonde rushes across the room and Rashad winds his arms round her, his face almost breaking up with pleasure. Saudi couples normally don't even touch in front of other people which makes this a very rare show of affection indeed. Madame, mother of five, grandmother of several, is not what you'd expect of an old war-horse's nag.

Next morning, Rashad goes off to the king and Jamida settles down to plates of sticky cakes, a long chat with me and the telephone. It rings all the time. Madame is very popular; probably because she's one of those women who make the best of everything and has no time for Moaning Annies.

When the air-conditioning breaks down in most homes (and it does, frequently) there's histrionics. It breaks down here and

Jamida beams at me. 'Isn't that good? Now we can open the windows and talk without that noise.'

At one moment she talks of her daughter living in Paris, the next of flying to Rome in a few days for a cousin's wedding and then she's on about the time, years ago, when Ibn Saud was wounded in battle and Rashad rushed off to treat him. He came back many hours later. The wound wasn't much but Ibn Saud had been reading to him the chapter of each of the thirty-six scars on his body, an anatomical history book of his conquest of Saudi Arabia.

Jamida tells me that her son Raith will talk to me too – I know that if she says so, he will. Raith Faraun is another of those Saudis who, in some ways, is far more interesting than the Khashoggi legend. Raith has the money and the international deals (his empires straddle the Middle East and reach across the Atlantic: shipping, insurance, petrochemicals, arms, you name it). He has the requisite private jet but he also has a blanket of security around him.

Every summer all the Farauns go to Raith's villa in the hills above Cannes. No one hears about it. They don't need publicity and they do want privacy. Apart from anything else, Raith has children and fears kidnappings. In the winter all the Farauns go ski-ing in Megève. They give parties for friends but gossip columnists don't get in. No one reads of their gatherings as they do of Khashoggi's caviare fling for fifty at Gstaad.

The Saudis are now using Khashoggi's willingness to endure publicity and his popularity with Western newspapers as a decoy. They would dump him if it suited them; already in some fields he's a figure of the past. Not in the West, where he's expanded fast. But here, where it counts, where the big money is. If you read any profiles of Khashoggi in which he's had a chance to chip in with some information, notice the ways there's always mention of his houses in Saudi Arabia. Mention those to top Saudis and watch the flicker of amusement. To them AK's based outside the country: his father (who was once another personal physician to Ibn Saud) is also out, almost permanently in London. In a country like this, you're only in when you're really in.

The Saudi's have a trump: their names. Newspaper readers couldn't keep up with them even if newsmen could get them right. Khashoggi is one they almost know. Reams of reporting on Khashoggi draws the flak away from Saudi's inner circle. And if they ever think he goes too far, the Saudis will soon send word to AK.

If he wants to allow himself to be persuaded to fly around with an NBC film crew including Caroline Kennedy on board as a researcher, exposing his importance and his proximity to attractive women on American television screens – that's fine. But when he wanted to break into the world of movies and hired Anthony Quinn to star in a multi-million-dollar production, about Prophet Muhammad, scripted by Harry ('Battle for Anzio') Craig, that was different. Filming was already under way in Morocco when King Faisal sent word. Hundreds of film crew checked out of the Holiday Inn and other hotels in Marrakesh.

Raith Faraun has to be another kind of operator; his father sees the king every day, after all. We're sitting on a terrace in Jiddah. Behind us there's another of those parties going on where the country's fat cats purr at each other. Faraun, baby-faced, friendly (because I mention that his mother, a major shareholder in his corporations apart from anything else, told me he would be) looks like an important man's secretary.

I'd hate to be on the wrong side of a negotiating table from Faraun. He's filling me in on a meeting early in 75 in the Pierre Hotel, New York. James T. Barnes Senior, chairman of the Bank of the Commonwealth in Michigan, is there to see lawyers from ex-Secretary of the Treasury John Connally's law firm in Texas. The lawyers and Barnes have been negotiating a multi-million take-over for his shareholding in the Detroit bank. A nameless Middle East client is involved. In the anonymous comfort of the hotel suite, James T. Barnes Senior is about to meet the man who's buying him out: Raith Faraun. It's a deal Faraun has spent months planning down to the smallest detail; it slips through smoothly.

At about the same time as that Pierre Hotel meeting, Khashoggi had been thwarted in his attempt to acquire his third bank, the

First National of San José. It isn't as if he's buying Wall Street, after all, but there's still a national stink. Democratic representative Fortney H. Stark, who had sold him a bank in Walnut Creek, announced in public that he wished he hadn't done so. Mostly the opposition is gathering around the disclosures about Khashoggi's arms commissions. Get down to the nitty-gritty and it might have gathered anyway. Arms or no arms, he's Arab.

Faraun doesn't hide his regret at the way Khashoggi handled the affair. 'He should have withdrawn his offer in San José the second he realised there was local opposition. Suppose he'd pulled out, I reckon the people in the town would have got worried that he'd seen the bank's financial position and decided it was unsound. The board would probably have ended up begging him to buy it. He'd have got it cheaper that way too.'

Race against prejudice

Raith Faraun got his bank in Detroit exactly as he'd planned it with none of the fuss. 'I wanted an American bank in the centre of an industrial city, not a small town. Saudi Arabia's buying in technology and industry, not tennis clubs. A small-town bank with not enough capital assets wouldn't have been the right vehicle for me. It had to be a bank with one major shareholding and not too high a percentage of Jewish money on deposit in case of a run after the take-over. My lawyers went through every bank in the States that could be up for sale. I went through their list, found four that met my particular specifications and settled on the Commonwealth.'

The Jews withdrew their money; now it's flowing in again. Jewish employees weren't fired (the first question everyone in America raised when the take-over was made public) and no orders were given against hiring them. The only change made on Faraun's insistence was that the bank had to move into the black areas of the city. 'Firstly, it's a public service. You can't refuse black people banking facilities. The board argued against it on a question of security. I said, "Buy security guards but open those branches." It's not just altruism. Blacks work; those branches make money.'

Nothing flames American paranoia like news of Arabs taking over banks. As a kitchen is to a home, a bank is to its community – a symbol of security. But nothing stokes Saudi paranoia like the resulting snarls of protest organised by local merchants, usually Jewish. It's a vicious circle.

Every time the Saudis try explaining themselves to America at large, they make matters worse. No sooner had the new Saudi Ambassador to Washington presented his credentials than he got dumped with the potential scandal that there was a 'no Jews' clause in a twenty-five-million-dollar highway-building contract his country was discussing with California state. How did he get out of it? By issuing a statement that anyone, even blacks and women (whatever next?), could come and work in his country unless he/she adhered to Zionism.

So when is a Jew not a Jew? Answer, when he's a Zionist. But how and who is going to judge who's the 'good Jew' and who's the 'bad Jew'? The American press has started to worry away like a dog with a bone at the question of whether Saudis get Jews pushed out of companies they're dealing with. But behind this concern about who can stay on the board and who can't lies the crunch question: have the Saudis really got it in for Jews?

I'm in Saudi only because I've 'proved' that I'm a Christian. It isn't true; I grew up in an orthodox Jewish home. Yes, I do have a nasty shiver when a perfectly intelligent, Western-educated Saudi tells me in all seriousness that every practising Jew has to drink the blood of a Muslim once a year. But this is only one man. And I had the same shiver of revulsion when a Jew told me equally seriously that every Arab wants to slit the throat of every Jewish woman and child in the world. Both are bigoted nonsense. But there's always been that kind of nonsense. It's nothing like the pogroms in Russia or the hideous happenings in Nazi Europe. It's more like the situation in 1815 when the ship carrying Napoleon into exile on St Helena anchored off the coast of Britain. Hundreds of people went out in small boats to see whether Napoleon really had horns. The English had been cut off from France for a whole generation so of course there were some who believed tales like that.

Saudi Arabia's in a filthy position. Officially it's in a state of war with Israel. How much did Britain trust Germans who happened to be living here during the last world war? And yes, I do meet some Saudis who because of Israel now have it in for Jews full stop. But there's one vital difference from any anti-Jewish feeling I've known or heard about. Arabs and Jews are much more alike emotionally and culturally than Arabs and Westerners.

I stay with Saudis who are astonished that I, a 'cold Britisher', am so at ease with their noisy families. How can I tell them that every night is Passover night to me here? That comparison is probably in particularly bad taste but I'm sorry. Of course I'm at ease with the strong, emotional mothers of Saudi Arabia, the enveloping warmth of their homes, the undercurrents. It's what I grew up with. There are moments when I'm instinctively afraid of being surrounded by so many Arabs. I've unconsciously absorbed fear: four Middle East wars have seen to that. But I'd rather have the overt, angry, hurt anti-Jewish feeling of the Saudis when I come up against it than the understated, sarcastic anti-semitism of some of the British Establishment.

I meet only the élite of Saudi; when I run into a Jew-hater I know it. It's out front. I can remember enough dinner parties in London where someone has made a remark about a man with an obviously Jewish name and then without actually putting prejudice into words (that's bad manners, after all) dropped poison on him in a way I can't pin down and mustn't challenge (that's bad manners too).

When it comes to the average Saudi attitude to Jews, you couldn't find a better example than the Saudi Ambassador to Washington when he's 'off duty'. Abdullah Alireza heads a family corporation that has the agency for Harry Winston in his country (the Jewish American jeweller). He has nieces, nephews and cousins who all went abroad to school and are sophisticated. They can and do distinguish between Israel and Jews. That's what makes this story even more upsetting:

The Alirezas were exceptionally close to King Faisal. The day he was killed a large group of them were in London. Their shock and sorrow left them stunned. That evening they gathered in a small Italian restaurant for dinner. As they were leaving, one of the ambassador's nieces, Hoda, asked her husband whether they could buy some of the oranges decorating the ceiling, to take back to the flat. A large party of Americans had been sitting at the next table. As Hoda put up her hand to the oranges, one woman yelled out: 'Go ahead, enjoy them. You know where they come from, dear? They come from Israel.' This wasn't the first time Hoda had been on the receiving end of remarks in public from Jews hearing her speak Arabic. Normally she would turn icily away.

This was the wrong moment: she took down an orange, slung it in the woman's face as hard as she could and shouted back: 'You want to enjoy the Israeli orange? Why don't you catch it?' I have become close to Hoda in Saudi Arabia, as I have to many other women. I see how burned up she gets as she tells this story. That's how hatred festers; it's the sadness and the threat of the Middle East.

The Saudis used to allow Jews in to work with Aramco and other companies. They still do let them in if there's no fuss made, if it's handled discreetly and if they trust the firms concerned. They asked me to produce a baptismal certificate. But one of the top Americans with Aramco told me that a while back several Jews in the company were 'thought' to have direct links with Israeli intelligence. They left and the Saudi and American governments hushed it up. There's been a nervous, 'official', 'No Jews need apply' ever since.

I used to wonder at the Saudis' anti-Zionist mania. King Faisal in his lifetime made a big deal about his wish to pray in Jerusalem. At first I got a kick out of asking Saudis how often he prayed there when it was still in Arab hands. No one could be certain that he ever did. I don't wonder at it now. Without their backing, that Egyptian-Israeli first tottering step towards peace would never have come off. President Sadat wouldn't have dared make an agreement without Saudi behind him; much of the Arab world still hasn't accepted it. And every time Saudis look at the American press, the only coverage they see of their country is rosy-hued rubbish from the Arab lobby (which does them no good at all – who believes it?) or inches and inches about bribes and how they attack Jews in companies they deal with.

Unless they're forced to (by pressure from Palestinians, publicity, who knows?) Most Saudi businessmen would rather not operate a Jewish boycott. Raith Faraun certainly doesn't want to. 'Fire Jewish employees from the bank in Detroit?' he laughs, 'I might lose some of my best staff.'

But the Faraun family have under their umbrella an interesting example of the insecurity working the other way round. I discover Ghazzam Faraun, Raith's cousin, by accident.

My teeth need cleaning. After all those cigarettes, they're as furry as a small bear. Friends direct me to the only decent dentist in town: the entrance nearly puts me off, it's like an old block in Whitechapel. Upstairs is this snazzy dental clinic – orange and white colour scheme, deep-piled carpet, the very latest equipment. A beautiful black nurse from California restores my teeth and charges me 50 riyals. I'm pleasantly relieved; the daughter of my friend is having orthodontics here; her bill is nearly 12,000 riyals and work's hardly started. On the way out, the name clicks – Faraun.

That night at a party, a flat, cheerful, booming voice behind me starts to make my ear tingle. Among the elegantly rolled 'r's' and precisely moulded vowels of top Saudis who've grown up almost bilingual is this unmistakably flat English accent. I turn round to see a young man with the appearance of a medical student and the confidence of a Saudi. It's most confusing. No foreigner behaves like this here (it's impolitic). But no Arab dresses like this either. He's got a mop of untidy hair, no jacket and an open-necked shirt with three buttons undone. He beards the room with his happy-go-lucky manner and hairy chest as if it were a beer hall full of his medical school chums.

Around him swish the long dresses (both men's and women's) and he has in tow a pretty little blonde girl in a trouser suit. This is Ghazzam Faraun with his girl friend, Debby, who teaches at the American school. Ghazzam grew up in England – he was only three when his Arab father and English mother moved there. In those days he was just another London kid with nothing Arab about him but his name and his relations who dropped by now and again.

After he went through Guy's medical school, he was doing rather well as a national health dentist earning £3,500 a year. Then his peaceful, middle-class life in Wimbledon was interrupted by the October war. 'I've never thought of myself as Arab in my life but when the war broke in 1973, the Arab in me leapt right out. I suddenly found I was incensed by the pro-Israeli stand of the English press. That took me aback. And it just so happened that my cousin Raith was in London then; I went to see him at the Hilton hotel and there he was, the same age as me, with his own suite and people at his beck and call. I was thinking "hey, that could have been me" when Raith asked me why I didn't come to Saudi Arabia. I left London there and then.' His comparatively restricted life isn't easy. 'It's hard being a Faraun here.' But he wouldn't change it now.

The closed book

I have fallen into Saudi Arabian society: businessmen on the outer rims of influence, insiders, royals, princesses and cameos worthy of Oscars of 'supporting actor' roles. But there's always that closed book – the women.

Their husbands can't explain what makes them tick to me; they don't know. One woman can't help me to understand another. I begin to think that the only open, unguarded wives are those imprisoned in the past – uneducated, untravelled, unquestioning. They live in rabbit warrens of women and children (more than one introduced a friend saying, 'our children have the same father'). They make lots of noise, grow fat and don't know what their husbands do when they're not in bed.

Then one day, the threads of the educated women that I have met and got to know better begin to weave together. Many of them are beginning to wonder who they are and what they want from life. Education has given them the tools to search inside themselves. Again I can't identify them, but what sets them apart in this country, where so few ask direct questions, is that these women do again and again. Just as I want to fathom and understand their existence, they want me to explain mine.

'What's it like being divorced and not going back to your family? Does it make you feel ashamed? Aren't you ever frightened of dying alone?' asks one. Divorce has no public stigma here but it's unthinkable for a woman not to return to her father (or her brother). And wanting to live alone, even wanting to be alone, few Saudis can comprehend. Bedu culture is too deeply rooted inside them. To be alone to a desert nomad means death. Outside the patch of shared life there's nothing – no water, food or shelter. The sick are left alone; to die. A new generation of women are discovering about being alone. Servants do the work; children go to school. Many of them plug the gaps with sisters, friends, tea parties. Others use the experience to look inside themselves, and to look hard at their husbands who, in their frenzy of money-making, don't have time for self-examination.

When I first met Ayisha I thought she was hard and brittle. She was at one of those table-laden tea parties where everybody shouts at one another at once and it's considered anti-social to move your chair out of the circle for a confiding chat. Women's parties fall into two categories. There are the ones like a hockey team having its tea break. At these, women bellow across the room, their raucous voices curiously at variance with their studied 'femininity'. At one such gathering I can't stand it any longer and pull myself closer to the next woman – to hear something, anything, of what she's saying. Everyone, but everyone, stops talking and eating (this isn't a tea break; correction, it's a dorm feast) and stares at me until I push myself back again. I might have thrust my hand down her tea gown to judge by their reaction. And there are the others: women dress up for one another, flatter and flirt, even dance for one another and the lesbian undercurrent sends waves of tension down the back of my neck. I met Ayisha at one of these. Here and at dinner parties later, she seems another of those beautifully bound, closed books. She seems to have everything: money, powerful husband, children.

One day I see her alone and we talk for hours. 'I would give anything to leave my husband but he'll take the children and never let me see them again. He can under our law. I hate him and at the same time I know it's not his fault. I was a virgin when we married and I expected him to teach me things. Nothing. The first night he rolled on me and two minutes later it was over. It's been the same for twelve years. I found out quite early on that he was going with other women, three, four times a week, and me – once a fortnight, once a month.

'He can't make love to me because I'm his wife. Can you imagine? His father drilled into him the idea that a wife's a man's most precious possession, the mother of his children. To him what he does to me in bed dishonours me. You Westerners think that Arab men are great lovers. Ah yes, they talk a lot about it and they pride themselves on being as strong as horses but most of them believe that a woman is there to serve a man – is that being a lover? I begged him to let me be his wife and his prostitute too. He wouldn't even discuss it. So I read books and saw blue films; after all he's my husband. Wanting him to make love to me isn't a crime. One night I did something to him that I had read about. It's the only time he has ever hit me. Then he cried; he was so horrified at himself and at me.

'It's still the same. And I've nothing in my life but him and the children. Would you believe that he finds ways for his girl friends to see me? He says he wouldn't dishonour me by letting them think I'm ugly. Whose honour is he worrying about – his or mine?'

Many women are sexually frustrated. It's another of those Saudi contradictions: most Arab men believe that if you leave a man and a woman in a room together they (probably she) will rip their clothes off; that's the reasoning behind segregation. At the same time they believe that men take pleasure from a woman physically, they don't give it. It's still true of many educated men. In the old days there was dishonour and shame. In these sophisticated times there's dishonour and guilt. It's still often true of the most educated men who've had more open, giving relationships at university in Europe or the States. Western women are one thing; their own are another.

Education for girls opens some horizons but it closes others. Girls' education has been as emotional an issue in Saudi Arabia as busing in the United States. When the first girls' school opened in the sixties, King Faisal had to call out the National Guard. To appease the country's conservatives, school girls spend over twenty hours a week studying the Koran.

Nadia's not the kind of woman I would have expected to question her country's code, but she's frightened that so much Islamic tuition is exposing her daughter to things she isn't ready for. 'It's all right for some girls, they learn parrot fashion. My daughter's intelligent, she thinks about things. The Koran says that men and women must wash immediately after intercourse. My daughter came home from school one day very upset and asked me if we wash because what we do is dirty. What could I say? I told her, "No, it's more hygienic to wash." To her, rubbish is unhygienic, open sewers are unhygienic. At ten she's already convinced that if our religion says you must wash after love then the act itself must be dirty.'

Nadia took a long time to get her next words out. For a Saudi woman to admit to adultery needs a great deal of trust. 'It does do something to you when you both get up as soon as it's finished and go to the bathroom. I'll never forget the first time I made love to a European man and he stayed there and held me. I felt closer to him than I have ever felt to my husband just because of that.' Nadia goes to Europe, pretends to be Italian and picks up men. She wants sex, affection, and she knows the risk she's running.

Sex matters because there's so little else to think about or do. After marriage a woman's freedom is completely in the gift of her husband. Suppose she wants to work; she needs a letter of agreement from him to get a job. And even the most understanding of Saudi husbands have a cut-off point that leaves their wives stranded in frustration.

I'm with a couple who are unusually close. They're first cousins and grew up together. He tries hard to give her as free a life as possible, right out to the limits of what their traditional and prominent family can tolerate. She travels, goes out with him in Saudi, he discusses business with her (that's rare) but we've just come to his cut-off point.

He and his wife spent a month together in London. She came back ten days ago because of the children and he got back yesterday. He's puffed up with pride; he's got a surprise for her. It's an £80,000 plus flat in London. He saw it last week and bought it on the spot. She's furious and won't talk to him. He's bewildered.

Not for the first time, I find myself caught in a curious man–woman confrontation that I'm not used to or prepared for. The husband takes me aside. For a moment, it's almost as if I'm one of the men. 'You're a Westerner, you're independent, but does that mean you wouldn't be delighted if your husband presented you with such a present? Tell me – why isn't she happy? Don't you agree she's being childish?'

Every fibre of me is tuned to his wife's fury. Of course she's angry. Of course I think she's right. I try to explain in idiot's language: an intelligent wife like his might have liked the pleasure of choosing the flat with him. It hadn't occurred to him; after all, it's his right to buy what he sees fit. It's nothing to do with his wife unless he decides it should be. He dismisses me sulkily and sends me back to the women where I belong.

I feel for him: he's as disappointed as a small boy whose mother tells him to go out to play and then yells at him for bringing her his prize worm from the garden. I feel for her: she's as hurt as a small girl whose father decides she's grown up enough to have her own allowance and then tells her she's too silly to spend it. Most of all I feel for them both: few Saudis are alone (their home either has relations living in it, next door to it or dropping in on it) long enough to make up these misunderstandings in a hurry. Issues like this flat have caused five-day marital silences often enough before now. And the crazy thing is, she wants this flat. Why? That's the knock-out: 'Because in London, we'd be able to stay in watching television and I could sit between his knees and he'd hold my hand. That would mean very much to me. In all the years we've been married, he's never once sat holding my hand at home here. In London, yes, in Saudi, no.' Stuck in this rule-bound place, they can't but help swing without warning from adult to child, from new freedom to old tradition.

Inevitably, some of the women trapped between the old and the new become bitches. They use their education as a tool to dominate their children. There have always been ambitious women here; they were locked away from the world, but they gained the power denied to them through their sons. Some worked negatively, some positively.

The most famous, the woman that no one will talk about (you don't talk about royal women, remember) is Hassa al-Sudairy. One young woman who knew her well finally told me the story of Hassa's remarkable marital career. She married her first cousin, King Ibn Saud, but they had no children so two years later he divorced her and palmed her off on one of his spare brothers. She gave birth to a son. The brother obligingly divorced Hassa and returned her to Ibn Saud. They remarried and she had seven sons and two daughters by him. She was the only one of Ibn Saud's countless wives to bring up her children herself. She may have been uneducated but she dedicated herself to her sons, forging them together by sheer will power. They're known now to diplomats everywhere as the Sudairy Seven, the pillars of the kingdom, Crown Prince Fahd and his full brothers. To the end of her life, Hassa drove through Riyadh rounding up her sons if they didn't appear at her table. No wonder they're close today.

The young woman telling me the story has been educated in a boarding school abroad but she takes Hassa Sudairy as her model. 'Can you imagine what Hassa would have been like if she had been born later? She brought up her sons to want power. They got it. I'm bringing up my daughters to want freedom. I only hope they get that.'

Women who won't fight for themselves will nearly always fight for their children. Tasnim has always accepted her husband's dictates as law. But much against his will, she's forced him to send their sons abroad to school. Saudi women aren't allowed into, or anywhere near, boys' schools at home. They can't go and talk things over with the teachers, who are men. Fathers are usually too busy to go, and wouldn't know what to look for anyway when their wives sense trouble. It's not uncommon for a boy to start losing weight and dreading school. His mother can rarely get out of him what's wrong. The moment a boy's old enough to know his mother is 'second class' and must 'be protected', his instincts usually hold out against confiding in her. It happened to Tasnim. She hates the emptiness of the house when her children are away and feels bitter that it's necessary.

'People from your country envy us. They say we're so rich. We're not rich. We can't even educate our own children here properly yet. Learning is wealth. We're people of the Book, not of the moneychangers. How could I stand by watching both my sons so unhappy when I couldn't even talk over the simplest things with their teachers – did they need more help with this, should they be doing more homework? I'm prepared to wait for the changes that make my life hard. But I'm not prepared to sacrifice my children's future.'

In public, this woman looks like any other Jiddah trinket. But she's searching for herself, uncertain and alone. She wrote this poem for her husband:

> There is so much beauty
> Hidden in me
> Close your eyes and reach within
> Beyond that mask
> Beyond that skin
> There is so much beauty
> You could share with me
> If you let me take you by the hand
> And see through my eyes
> You might understand
> I can sing with the wind
> Yet bleed with each and every wound.

I was there the day she finally steeled herself to read it to him. 'Yes, dear,' he said tolerantly, 'very nice.' I could have screamed for her. She said nothing. The book closed again.

Ahmad and the nurse

The casualties aren't all among Saudi women. There are Western ones too. I get talking to Nancy at the airline office and we go off for coffee. She's waiting for a flight home to England. In the way that you sometimes do abroad, she unburdens herself on me, a stranger. She's quit her job nursing at a hospital in Jiddah. She liked the job, the pay was marvellous but she didn't realise how different Saudi Arabia is.

'One day a young Saudi came into the outpatients' department. He was, literally, tall, dark and terribly handsome. He also spoke super English. I'd only arrived a few weeks before and I was terribly lonely. I didn't know what I was doing here and I longed for home.

'Then suddenly here was this guy who'd been educated in England. He's read the *Daily Mail* and shopped in Harrods. It was my world. He also made me laugh. I wasn't busy so we sat and talked and when he asked me out for dinner I accepted. Naturally, I liked him; he was the first decent person I'd met in weeks.

'One of the other nurses flew at me when she found out. She told me I was crazy. "If you're going to go in for that kind of thing why have you been putting off all those other men." You get propositions all the time in my job, you see, you get used to it. I told her she was like all the rest, cynical. I also thought she was a bit jealous. I wish I'd listened to her now.

'Ahmad gave me a marvellous evening; he couldn't have been more fun. And he was so unlike the English men I'd been out with. Everything he said, he was so passionate. We started going out together, for meals and round to friends of his. I've never felt so attracted to anyone in my life. It wasn't only that. He didn't seem to have anyone else to talk to. He had a wife. But I wouldn't have called her a wife. He never talked to her, never spent any time with her; never took her to visit his European friends. He took me.'

She keeps pushing her fringe out of her eyes. She has that white papery look about her face that people get when they're about to crack. I change the subject for a while and find out that she's the daughter of a doctor in Lancashire. She qualified at a London teaching hospital and stayed on there to nurse. She sang madrigals, went to the Proms and on a walking holiday with her boyfriend in Wales. She answered an advert for nurses in Saudi Arabia one day when she was fed up. 'Pure escapism; I never thought it would come to anything.' Her parents weren't happy about it and her friends made digs about her coming back with an oil sheikh or a jewellery box full of diamonds. She's going back with neither.

'Ahmad's wife didn't seem very real to me. He was unhappy and I wanted to make him happier. He was miserable at work as well. He used to turn up after work fuming at the humiliation of being at everyone's beck and call the whole time. He'd talk to me for hours about going into business on his own so that he could control his own life. He used to say that at thirty-five he felt he was being treated like a child.

'Of course we wanted to sleep together after a while. He did from the start and I was crazy about him. But it was one thing wanting to. Where were we to go? I was in the hostel and all he had was his home. In the end we told some old friends of his, a German couple, and they said we could use their house.

'No one's ever made love to me like Ahmad. It was fantastic. He was very strong and passionate. But looking back I knew something was wrong. I had the queerest feeling that this was some kind of performance for him. He kept asking if it was all right for me and he used words that must have come straight out of a European brothel. He also got angry when I wouldn't do things he said excited him.

'Anyway, the German couple couldn't keep their mouths shut. They told someone, and it was all over the place in no time. Ahmad dropped me like a brick. He never got in touch with me again. I didn't understand it at first. Now I do. You see, I *was* like someone out of a brothel to him deep down. And he was scared of his wife. He would never have given her up for me. The worst moment was when his brother came to see me. He warned me not to try to get money out of Ahmad. I couldn't believe it. It seems it had happened before and girls had tried blackmailing him. It made me feel so cheap and then he said there was no point, I didn't matter enough for anyone to have to pay me off. I thought I'd had a love affair, his brother treated me like a hamburger Ahmad had just had. That was it; I don't think I'll ever feel clean again.'

How can you blame her? How can you blame Ahmad? Nurses on contract have three options. They're sensible and find European boyfriends. They keep to themselves, save money and go home. Or they earn overtime 'seeing' Arab men. The Saudis hate it; they put guards along the roads near the hostels where they can and every nurse who takes money for sleeping with Saudi men confirms them in their opinion that all Western women are up for grabs. Another contribution to the mutual fund of distrust.

But in case I've given the impression that Saudi men are all lecherous monsters, I'd like you to listen to this man who's nearly forty. He has a high government position, travels nearly all the time and is still single. 'I want to be married more than you can believe. Not just to solve my sexual problems, although they're not easy – I don't like using air hostesses or nurses, the women whose bodies are available. So when I come back to Saudi Arabia, I switch off sexually. I block it – how do they say? Sublimate?'

'But where will I find a wife? I want a companion. I'm too old to settle for a woman whose only ability is that she can give me children. What's worse – to be married to an empty head and live without caring for her or to live alone in a hotel as I do? We work here from early morning until one and then all afternoon and at night until ten or eleven. Don't you think I'd work better if I was married, if I had a woman I could talk to?

'There are several of us like this in the Ministry. We believe in what we're doing and Prince Saud, our Minister, is one of the finest men in the country. You say there are women here who would understand, who are interesting. How am I to meet them? I'm too old to let my family arrange it all or rely on my sisters' reports from their tea parties. No Saudi woman can show herself to a man who isn't her husband so what do I do?

'I would marry a foreigner, but what kind of foreigners do we meet? Seriously, what kind of women go out with Arabs in London or New York? I need a Western woman who's looking over my shoulder at our money less than I need an empty-headed Saudi. Suppose I met a respectable woman abroad. We'd have dinner together for a few days and then I'd have to leave. Months later I'd be back, that's no use. I'm alone and it's a cold life. Find me a wife, I'll be grateful to you. As it is, men like me, we smoke a lot, we work a lot, we spend our time together. We're trying to build something. Not everyone's out for himself, you know. Some of us work like hell and we don't have private businesses, we don't have "extras". We do it because we believe in Saudi Arabia.'

He's such a super man, my match-making instincts go into overdrive. I've met so many women in Saudi who are desperate to meet a man like him but he'll never know about them. There's nothing I can do. Advertise? Broadcast? Drop hints? Not on your life. He's also a casualty. And I believe him completely when he says: 'Working for our country takes all the hours, all the energy of everyone in the foreign service. If I won't settle for second-best for my country, how can I settle for second-best for myself?'

A modern babel

It isn't done to talk about oil in Saudi Arabia any more than it was to discuss coal in the drawing rooms of Victorian England. The stuff comes out of the ground in the east, where Aramco laid the foundations of American suburbia. It underpins the government capital of Riyadh, where concrete flattens the lumpy desert. But for sheer wealth, it's Jiddah that counts. In this major commercial centre on the Red Sea a plot of land that cost 2,500 riyals two years ago has just changed hands for 700,000. Nor is it done to reminisce about the 1920s; all that rape, murder and pillaging in Taif by the fanatical Wahhabi troops before Ibn Saud arrived and the two years' siege before Jiddah fell. That was fifty years ago and it's another 'politically sensitive' topic.

When I heard about Jiddah in Riyadh it sounded like Paris. 'Ah but wait until you see Jiddah,' people would say wistfully. Yes, it's different. It's got a few hundred thousand more people, for a start. It's no use asking how many more than Riyadh; it's one of those things no one knows. For once this vagueness is excusable. This port is the last call before Mecca, the hotline to Allah.

Hundreds of thousands of Muslim pilgrims from all over the world arrive here every year on their way to Mecca, fifty-five miles away. Many stay on, poor, possibly diseased, sleeping rough. The Hajj is the season for burglaries; there were 500 last year, a scandalously high crime rate, incomprehensible to the Saudis.

Jiddah is an ancient port. Foreigners have poured in for the Hajj and merchants have set out to trade for centuries. In the Najd, Arabs boast of their pure blood. Hijazis have always married foreigners from all corners of the Muslim world, and besides that the Ottoman Empire left some mixed blood behind.

Jiddah's the only town in the world that houses foreign embassies and isn't a capital. The Foreign Ministry, more of a wedding cake than a building, is a copy of the Hijaz railway station in Damascus, built by the Turks. It looks over one of the best and one of the worst views in Saudi – the sparkling sea that delights after desert-bound Riyadh, and the road between packed with cars and dangerous drivers.

As one Arab remarked: 'Saudis drive their cars as they drove their camels. They look neither left nor right and they beat it until it goes faster.' They couldn't look left or right if they wanted to; they're blinkered by their head-dresses. Add to this the natural exuberance of Jiddah and the traffic's a disaster – unless, that is, you're a pedestrian.

If a driver kills a pedestrian, at best the law will get him with a 32,000 riyals fine. At worst the family will insist on blood money and a foreigner can get stuck in prison until the price is agreed. It's a driver's hell, a pedestrian's paradise. I just put up my hand and cars screech to a halt to let me cross especially if it's a foreign driver who reckons me for an Arab. A really troublesome family can be a right headache for a pedestrian-slaying foreigner (and it's not hard to be one – the roads are anarchic).

At least it's not as bad as the story I heard one Western business-man relaying to a newcomer. According to this 'authority', if a foreigner kills an Arab, he has to lie down in the road and let someone run him over – family revenge and all that. Rubbish. Most stories you hear like that are rubbish. Er, nearly most stories. Well, that one is anyway.

The stories about how much money's made in Jiddah certainly aren't rubbish. It's very obviously the government's money centre. You can sense the hidden world inside the Saudi Arabian Mone-tary Authority in the middle of town. It's from here that the orders go out to Aramco telling them into which banks to pay the oil revenues. Then huge amounts are checked into current accounts in chosen American (like Chase Manhattan, Morgan Guaranty, First National City) and London (like National Westminster, Lloyds, Barclays) clearing banks. Moments later, exact instruc-tions arrive from SAMA directing dollars, converting sterling, moving millions. Result: a disproportionate number of banking gnomes in highly polished shoes (if they're American), baggy trousers and braces (if they're Brits), carefully darted shirts (if they're Swiss), standing around in my hotel – the Kandara Palace, an institution not a mere hotel.

Its scruffy grandeur reigns over Jiddah life. There's no postal delivery service, only unreliable PO Box numbers. The Kandara acts as *poste restante* for a large part of the city. Nearly all Saudis who matter in Jiddah (men that is) will spend some time in the lobby here during the week.

I arrive in my nightdress from Riyadh, looking silly again. There are so many foreign women in Jiddah that it's back to short skirts. A top man from the Union Bank of Switzerland is sipping coffee with his team waiting to go to SAMA; his bank is an official adviser. A big noise from Credit Suisse, White Weld, another SAMA lot, is bullying the one switchboard operator to get him London in four minutes. Some hopes.

My one consolation is the sight of the aquiline figure of David

Douglas-Home, son of former Prime Minister Sir Alec, city banker with Morgan Grenfell. He's slumped in an armchair looking just like a man with a firm reservation but no hotel room. He is. During the oil embargo days, David Douglas-Home was pilloried in the press as an 'Arab lover'. He got no less than 900 letters of abuse (from the United States alone) for his putting together a loan for the Arabs (Abu Dhabi, actually) during the October War. Those correspondents should see him now. He's sent his ADC, Rupert, son of Lord Carrington, to do battle with the switchboard and phone for a bed, somewhere anywhere in town. Unlike lowlier fixers, the men who are completely trusted don't feel the need to fawn all over Arabs. 'Fred,' he calls the waiter, 'bring me a drink.'

Douglas-Home is fed up to the teeth with Jiddah. 'You couldn't do business here if you were a romantic Arab-lover. You'd go out of your mind. Nothing works. Not the telephones, not the hotels, the roads are abominable. It's collapsing around us.'

He's here to see a client who is a diversified concrete king ('every time he does a deal he turns over twenty to thirty million dollars'). He goes into a beauty shop; there's the owner, his client's brother, Salim. The youngest brother is on the till 'wetting his fingers in business' explains Salim. Douglas-Home stands around, hands in his pockets with the air of the head master visiting the lower fourth. His aristocratic hauteur goes down well with Saudis; they understand it. He feels sad what's happening to them now the cowboys have ridden in. 'Two years ago the place was deserted. Now look at it, a shambles.'

He's right of course. This Paris of Saudi Arabia doesn't work. It's rumoured that there's a garbage removal service; most people rely on stray goats. 'It's the west today,' is the kind of snippet I overhear at coffee mornings. It doesn't mean the wind. It means the telephones of the entire western section of town have been unplugged, or hit through with a pick-axe by workmen. A quarter of Jiddah's phones are out of order at any one time.

The princely merchants have found a way round the problem of international calls (four days to London? six to New York?). They know all the international operators at the central exchange personally. The telephonists bring their problems to them (money problems usually). The merchants solve them and, coincidentally, they get their calls abroad at once. As big, as sprawling as it is, inner Jiddah still works on a personal basis. I asked one such merchant prince, whose investments are now in Luxembourg and Lichtenstein-based companies, why he doesn't operate in Europe permanently.

'I couldn't bear to walk in a street where I don't see people I know. I'll never forget staying in a Paris apartment once when an old lady died. When they came to take her away, no one in the whole block knew who she was or remembered talking to her. That couldn't happen here. I'd rather put up with a telephone system that is, I admit, useless. But please don't quote me by name, I mustn't be heard criticising the government.' Saudis are real forelock-tuggers.

Until the apparatus of a modern commercial centre arrives (the telex only got going in 1973 – security reasons), Jiddah relies on the oldest form of communication known to man – word of mouth. Getting an invitation to someone, making an appointment, is an adventure. It means relaying information via any intermediaries who might be in contact with other intermediaries. As a result everyone in Jiddah expects everyone else to turn up for something at any time. It may be yesterday's lunch today or tomorrow's dinner party the day after.

It also means that there's twice as much traffic on the roads as there need be. Everyone's sending notes with their drivers to someone else. Outings are further complicated by the fact that there are no street names and, unlike Riyadh, no visible town planning. Directions for dinner go something like this: 'Tell the driver to go to the school. I don't know its name, it's the boys' school. Take the second turning, go over a hill, but mind the oil drums, look for a yellow gate then count seven on. You'll know if it's the right one because I'll have someone standing there.'

There turn out to be several boys' schools in the area. The oil drums are a mound of building rubble, the gate has turned brown in the sun and every entrance has a crowd around it. That's assuming the driver has negotiated the rutted, craterous mud tracks that lead off the new tarmac road to the expensive residential areas.

So how and why does anyone bother to do business in this city where communications approximate those of a medieval town? Because, answer the bankers, well-briefed on SAMA's accounts, there's nowhere else (Kuwait and Abu Dhabi included) where the profits are big. Big? The chief assistant to one government prince is dismayed at the sums involved. Five years ago, this foreign Arab (who picked up his prince while eking out a living as a Paris pimp) would take a cut of 100,000 riyals to get his boss's signature on a contract for a foreigner. Now he has to think twice about it unless it's worth a million to him. I know. He told me this most seriously over coffee.

And why go out to dinner when every drive is a fight past the twin monsters of logistics and directions? Because the people of Jiddah, when you have finally arrived, haggard and neurotic, compensate by being the most generous, hospitable and outgoing there are.

One long party

When a Kuwaiti official, let alone a Bahraini, says something about continuing separate development for women, it's said almost for the record. He doesn't actually believe it. Foreigners have been around the Gulf too long, eroding traditional values by their colonial presence. But the Saudi does believe it. His country was founded on and still lives by the ideals of Wahhabi Islam.

It's beside the point that it makes no sense (not as far as manpower, let alone human happiness, is concerned) to keep one sex locked in a box in a country while the rest of the world capers around believing in a different way of life. No where else is there the same discrepancy between how things are meant to be and how they are. The Saudis are afraid that if they let up one tight set of controls and officially say goodbye to one part of the ideal, anything could happen. Absolute monarchy isn't the political fashion of today. You see the hypocrisy of running a country on a double standard most clearly in Jiddah. There's a growing number of men too educated, too cosmopolitan to accept the all-in emotional package called 'the Saudi way of life'.

There's a set in Riyadh, there are sets in Jiddah. At the very top, there's only *the* set. Ma'amun and Lita Tamer are part of it. They're having a soirée. Ma'amun owns the biggest chain of pharmacies and beauty stores in Jiddah. One look at his house and I know that he makes money.

Of course he does; all the women are covered in costly war paint and drenched in the most expensive scents in the world. As I go round the room shaking hands with everyone (yes, they bob up and down here too) I feel like a dog let loose in the park. I go from one interesting sniff to another – only instead of trees, mongrels and trouser legs, I'm sniffing Joy, L'Air du Temps and Calèche.

When I say the Tamers' house is elegant, it means it's so unobtrusive, I can't even describe it. The tones are discreet, the sofas low, the picture windows in the split-level drawing room look out over the lushly landscaped swimming pool. It isn't unusual for Jiddah and that's the first difference from Riyadh. Here the million-dollar look means restraint. They've long outgrown vulgarity.

Compared to those stiff Riyadh parties with split-level men and women, suffering from prickling awareness of each other, this could be London. The women wear thin-strapped dresses, low cut, sometimes short to emphasise their chic and daring. The better the Jiddah name, the less flamboyant, the plainer the material the finer the cut. Only the blue–white rocks betray the accumulated wealth in the room. None of it's insured; all of it's real. No one would dare burgle the names here and it doesn't travel.

One woman nods towards an Alireza; the family firm has the agency for jeweller Harry Winston. He should be pleased with himself. I'm told Harry Winston sold six million riyals worth of jewellery between here and Riyadh last week. Jiddah gossip on this level is rarely wrong.

The whisky flows unselfconsciously. No one's surprised that I don't drink as they are in Riyadh. Because alcohol is taken so much more for granted here, it doesn't have the same obsessive attraction. There are no knots of women or men tied together. Everyone mixes freely. There's the same polished, flirtatious bantering that goes on wherever the international rich meet. In one corner I listen to a surprisingly intimate discussion about who's sleeping with who in London society. But this is Jiddah, so flirtatious gossip can't stretch to who's doing what to whom here. Not much actually. The Set's too small. They need each other too much.

One woman holds forth to me at length about how the Gulfies are ruining London. 'Claridges is still all right, they haven't discovered that yet. And we always go to the Dorchester. But have you been to the Grosvenor House recently? It's humiliating. Those Gulf women sit in the lobby, masked and veiled from head to foot, surrounded by half-dressed children. But that's not the half of it. I'm told when they've gone, the bedrooms have to be redecorated. They look as if the locusts have been through. Those people have never used a lavatory or a chair in their lives...'

I break away to another corner where more serious talk is going on. Medical talk. Outside a convalescent home, I've never met so many people who talk so much about their doctors. For some women it's a way of filling the boredom. The men's passion about their health is harder to plumb. 'It's simple,' confides one woman with catty delight, 'Once they've been rejected by three air-hostesses in a row they become vulnerable and then the only fumble they're likely to get is in Harley Street.'

What separates this party from any of the snowy gatherings in St Moritz in the sixties or exquisitely well-bred black tie affairs in London or New York is not the white thobes and head-dresses of the men. It's the staggering warmth of the people. Once you've been accepted, there's a flood of invitations, all genuine. None of the 'you must come over and see us sometime' variety. Come to stay, come for the weekend, come round any time.

But after a while with The Set I see another glaring difference, this time from Riyadh.

Look around the room at any Jiddah party. There are some Saudi men married to Saudi-born women, mostly first cousins. Because these women live right at the top, they've grown used to going out with their husbands; they've long since dropped the veil proper. But they live on a tight-rope. They're poised on the life-style their husbands want them to lead. Way below them is the chasm: that's where her family and his still live, observing their rigid ideals of what's honourable. Few of these women would dare to smoke in front of their family elders; none would drink.

Then look at the wives of the other Saudi men here. Most of them are foreign. Lita Tamer, sloe-eyed, lovely, is Christian. Jiddah respects her for holding to her religion but in this country where people go on and on about Saudi for the Saudis and all that pure blood stuff, Lita Tamer is Greek.

Abdullah 'Ali' Alireza, ambassador to Washington, is holding the floor with his very own switched-on charm. The Alirezas are one of the top families, bankers to Ibn Saud, faithful to Faisal but I often hear them called: 'non origin'. That's because generations ago they came from Iran where they'd gone generations before that from Jiddah. Dammit, the Alireza family was trading with Egypt from Arabia before the Prophet was born – is that 'non origin'? Ali's first wife was American. His second, Jugette, exotic, with a vivacious gypsy face, is Lebanese. Their marriage is one of Jiddah's successes. But then she can lead pretty much the life she wants here. Her restrictions are her luxuries. She can't drive? Why should she want to with a driver permanently on call? She can't work? She's far too busy being social.

Her husband's appointment to Washington occasioned a flood of tears from Jugette. Far from leading the free, Western-style life she's used to, it means acting out the kind of life that a Saudi woman is supposed to lead. If she's representing Saudi woman-hood abroad, it's goodbye to Jiddah's intimate parties where men and women meet with a peck on the cheek, the arm around the shoulder. It means staying at home in Washington while her husband gives male dinners and goes to receptions alone. They may be called Saudi now, but most of these wives were born Egyptian, Jordanian, Lebanese. The West may lump them together as 'Arabs' but the Saudis can tell them apart.

The whole kingdom is structured around a xenophobic ideal and yet more and more Jiddah men deliberately choose foreign wives. It's their way out. It's not a question of finding an educated woman; Zaki Yamani wasn't the first to send a daughter to a Californian campus. Saudi men here marry foreigners to escape the awful problem of what a Saudi-born wife can and cannot do. One family's expectations are enough. Two families impose an unbearable weight. The man who chooses an Egyptian, Lebanese or even European wife might have to fight like hell to get his father to accept her, but after he comes round the son can make his own way of life.

So here I am in a country clinging to its ideals like an unsure virgin clinging to her nightdress. There was a right old fuss in Riyadh when a certain London newspaper report came through. Gracious, the new Saudi Minister for Industry (note: a German wife) 'showed a readiness to enjoy certain local customs such as a stiff bloody Mary' during an interview at Claridges. Yet at every party in Jiddah, everyone drinks openly. When I go home what do the Saudis imagine that I'm going to say? That I saw consumed only large quantities of Coca Cola (correction: Kaki Cola, Coke's on the black list)? The answer, alas, is yes.

Dinner is served on the terrace around the pool. I share one of the sidewalk café tables with Abdul Aziz Sulaiman. He's forty, compactly built, jet black beard, jet-hard eyes, boss of a trading empire turning over several hundred million dollars a year. They don't come more Saudi than Abdul Aziz. He's Najdi; his father was King Ibn Saud's first finance minister and the man who signed the historic Saudi-American oil agreement in 1933. Abdul Aziz is just back from New York where he's negotiated to build new Intercontinental hotels in Jiddah, Dhahran, Jubail and Cairo. We chat about the City of London, where Abdul Aziz has merchant bankers, Arbuthnot Latham, as partners in an investment company, Oryx. But it's late and time to go. Abul Aziz's wife comes over. Intelligent, fashionable in every sense. She's Lebanese.

As we swish out of the circular Tamer drive on to those muddy tracks, we go past the Sulaiman's five-acre estate with its white twenty-roomed palace and four outhouses. Then on past other Jiddah mansions, walled in, greened off. There's an equally muddy confusion in my mind about what being Saudi is going to mean after the influx of more foreign wives, of more oil millions.

Right now, I'm reminded of Nassau in the heyday of the sixties. There's the smell of laundered money in the evening air.

Intelligence at work

I met a man in Kuwait. He was sent by another who took four days deciding whether or not he could trust me. Abdul Aziz Muammar stumbled on me and spent two hours trying to make me tell him about Saudi Arabia. He was desperate to talk. His eyes half-unseeing, his brain barely comprehending, he had the wild look of an animal that has just fought its way out of a cage.

Muammar has spent twelve years in solitary confinement in a prison in Hoffuf in Saudi Arabia. King Khalid let him out; his government is paying to send him to Boston to see the finest eye specialists. The darkness has left him half-blinded. He says that he was kept in chains; those who know confirm that it is likely. His crime? No one knows that. He says he was never told himself. 'They' say that he had 'reforming ideas'. No one suggests that he was plotting against the state. He wouldn't have survived if he had.

In King Saud's time, Muammar was leading the good life as Saudi Ambassador to Switzerland. Faisal took power, recalled Muammar, had him arrested, imprisoned without trial. He was released without warning when Faisal died. He sits in my room wearing a faded suit, against the incongruous luxury of a Sheraton Hotel. There's nothing I can do for him; nothing I can tell. We've come out of two separate Saudi Arabias.

Muammar says there were about seventy prisoners like him in Hoffuf. And that was only one of the country's jails. When people who are interested in the country find out that I saw him so soon after his release, they react. They want to know about him, where he is now. I don't know. The man crossed my life without warning. He disappeared from it leaving only the memory of his pain. The years taken from Muammar is the other, secret side of Saudi Arabia. Its security can work efficiently and incomprehensibly.

No one says or does anything to frighten me in Saudi Arabia. And yet I become so infected by the atmosphere that when a friendly official offers me his beach house to write in, I sit in my hotel room and howl with fear and loneliness. His house is miles from anywhere, has no phone and I have visions of being found 'accidentally drowned'.

Security is part of the way of life here. On a silly level it means that newspapers from abroad arrive on book-stands a mass of tiny holes, like lace. An army of censors go through each one like silk worms in mulberry bushes. They cut out everything objectionable, like the word 'Israel', any obviously adverse comment and endless other surprises.

In September 1975, British Embassy staff in Jiddah sat around trying to puzzle out why 2,800 copies of an inoffensive (yea, sycophantic) London *Times* supplement on the country, puffed out with adverts, had ended up on a government bonfire. It took a Saudi official to point out to me the most probable gaffe: an over-enthusiastic education correspondent, trying to show helpfully that Saudis aren't all that different from the rest of the world, had written a story headlined: 'Mixed classes at schools promised in two years.' Bosh. But even if it was a possibility, saying it out loud almost guarantees that it can't happen; that's Saudi for you.

On a more serious level, security runs the gamut from snatching men like Muammar to carefully screening labourers from abroad who might foment political unrest. The men from Yemen have the rawest deal; they come over the border from the impoverished republic (no, not the communist one, the other one) to build roads and mansions for the Saudis. Among them are bound to be left-wing agitators. The cabinet has been so worried by it that they recently persuaded the Religious Research Unit (made up of the ultra-conservative Wahhabi leaders) to allow women's photographs to appear on passports. You can't imagine what a step this is for the Saudis – men officials will have to unveil strange women. It's no use having passport snaps unless you're sure the faces match. Why did the religious leaders agree to this horrendous change? Because the Saudis knew that troublemakers were slipping in with Yemeni labourers disguised as women under black cloaks and veils.

It's safer not to know any details of the networks of paid informers, the men who do the dirty work, the onion skins of watchfulness. And I don't. But I do know that if any Yemenis come under suspicion, they're deported at once – and that's getting off lightly. The system is all part of keeping Saudi Arabia for the Saudis, safe and secure in its status quo – and the oil flowing to the West.

Now the ultimate Saudi contradiction must surely be the fact that the head of intelligence and national security affairs hasn't a drop of Saudi blood in his veins. It's one of these more exquisite ironies that you might find hard to swallow. But no, it's true.

Kamal Adham, the man who heads the intelligence system, is half-Turkish and half-Albanian. How did he get to this exalted position? An unbeatable combination of natural ability and nepotism. Adham is the adored half-brother of Queen Iffat, the adored favourite wife of Faisal. During King Faisal's time, Kamal Adham was closer to the throne than anyone. When Khalid acceded, Adham's enemies waited gleefully for him to fall; far from it. He grew far too powerful under his late brother-in-law's rule for King Khalid or Crown Prince Fahd to push him out now, even supposing they wanted to.

Queen Iffat was also 'non origin' – Saudi by descent, Turkish by birth. She returned to her native country in 1933 unveiled (the reforming leader Ataturk had ripped the veils off Turkish women) and went to petition Prince Faisal for the return of her family property. Faisal took a look at her – which is more than he got of his former wives before the wedding night – and he married her. It infuriated King Ibn Saud who, for years, nursed the grudge of her Turkish upbringing against Iffat. (No, that's not mentioned in polite company these days either.)

Kamal Adham, Iffat's half-brother, came to join her as a boy; she brought him up as her own son. Are you still surprised at his position today? And all that's Saudi about Kamal Adham is his adopted nationality – nothing else, least of all his personality.

He's secretive, shadowy, moves around the world almost without disturbing the air. To the merely curious he's as accessible as Howard Hughes was. He travels not just on government business; he controls an intricate financial empire and manages a hefty chunk of the private fortune of his dead brother-in-law's family. And even a chunk would be very hefty indeed.

Adham's wells of power bore deepest in the connection he made with Egypt when, as the most trusted of Faisal's servants, he was go-between for his country's reconciliation with Cairo after years of feuding and a war fought in Yemen. King Saud once wasted £2 million trying to have Nasser bumped off. Nasser almost certainly returned the compliment to brother Faisal.

Today, Adham is still Saudi's Mr Egypt, in close contact with President Sadat, channelling millions to him for arms and aid. Adham has an organisation of his own in Saudi that can bypass officialdom. If anyone runs into trouble in Riyadh or Jiddah, Kamal Adham would be the man to go to – he has the power to make decisions and the sophistication to weigh up the decisions he's making. Anyone with a less than clear conscience should stay away from his X-ray eyes.

But there's another Adham, 'a proper gentleman', as a friend puts it. He's the top of Jiddah's top set. When he's at home he entertains. There are no invitations; you're either in or out.

Dinner with the head of intelligence

Kamal Adham lives behind walls that seem to stretch for ever. His garden is the first signal of his position. It's green and jungly, like a painting by Douanier Rousseau.

Green is the greatest luxury in Jiddah. Well-kept green is an even greater luxury. Their desert past never taught Saudis about upkeep and many's the rich man who's planted a garden here, didn't read the back of the packet and never thought to ask if these things need after-care. Adham must run an army of horticultural commandos. This is winter and it's steamy hot. In summer it's humid hell. But here there are generous trees, flowering plants and spot-lit greenery everywhere. Parked on the wrinkle-free drive (no rubble here) are a few visiting cars, nothing racy, expensively solid.

Adham's driver dozes over the wheel of a Rolls in front of the door. As I walk in, it's the only time I feel relieved at being able to hide inside the one smart dress from my suitcase (packed for Kuwait; who would bracket Saudi Arabia with *Vogue*?). I know I am somewhere sophisticated, but spooky. There are marble floors, white walls, beautiful carpets and Chinoiserie. It isn't splashed about the place as proof of wealth. There are stunning museum pieces without the museum atmosphere. Not a lapse anywhere. In the large, low rooms The Set wander around, starting at the bar. It's the usual crowd, talking quietly among themselves, but all the time everyone is aware of the presence of the round, blue-eyed Buddha in repose in front of his videotape set. Adham spends most of the evening glued to it.

The house, a mixture of exotic and calm, is an extension of Adham himself. He has a way of manipulating his acolytes. Every now and again they approach tentatively, drawn into talking at him. He takes in all and gives back nothing, just that gentle, all-knowing smile. Every now and again he addresses a question to someone. It sounds like a riddle from an oriental sage; it may be nothing more complicated than an enquiry about a recent trip abroad. The complex and active mind of this guardian of Saudi Arabia seems bored by his toadies. And yet he's pleased at their presence. Most of them perform a service for him in one way or another. Under the grandeur and charm, I sense in him the Turkey where he was born. It was a sick dying old lion watching its empire disintegrate. It was rampant with cunning, treachery, decadence; at the same time there was learning and a passion for reform.

Kamal has decided to give me a treat. He'll play the videotape of his nephew's first major television appearance, on 'Meet the

Press', the hard-hitting American interview programme. Prince Saud bin Faisal, Minister for Foreign Affairs, makes Yamani's interviews seem as subtle as the deodorant adverts that punctuate Saud's sparring match. The acolytes, who talk and cluster around the drawing room during Adham's customary feast of movies, know instinctively that this is the moment to fall silent in admiration.

When I asked anyone else in Saudi Arabia why Prince Saud spoke for his country on American television sporting natty Western clothes instead of the all-important national dress, I got any amount of evasive answers. Adham has the confidence to tell me the truth. Some time before, an in-group had sat down with Adham and examined Prince Saud as a 'marketable commodity'. With his Princeton command of English, his economics and petroleum background (he was Yamani's number two before taking up foreign matters), he seemed a good bet to overcome that ubiquitous image of Saudis as hawk-eyed predators in white sheets. Yamani had worked as an experiment. He appeared at OPEC press conferences in a suit, he looked 'normal' to Westerners, they trusted him. Having put the commoner's toe in the water, time was right for a royal dip.

Cover Prince Saud's dark features with a head-dress and he looks (as his father did) a 'heavy'. Leave his head uncovered, get him a good hair cut, allow his stylish sense of Western dress to come through – and he makes an impact. Slowly but surely the plan is working. Saud's growing used to television. He knows when to make the solemn, carefully worded reply. He knows when to bite back, when to allow a personal show of emotion or humour to seep through. At last the Saudis are learning to stop bleating that the devil (Zionism) has the best tunes. They've found one of their own. Prince Saud wins 'Meet the Press' on points.

Adham savours his nephew's celluloid success. Prince Saud is good but doesn't quite merit the ten-minute eulogy that follows from Kanaan ('I'm named after Canaan, it flowed with milk and honey') al-Khatib, dancing round the room in his black silk thobe, tailored in Hong Kong. He's praising the prince with the same fervour with which he once recited one of his poems before a crowd of 54,000 at a state affair in Algeria. But al-Khatib, in his seventies now, stands out from the toadies. He was Faisal's court poet, there to praise the heroes and ignore their warts. His heart is worthy of his name and, noticeably, he is the one man in the room Adham doesn't cut down to size.

When Kanaan's flow of adulation finally runs dry, Adham continues his tale. He fills me in on the background to Saud's appearance at the opening of the last United Nations' General Assembly. Nearly a bad moment, there. Adham and Saud were ironing the British speech in their Waldorf Astoria suite. Someone, at least, remembered that Saudi Arabia had just led the battle to get Arabic recognised as an official UN language. The political ramifications were obvious. Prince Saud addressed the UN in Arabic, to the inevitable boredom of the press corps gathered round their closed circuit television in the smoke-filled window-less room above. Adham was disappointed; in English, Saud's charisma could have been irresistible. Never mind, there's time.

Slowly I become aware of resentment rolling across the room towards me. The attendants feel I've had more than my share of the Buddha. I retreat, regroup and corner al-Khatib. Is there anything this adorable old man hasn't done? He's had the distinction of teaching five British ambassadors to the Middle East at a Beirut university. Later he went into oil exploration, lost seven friends in three plane crashes, was the only survivor of one and saw some of his closest friends burned to death. He prefers to remember the good days. Like the night he met Paul Getty at a cocktail party in Paris and was persuaded to be his representative in Jiddah. He turned in that job when Aristotle Onassis passed by and enlisted his help. The Greek was negotiating an agreement with Saudi Arabia to control the country's entire oil shipments (a deal undermined by the CIA egged on by the oil companies).

Al-Khatib enjoyed working for Onassis, nearly as much as working for Texan oil billionaire, H.L. Hunt (Bunker's dad), but while he was enjoying that job an order came from the Saudi court: 'Return and work for Faisal'. He stayed by the king's side until his death. He seems to have been Faisal's book picker: 'I came across him reading Karl Marx one day. Not my idea; he said he had to understand the man's inferiority complex.' Once a year he composed a poem for the Hajj in Mecca and he spent many months in London minding Queen Iffat when she was having a hysterectomy. 'She had two of her daughters with her and they were always dying to go out. They danced me off my feet.' Impossible, he's still too full of energy.

It isn't polite to glue myself to one guest so I look round the room for other possibilities. Where's Fuad Rizk, the Lebanese smoothie who made good, very good and is now so rich that his arrival at Adham's London office is treated like a holy visitation? Here he's a creepy hand-kisser, watching Adham with the anxious attention of an ambitious office boy. Fortunately there's no sight of Rizk. And Phillipe Trad? A solid, humourless, neckless bull, another of Adham's small fry who seems so important away from The Presence? He's playing bar-tender.

Eavesdropping is far more fun. 'Poor old Muhammad; that huge motor cruiser of his in the Creek and no one, absolutely no one, will go near it. Well it's such a bother. I'd rather sit round the pool. And do you suppose he's ever sold a Stutz? He's given four already to King Khalid's son.' Muhammad Ashmawi has the Rolls and Stutz agencies. Stutz, Elvis Presley's favourite, is the world's most expensive car, gold-trimmed, mink-rugged, but these Saudis think it's showing off.

On I go. 'Where's Kanaan living these days? Oh, the Kandara. He's let his house hasn't he? But then who wouldn't? I let one of mine to an embassy six months ago for 175,000 riyals a year and now I wish I hadn't. I could get 250,000 for it today.'

No one talks about problems in the abstract. It's all money, possessions, swapped anecdotes, children and, inevitably, doctors. Beirut is being ravaged. There's hardly a person in the room who doesn't know someone who's been killed. It's passed off with: 'Isn't it dreadful. How many died today?' It's a wariness of politics; it's also a reflection of a society where people are brought up not to ask questions. Business is where they shine; all that Levantine intrigue is perfectly safe.

At one o'clock it's time to move into the stately dining room. Kamal's 'at homes' are a new development instigated by Mrs Adham. She was once a great beauty; she's now an attentive, sad-eyed hostess. For years, Nadia Adham was left alone night after night while her husband went off to visit the men. A few years ago she suggested that he bring his friends and their wives to the house.

It means catering for a multitude: ten or sixty may turn up. It means staying up until three or four in the morning while Kamal wastes his stamina watching one videotape after another. It means having some of his entourage, whose company Nadia Adham would surely not seek out otherwise. But it's brought her husband back home. He treats her with the greatest respect. She treats his guests with the greatest kindness. 'Goodbye, I do hope you enjoyed yourself,' she says as I leave. Far more than she must have done. The sound of yet another movie fades as the door shuts behind me.

The film strip

Muhammad Ashmawi is Jiddah's movie king. He lends films. You can't imagine how important that makes him to The Set's social life. It's just as if he controlled the biggest stash of cigarettes in a prisoner-of-war camp. I see more movies in a week in Jiddah than in a year, maybe two, in London. Everyone into video. They don't bother with their local television station; they gobble up cassettes at the rate of two or three a day. That's where Muhammad comes in. He doesn't have a large collection of films; he has a library.

'Oh no, not *Serpico* again. Ring Muhammad, see what's new over there.' I have by now heard so much about Muhammad that I can't resist a visit. So far I've only glimpsed him at parties.

By the time his phone directions have, as usual, taken in a gasoline station and a set of traffic lights, one permanently on green, the other on red (typical Jiddah), we both give up. He sends a car over for me, or rather, one of his cars. The fur-lined navy Lincoln parks outside his house next to his Bentley, his Rolls, his 'Cadi-Rolls' (a mongrel of dubious ancestry), his Stutz and, his favourite, a yellow Dino Ferrari. It's four o' clock in the afternoon. I've just left a lunch party; Muhammad is sitting down for lunch with his children (his German wife Elfrida is delivering again in Munich) and an unspecified air hostess. I get the feeling this isn't the best moment to arrive but nothing will satisfy Muhammad's hospitality until I join in yet another lamb feast.

His son Ahmad, twelve, and daughter Naveen, nine, have discovered Harvey's basket, overlooked in the juggernaut-loads of furniture and packing cases that have arrived from Munich. Muhammad's wife has been looting department stores. Harvey arrived with the baggage, locked in his basket. He's glad to be allowed out at last to stretch his titchy legs. Harvey's a chihuahua. A nasty, twisted looking thing that once had an accident down a flight of stairs. I wouldn't blame the person who kicked him. Nor from the expression on his face would Muhammad. Like most Arab men he shrinks at the thought of a dog in the house. But it's 'the thing' for women to have now. I keep finding these small ferocious creatures glaring at their mistresses' husbands. A glare by proxy, so to speak. The Koran has rules about dogs. No dogs; they're unclean.

Yes, but Islam forbids men to wear gold too, and Muhammad has a gold watch on one wrist and gold cuff-links on both. Nobody seems to have one gold watch in Jiddah; they have a wardrobe of them. The ones with a troublesome Koranic conscience have a wardrobe of platinum watches instead. But considering how little sense time makes, watches are hardly functional utilities here. They seem to fill some ceremonial niche.

Muhammed, however, is getting very concious of the passing minutes. Could it be that I am playing gooseberry? Muhammad's an attractive man. There's no getting away from the fact and the admiring air hostess isn't trying to. He's forty, as smooth as easy-spread margarine and can hardly rely on a couple of car agencies and a lending library of movies for a living. He doesn't;

he isn't here to dole out cars and films, he's not a service centre for the jet set. He plays up to the role but he's only another of those entrepreneurial conjurers whose tricks are many and mysterious.

Jiddah airport is one of his money launching pads. He refuels half the aircraft landing there ('over a million gallons a day during the Hajj'). He only refuels half because he has the Shell concession and someone else has the other half for Mobil. A million gallons a day isn't bad, and that's only one of his outlets. They shell out enough for him to have homes in Munich and Beirut, and four houses in Jiddah: Four? 'My mother lives in one, my sisters live in one, you're in the third now and then there's my favourite. It's a comfortable little house where I can turn off the telephone bell when I don't want to be disturbed.'

The telephone in this brocaded, tasselled Vienna thirties house does ring however. It's someone else after *Jaws* (*Jaws* opened here before it opened in London). Muhammad promises to look and gets up swishing his thobe with the finesse of an expert. Don't be misled into the notion that a long dress makes a sissy out of a man. It turns male deportment into an art of self-representation.

Muhammad pops over to see what's on the shelves of the library. The famous Jiddah film library has a house of its own. A dishy secretary-receptionist who would look at home in a Madison Avenue advertising agency sits at her desk by the entrance, answering the telephone, keeping the catalogues of in-coming cassettes and outgoing borrowing. It's a full time job. After the chaos in the house with Harvey scooting under the fridge and the chaos in the yard where the swimming pool will be once Elfrida's loot has been unpacked, the cassette library is organised as systematically as a college archive.

Jaws isn't in. There are six unedited versions of *Emmanuelle* doing the rounds of Jiddah at the moment. But not from Muhammad. His shelves stock more wholesome entertainment, but these are for his friends' family gatherings.

Another of those ubiquitous Saudi contradictions. I'm watching one of Muhammad's films after dinner with friends. It's a harmless action-packed thriller with blood spilling everywhere. So far so good. Nothing wrong with gratuitous violence. Dissolve to a naked woman climbing on to a battered man to offer solace. Grandma in the back row of the sofas yells into the darkness: 'Cover your eyes everyone; you mustn't watch.' We spring to attention.

In Muhammad's library, there's a prominently displayed notice: 'Please return films in four days.' Does everyone obey the rules? The secretary turns her eyes to the ceiling. 'I only wish they would.' I ask if he charges a lending fee. I choke on the *faux pas* as soon as it's out. 'Charge my friends? Never.' His grey hair and smiling brown face turn to frost. The moment passes when I remember that Ashmawi is another old boy of Victoria College, Cairo (along with those other tycoons, ministers, presidents and kings) and hurl that into the conversation as a cover-up.

Surprise. The car salesman patter grinds to a halt and Muhammad tells me of his time at a proper English prep school, Picton House, Fordingbridge. He recalls its setting in a green sward in rural Hampshire and trips to the Abbotsbury Swannery. From there he went to another English public school, Tonbridge. Presumably he progressed to university? Back with a bump to the unexpected that I'm always expecting. 'University? I didn't think it necessary. I did a Pitman's course in shorthand and typing.'

This ex shorthand typist is more than ready for a nap. He's sending me away in a Rolls this time ('last year I sold seventy'). I look longingly at the Stutz, all £60,000 of it. 'No, the Rolls for you. The Stutz is too ostentatious, it's more of a toy really. Another time, though.' Of course, there's always another time with The Set, if not in Jiddah in London. The Rolls carried me off to a birthday party with some more friends. As a treat there's a film show. A Robert Redford movie. Also from Muhammad.

After Jiddah you realise how simple it is in the West to guess about wealth – who has it and (mostly) where it comes from. Here there are no recognisable clues. If a banker so much as breathes a word of his money on deposit from these secrecy-loving millionaires, he'll have lost the account before the words are out of his mouth. No one's in any particular business. The age of the specialist hasn't dawned here; specialists are what you hire from abroad on short contract. Possessions are no guide. The Saudis spend a fortune just to live passably well in Jiddah. Inflation runs higher than fifty per cent. That's why those London apartments go for such outrageously high prices; they're rock bottom compared to Jiddah.

Muhammad Ashmawi lives in a home that would suit a sub-urban doctor in his sixties. How much he's worth is anybody's guess. There's no exchange control here, no band of nosy taxmen with their detailed returns, no taxes for that matter.

So a man works for the government; it doesn't mean a thing. I'm with a fairly lowly official; he's so lowly that I don't like to watch him pay the bill for the Kandara's over-priced coffee. Then he reaches in his pocket for a handkerchief (he has a cold and many homeopathic remedies for it) and out tumble a three-carat canary-yellow diamond, even larger blue-white marquises and a good five-carat solitaire. He's a bit of a diamond dealer.

He's having trouble with his builders, he tells me. No, they're not building a house for him to live in; he's seen to that already. They're working on a few of the plots of land he has in Jiddah and Medina that King Faisal gave him. Anyone hanging around the court for long enough gets something for his services. And anyone hanging around in Government can get to hang around the court some time. When he gets through with cursing the builders, he starts on the cost of food. It's just like home. Two years ago a whole sheep, essential for those hospitable soirées, cost seventy riyals. Now it costs 350. When he starts on the problem of finding a reliable plumber, it has an even more familiar ring to it.

The only place the Saudis do well is in the domestic quarters, where other Arabs end up doing the dirty work. The Saudis treat their servants without a trace of snotty stand-offishness. They feel as responsible for them as they do for their families. And they're as mean as hell with their paychecks.

A gardener gets 460 riyals a month, a cleaner gets 250, cooks come more expensive at 800. But those all-important drivers now command the impressive salary of 1,000 riyals a month. Although they're foreigners, mostly Yemeni, a certain money militancy has entered the ranks of the sought-after men behind the wheels. Where would the women be without them? Driving, if they had any luck.

But even knowing how much it all costs doesn't help you place a Saudi. There's no class structure as we know it here; there's rich, very rich and at the top there's very rich close to the Right Ear.

What can you tell from a man's thobe? In the West you can weigh up the cut of a man's suit, the material, perhaps the old school tie. A thobe is only a negative give-away. It doesn't tell you if a man's rich; you know he's poor when he turns up in the afternoon in the same thobe he wore in the morning. Everyone else changes several times a day. Even those expensive watches and cufflinks don't necessarily tell you anything. They may be something he couldn't resist in Cartier last week; they could equally well be a gift from some higher being.

But the wealth is there alright. It's what brings home the young men who have tasted the freedom of the West at universities in America and Britain. They know they'll be able to pick up enough money in Jiddah to buy their way out to the high life, or the highbrow, whenever it takes them. Some young men come back and kick a bit at first. I'm in a family living room with a new Ph D of twenty-five who's making rude noises about the gangsters shooting it out on the videotape. 'I don't watch rubbish, Buñuel and Bergman are more my thing.' He sniffs with disgust at the latest Harold Robbins his mother's digging into. 'I'm reading an interesting book about Libya by Ruth First.' But isn't she a communist? If so, he can't be caught reading her. 'Oh really? I had no idea. I'd better throw it away.' He's learning.

Umm Khalthoum then the Beach Boys go on to the hi-fi: 'I don't know how they can put up with that noise.' What does he like? 'Chamber music is more my thing, but I do enjoy Mozart, his Eroica symphony'. As he sits hankering for his liberal Western newspapers ('Oh, for the sight of a *Guardian*'), he's indulging in that Saudi weakness: playing another role. It's those small mistakes that give it away again (Mozart's Eroica? Come now). While all this is going on, his family is worrying needlessly about his future. Sooner rather than later he'll settle down, learn to make money and, relinquishing his last gesture of defiance, marry the first cousin ear-marked for him. Or he'll marry a foreigner but they'll patch it up somehow. This boy chose to come home.

Salim bin Ladin didn't plan on coming back in a hurry. He was having a marvellous time with the friends he'd made at his English public school, Millfield. He was chasing around London talking about becoming a doctor, and doing some female anatomical research on the way. That was 1966; he was the son of the largest construction man in Saudi Arabia and enjoying the proceeds of the palaces and roads his father built. Bin Ladin Senior died in a plane crash. Salim came back to take over the firm and play surrogate father to his fifty-two younger brothers and sisters, one of whom wasn't born, two of whom he had never met.

Nobody in their right mind would take Salim for a multi-millionaire. He's a skinny Peter Pan who looks about seventeen, is thirty-six and lies through his teeth about his age. 'Everyone has one fear. Mine's the fear of growing old.' He's sitting on a deck chair overlooking the Red Sea in his parents-in-law's cosy Creek house. He's wearing a swimsuit and there isn't a hair on his youth's body nor an ounce of spare flesh. You have to know how exclusive the Creek is, how only the very top people have houses here at all, to appreciate what an Establishment signpost this modest house is. He's drooling over his baby daughter, being unexpectedly smashing to his wife. Sheikha is frail but intense with deep pits under her eyes. Salim looks like any young man from Selfridge's shirt department having a day's outing by the sea.

Sheikh Salim (as he's now called as boss of both the family and its business) didn't want to come home at all. He couldn't have been less interested in being a merchant prince. It wasn't his fault that he was the eldest son of a man who started life as a semi-skilled bricklayer and died at the age of forty-seven, leaving an empire with 5,000 employees. It wasn't money that pulled Salim back to Jiddah. It was that Saudi conditioning that forced responsibility on him. 'I must decide what schools my family should go to, how much money they should have to spend. I have to decide who my sisters can marry. My father was a great man, he was illiterate to the day he died, but in his own way he was a genius. He was a very religious man, worked fifteen to seventeen hours a day and he never had a holiday in his life. I'm nothing compared to him, nor will I ever be. I don't want to be a slave to money or work. I like having a good time.'

He gets by. He spends at least six months abroad, not always on the hunt for new contracts. When his father died, King Faisal put the firm under the control of a board of trustees, and he has younger brothers, who tower over him, to keep things going. When he's at home he plays with his four private planes. 'It's so peaceful up there; you look down on the whole world and you're as free as a bird. Why should my father's crash stop me flying? In our religion we believe it happens the way it's meant to. I'm even teaching my wife to fly, She isn't allowed to drive, but there's nothing to stop a woman flying.'

And he stays away from the office as much as possible doing most of his business on the phone from home. One night, when I'm in the office with him, a bevy of Americans arrive, hot foot from the airport, dazed by jet-lag. The expression on their faces when they finally get to meet the man they've crossed the world to see makes the irreverent Salim even merrier. They have to swallow their pride at being confronted with this tiddler. Trustees or no, Sheikh Salim counts.

He doesn't take much more sense of solemnity along with him to the Dutch ambassador's celebrated Monday musical evenings, high point of Jiddah's cultural life. Salim's regular offering is a cherubic rendering of 'Where'er you walk'. They're lucky to get off with that. He usually turns up to official receptions with his harmonica, which stunned one bunch of American corporation presidents hosting a banquet in his honour in the States. He did an unexpected puff and blow job on his mouth organ instead of giving a speech. He doesn't like to take life seriously.

His father helped to build this country. His money gave Salim bin Ladin a taste for what it could buy. He's aware that men like him will change the country that drew him back. 'We, the younger generation, have nothing to be particularly proud of. It was given to us. Maybe when I'm dead, my son might say "you know, Salim wasn't a bad guy." That's all I deserve. It was the old guys who made what we have today.'

Salim has millions of pounds, a few more sisters to marry off and a burning ambition to own a Battle of Britain Spitfire. And sometimes his high jinks are even appreciated. A little while ago he arrived in Cairo to find there was no room at the five star inn. No amount of multi-millionaire's sulks could have budged that situation, but they're not Salim's style. 'If I play the French National Anthem to you on my harmonica,' he asked the surprised room manager, Monsieur de la Porte, 'will you give me a room?'

'That's a funny way to get a room,' said M. de la Porte.

'It's the only way left,' answered the pragmatic Salim. He played the Marseillaise and slept well that night.

Goodbye to all that?

If I have to explain to anyone why I feel drawn back to Saudi Arabia, I know that it has something to do with the Alirezas and what they represent.

On the left-hand side of the Mecca Road spinning out of Jiddah, there's a particularly forbidding pair of gates. They open, rarely, on to a tree-lined drive leading to a wide sweep with an island in the middle facing the Arab version of a baronial hall. Scattered around it are a collection of other, lesser houses which have been run up over the years as the Alireza family expanded.

This is the scene of that particularly Saudi institution: the family compound, base for a whole clan of brothers, cousins, uncles and their off-spring. It's the outward, visible structure of a deep-rooted binding magnetism that brings home those foreign-educated young Saudis for whom money and obligation would not be enough. There are few such compounds left.

Early in the morning, the steamy heat of Jiddah hangs over the silent compound. A few servants, many of them former slaves (slavery was abolished in 1962), go about their business. At about ten the families stir, mingling over any one of a variety of break-fast tables.

Going to the seaside is something that happens every weekend. Even so, it still takes two and a half hours to get everyone mobilised. There are problems. Hayyat, hair awry, arms flailing, mother figure in residence for all and actual mother of some, is panicking as usual. At least she's reassured that the food did go off hours ago with the servants, cleaning instructions went too and the lorries are on their way to deliver the desalinated water. In all this babble of excitement, Fahd, twenty-eight, is looking unusually surly and threatening not to go. There's a rumour that the generator has broken down. What, no hot showers after swimming?

It's an unpromising start, but at last we're off. The Creek is a special place indeed. It's not only the fabulous strip of blue water teeming with exotic fish, it's the exclusivity of it all. For love or money, you can't buy into the Creek. A large chunk is owned by the king's elder brother, who has a fortress-like place of his own and keeps the rest as a public beach, although no Saudi who is anybody would be seen dead on it. Crown Prince Fahd owns a chunk, naturally. It's another fortress.

What's left belongs firmly to a few families – like the Alirezas. Their fenced off compound embraces yet another cluster of homes centred around a large, terraced waterside residence under the trusteeship of Sheikh Ahmad, white-haired, dignified. He's acting head of the Alireza clan in the absence of cousin Ali, Ambassador to the States, and cousin Muhammad, Ambassador to France.

In their absence, he's also minding the family firm. The Alirezas are old money. They were rich long before oil. They have been

1 King Khalid of Saudi
Arabia

2 Crown Prince Fahd of
Saudi Arabia

3 Sheikh Yamani, Minister of Petroleum and Mineral Resources

4 *Below left* Sheikh Hisham Nazer, Director of the Central Planning Institute of Saudi Arabia

5 *Below right* Sheikh Abdullah Alireza, Deputy Minister of Foreign Affairs

6 Jiddah

7 Prince Saud Ibn Faisal

8 Adnan Khashoggi

9 *Above left* Sheikh Isa bin Salman al-Khalifa, Ruler of Bahrain

10 *Above right* Sheikh Sabah al-Salim al-Sabah, Ruler of Kuwait

11 *Below left* Sheikh Saud Nasir al-Sabah, Kuwaiti Ambassador to Great Britain

12 *Below right* Sheikh Nasser Sabah al-Nasser, Governor of the City of Kuwait

13 Sheikh Rashid of Dubai

14 Feast given by the ruler of Dubai, Sheikh Rashid

15 Ruler's palace in Abu Dhabi. *Centre:* Sheikh Zayid; *Right:* Sheikh Rashid of Dubai

16 Sheikh Zayid's Rolls-Royce and accompanying guards. Note the chrome-plated automatic rifle carried by guard on the left.

17 Sheikh Khalifa bin Hamad al-Thani, Ruler of Qatar

18 Sheikh Sultan bin Muhammad al-Qasimi, Ruler of Sharjah

19 & 20 Modern development in Sharjah

merchants for centuries. There's a high-rise Alireza building going up in the centre of Jiddah to house their multifarious interests. Their entrepreneurial emporium stocks insurance, shipping (four 8,000 tonners), agencies like ITT and that Harry Winston connection, of course. While we frolic in the Creek this weekend, a three-million-dollar diamond and emerald rope lies smouldering in Sheikh Ahmad's office safe. It'll be sold by the weekend.

Doing business with the West is no novelty to the Alirezas. In the 1930s another Muhammad Alireza ran a pearl empire stretching from Bombay to his shop in the Faubourg St Honoré, Paris, and his suite in Claridges that in its time attracted the world's top jewellery dealers. Then came the Depression; the pearl trade crashed with it but not the Alirezas.

What is remarkable is that throughout all these cosmopolitan dealings, foreign marriages and three generations now educated abroad, the Alirezas, as a clan, have preserved their intense traditional family life. No matter that some of the family are half-American (Ambassador Ali from Washington married from California before he married from the Lebanon), no matter that the whole family still bears that 'non origin' label from their generations spent in Persia. Plus royaliste que le roi: the Alirezas are more Saudi than the most pure-bred Najdis. One of the family's other Abdullahs, thirty-three years old, high up in government, was sent to Harrow and turned out from there as a proper little English gentleman straight into Fitzwilliam College, Cambridge. Friends say that when he came home he scrubbed his voice clean of its upper crust to help him fit back in. But today he's Saudi through and through, desperately fighting to keep his children protected in the family set-up.

At the Alirezas over the weekend, there's only family (and honorary family); no business entertaining here. There's a babble of children and a multitude of adults all of whom respond with the same immediate physical affection to whichever child happens along. It's taken for granted here that children scream and shout and get away with murder. But when they are told to do something they respond without question. It's easy to see why so many first cousins have married in a family like this. It's not because it's arranged for them; when they grew up the only members of the opposite sex that they remembered being free and happy with were the cousins of their childhood.

We all do whatever we feel like. I go thrashing in the sea – free at last. Motherly Hayyat is a demon at the backgammon board, trouncing whoever takes her on. She favours a flamboyant game with a lot of clacking of pieces on the wooden board and frequent explosions of triumph. She wouldn't go down well in the hush of the Palace Hotel, St Moritz, but she's marvellous to watch here. A procession of women go in to swim, modestly clinging to their wraps until they reach the water's edge. Swimming in front of men, even family, is still something of a risqué novelty; the Alireza women only do it in the comfort of a flock.

At night, there's the inevitable film, projected against a white screen painted on to the wall. It's three o' clock in the morning before I get to bed, not lapped to sleep by the noise of the waves, but drummed into it by the throb of the air-conditioning. At dawn, a hardy few chug off on a fishing trip before the sun gets hot. The rest of the clan don't stir until much later. It will be another relaxed day, punctuated by four meal times and five prayer times. The Alirezas are religious enough for praying to be personal and unselfconscious. At odd times, not necessarily simultaneously, they go off and fetch their mats, kneel in (I suppose) the direction of Mecca and pray. Everyone else carries on as if nothing is happening. One woman doesn't pray all day. I ask her why not. 'I can't. I'm having a period,' she says matter-of-factly.

It's a jarring reminder of how the Koran, the foundation stone of their life and kingdom, stresses the lowlier status of women. It's a status that in Hayyat's case has been intensified by some deep personal tragedies. Sitting here, her face full of animation and fun, she betrays no bitterness towards the past. But in the past, Hayyat was the first and only wife of Muhammad, the absent stern pillar of the family, now Ambassador to France. She is still his wife, officially. But in the fifties, Muhammad took another wife, Hamsa. Unlike many women, in that Saudi era, Hayyat couldn't face sharing her husband, so they lived apart. Not very far apart; she stayed in one house in the Mecca Road compound with her children by Muhammad. He and Hamsa lived next door with theirs.

Hayyat's eldest son died slowly of leukemia in an American hospital two years ago. One day he felt better. He got out of bed, took his wife (his first cousin, a usual Alireza happening), one of his sisters and his nurse out to lunch. He died the next day. And then there was the car crash in Paris. Ambassador Muhammad decided to take some of his family off to the sea. He ran the car into a tree. Second wife, Hamsa, sitting up front, was killed instantly. The wife of Hayyat's second son had her neck broken. An adopted daughter's skull cracked open and Hamsa's youngest daughter, physically unharmed, saw it all.

You can't begin to understand anything about Saudi Arabia until you appreciate the force that keeps an old-fashioned family like the Alirezas together. It's so strong that after the accident, it was Hayyat, the discarded first wife, who laid out and washed the body of her successor.

Bahrain

A Glimpse of the Future

Playing happy families

Sheikha Maryam is hot. Tiny sweatlets escape from her short, lustrous hair down her refined lustrous forehead. Last week she decided that it was time for winter (a short cold spell that interrupts Bahrain's perennial steam bath). Her summer clothes were packed away and 30-year-old Maryam is wearing the latest Paris layered look. She would be the picture of elegance if only she wasn't so hot that when she finally discards her mauve Chanel-style jacket, wet stains creep from under her purple silky armpits.

Even an al-Khalifa sheikha can't dictate to the weather in Bahrain. It may be time for winter in Maryam's mind but outside it's still boiling. As the al-Saud are to Saudi Arabia, the al-Khalifa are to Bahrain, give or take a few essential differences. The size of the place is one: Saudi Arabia has gorged three quarters of the Arabian peninsula. Bahrain amounts to a scattering of islands with one main one the size of the Isle of Wight with the population of Portsmouth. But Bahrain is al-Khalifa land, ruled by the family since 1783 when they swept out of Arabia, down the Gulf and over the eighteen-mile stretch of water to push the Persians off Bahrain and divide up the richest date gardens among themselves.

Sheikha Maryam is married to her mother's aunt's son (a common family knot), Sheikh Isa bin Muhammad. Since there are al-Khalifa Isas all over the island, you have to get the bin Muhammad right, or you might end up visiting any number of other Isas. Maryam and Isa don't live in a palace. It's not the al-Khalifa's way. They have a comfy two-storey house, the decoration of which can best be summed up by mention of the Louis Quinze telephone. They live in the suburb of Rifaa, the al-Khalifa housing estate where the family pile together about nine miles out of the capital of Manama. The focal point of Rifaa is the roundabout outside the ruler's palace (he's another Isa and it is undoubtedly a palace). Tubby topiary ponies trot on top of a neatly trimmed hedge around a ring of tidy green grass. It's appropriate; the al-Khalifas look like short, friendly ponies. There are some with big heads, some with saggy middles, and sleek economy-sized ones like Maryam.

She's in a quandary. Guests are coming for tea; there's no time to unpack the summer clothes, so she'll have to grin and bear it. No, grin isn't the right word. Maryam smiles. Anything larger would bare her only bad feature, a set of distinctly pony-like gums. The man servant, kitted in white trousers and jacket, is getting the tea trolley ship-shape. It's a work of art in itself. A gilt cocktail trolley by birth, it's now arranged with organdie-decorated plates of cakes, china cups and a silver tea service. The only thing that doesn't rise to this *Woman's Home Journal* standard of afternoon entertaining is the man servant's bare feet. He doesn't go in for shoes.

All this is in aid of Isa and Maryam's architect and his wife. They're bringing over the final drawings of an extension. By the time everyone has done justice to the cakes, Maryam and Isa have scrapped the idea of an extension in favour of gutting the whole house and adding a new wing. Fortunately there's a spare al-Khalifa roof going somewhere while two years' building goes on here. Fortunately there's no lack of available funds.

Maryam begins conversations with the Bahraini catch-phrase: 'We're not rich you know.' You might even believe her. The furnishings reflect more of a yearning for elegance than its achievement. But not her clothes: little numbers she picks up in London and Paris and San Francisco and Rio de Janeiro and then there was that time on holiday in Barbados. She was sunning herself on the beach and an American woman came up to find out where she hailed from. 'I told her "Bahrain". She was all over me. "So you're an oil sheikh. I've never met a real live oil sheikh." It was nearly as bad as the time in New York when I went to change a few thousand dinars in the bank and the cashier asked me how I get on with my husband's other wives.'

Most of the al-Khalifas have chucked in having several wives now. Trouble ahead. They still stick to marrying family and in-breeding isn't the best thing for blood-stock. In the old days, number one wife would be a first cousin but there'd be a foreigner or two among the next batch. Since they didn't hang on to these outsiders very long, the stock so far (apart from minor hereditary diseases like diabetes) has been bright and lively.

Sheikh Isa bin Muhammad, Maryam's attentive husband, is a good example. He's an able al-Khalifa so he's been drafted into government to be moved around wherever there's an empty desk. It seems a waste of a qualified petro-chemical engineer (London and Southampton Universities, England) but engineers can be hired. Al-Khalifas have to run the place. And no one's quite sure how many there are. A house-to-house count two years ago numbered them at 3,000 in all. 'To tell you the truth I was surprised; I thought we were at least 5,000.'

Once Nanny has found something cooler to wear, Maryam's week perks up. She doesn't do very much but she's happy looking after her two young sons. 'I don't want any more children. My mother had ten, but in those days they didn't know how not to have them. I must say, though, it did give us friends to play with.'

One of her friends, sister Sheikha (Sheikha Sheikha), drops by. She's Bahrain's Marisa Berenson, married with two children and taking a law degree by correspondence course. 'Poor Sheikha', says Maryam pouring a consoling cup of coffee, 'she always has her nose in a book. Imagine, I have two sisters and a brother studying law and my father was a judge. My mother and I sometimes go mad listening to them. We housewives have almost nothing to talk about.' She and Sheikha have something important to talk about today. Maryam's youngest, aged four, might be getting spoiled. 'Salman is car mad. He consulted me the other day quite seriously about whether he should have a Lamborghini or a Ferrari. What can I do with him? I blame my nephew. He gave Salman a ride in his new Lamborghini and now the boy thinks everyone has to have one.' The nephew is twenty.

Isa bin Muhammad comes home from work. He's thirty-seven, comely, quick-brained, gentle and very hungry. We go in to lunch joined by Isa's mother who lives with them and does the cooking ('I can hardly boil an egg,' says Maryam). This sophisticated couple, veterans of some of the world's most select watering places, sit down to lamb and rice. Maryam daintily uses her knife and fork. Her husband and mother-in-law forage among the dishes with their fingers, making a satisfying mess and a great deal of noise.

'If you're going to Kuwait,' says Maryam above the din, 'you must go and see my best friend, the ruler's daughter. She and her husband used to come and spend weekends with us in Bournemouth when Isa was a student. We had such good times together. Mind you, she doesn't have much style. The first time I went to stay with her in Kuwait, I jumped into the swimming pool before anyone warned me. Can you believe it, it was full of sea water? I said to her "how can you be so stingy? Your father's the ruler and you don't even have fresh water in your swimming pool."'

Emerald Isle browned off

At first it hits hard, all this ordinariness. Coming straight from Jiddah, it's like entering a decompression chamber. There's that helpless feeling on the first day when someone suggests that I take a taxi to a strange place. For a moment I have forgotten how. I go on being 'an Arab woman' – until suddenly the silliness of it dawns. I have been looking forward to Bahrain. Date groves, rambling gardens, green, green, green. Green to anyone from Saudi; brown, brown, brown to anyone reared in English orchards.

As if that isn't enough of a shock, I have also moved from the most Arab of Arab countries (which Saudi Arabia is in the sense of Islamic and desert traditions) to the least. Nowhere has the British character been so hard at work chiselling down the natural quality of a people within its 'sphere of influence' as it has in Bahrain.

In 1967 I spent a nervous time in Aden at the tip of Southern

Arabia. The British Army was signing off with a certain ignominy. Soldiers were sniped at, grenades lobbed, booby traps laid and a security handout at the military base began: 'The terrorists who carry out attacks are not noted for their courage.' Neither was I. So the arrival on the scene of Sheikh Isa, Ruler of Bahrain, had the romantic relief of Errol Flynn in the last but one reel. He presided over a regimental boxing-match as guest of honour. Word soon got round that after handing out the army's cups to the winners, he presented his own consolation prizes to the losers – cars all round. When I finally got out of the Aden hell-hole to Bahrain on the way home, it felt like arriving in a corner that would be forever Britain.

Since then Aden has gone communist (the People's Democratic Republic of Yemen), the British have pulled out of Bahrain and the ruler takes second billing to the new oil superstars of the Gulf. Al-Khalifas like Maryam and Isa bin Muhammad have settled down to nice, ordinary lives, trying in vain to keep up with the royals next door, and it all seems frightfully dull. A short while ago a cartoon appeared in the London *Evening Standard*. It featured Manama full of fat, bearded, gruesome-looking Arabs all in national dress, many touting daggers at their waist. The only woman was a wretch heavily veiled in black. What a farce.

The market place of Manama is actually full of European ladies with frizzy perms, stripy deck-chair frocks, sensible sandals and shopping bags. The distinguished international fixers that you find in Saudi Arabia give way here to low-grade mechanics and soldiers of lower rank who stayed on after independence for the good middle-class life they couldn't afford in Britain, for the cheap over-the-counter booze and cigarettes. Not for nothing has Bahrain been called 'the Welwyn of the Gulf'.

The few Bahraini men to be seen in national dress (and many don't bother with it) aren't loitering. They're going about their business and they haven't been near a dagger since they last saw one displayed on some collector's mantelpiece. The main attraction of the centre of Manama is the post office; this is the only place in the area where mail arrives from Europe without fail, sometimes in two days. What's more, the post office is almost entirely staffed by Bahraini women. The only apparent difference between them and the women behind European counters is that here they take time to be pleasant. Bahraini girls in mini-skirts and jeans work alongside men in offices and when the day is over, they climb into their own cars and drive themselves home. So much for the veiled wretch of the cartoon cliché.

The British left behind cinemas (the first opened in 1937) and, more important, driving tests. As a result the Bahrainis drive the same way they live; slowly and safely with both hands clutching the wheel. Notice the traffic lights; they work. If they're red, the obedient drivers stop. Notice the curbs, painted white, the pedestrian crossings, the alert traffic police.

Bahrain is having to work for a living now. In the 1930s it enjoyed a brief reign as the richest teenager in the Gulf when its oil came in before anyone else's. During this time, the crafty ruler acquired a considerable tract of land in Kuwait in return for loans to his impoverished fellow emir. It wasn't worth much in those days but it makes the present ruler the landlord of the Kuwait Hilton, the American Embassy and twenty of the smartest villas there. Just as well. Bahrain's own meagre oil reserves are running out. Its main source of income comes from refining Saudi oil piped across the sea.

It's quite a come-down for an island that once strutted confidently under the protection of the British military. That had its drawbacks too, of course. It meant getting stuck with a lot of bored army wives too pukka to make pets of sheikhly wogs. But the sheikhs, appetites whetted, took to flying in curvaceous bunnies from European rabbit hutches. Today the army wives have been superseded by not so pukka wives of limp-shouldered technicians from the north of England, an array of air hostesses, some 'resting', others working for Gulf Air, but many of the sheikhs stay home with their families.

At first sight, it's drab if reassuring. Any drama breaks the monotony, like the one that happens soon after I arrive. It's a day that will rankle forever in the history of the local fire brigade: the day the bank caught fire. At seven-thirty in the morning the electrical system in the two-storey Chase Manhattan building goes haywire. The building in the town centre goes up in flames. The Manama fire brigade trundle down in their vintage red engines to put out the blaze. No *Towering Inferno* heroics here. The firemen are so keen to keep away from the heat that their hoses never reach the flames.

They call out all the fire brigade from the airport; the £5 million airport has to close. Chase Manhattan burns on. In desperation they call in the oil company's fabled modern fire-fighting team from the other end of the island. Up they roar, raring to go. Their hoses are punctured. It takes half a day for the police to think of shutting off the road to clear the maze of fascinated onlookers and those slow-moving cars. It takes twenty-four hours to soak the bank's building into blackened submission. 'Isn't it typical,' mopes one Bahraini businessman, 'here we are trying to convince the world that this is the perfect service centre for the Gulf and we can't even cope with a little fire.'

But it's not that unfortunate lapse in the fire brigade's efficiency that disturbs the men in the penthouses of banking know-all. It's the creeping rumours about those black sheep who have imbibed Marx or plunged into the Baa'thist party.

The Jeremiahs have been predicting the downfall of the al-Khalifa for years. Few realise that Bahrain has the tightest security service in the Gulf. That's another British legacy: Ian Stewart MacWalter Henderson whose job it is to make sure it works. He's one of those colonial, hard-headed, under-stated types who won his colours as Superintendent of Police in Kenya during Mau Mau time. One of his jobs there was to walk into terrorist infested jungle. If he got his head blown off, the high-powered British negotiators in his wake would know that the Mau Mau didn't feel like talking that day. He survived with no less than two George Medals and 'a mention in despatches'.

Henderson leads an inconspicuous life in Bahrain but he keeps a weather eye on everything. When an American secretary was raped last year (a rare occurrence), his network of informants unearthed the culprit in two days. And if, as a result of his beady-eyed surveillance, a few locals go off on holiday to a small Bahraini island, at least the al-Khalifa sleep more soundly.

They have enough on their minds. Iran, the Aryan colossus across the Gulf, didn't drop its claim to Bahrain until 1970 (and that was after some secret international dealings). It still keeps a weather eye on the place. So does Saudi Arabia. Another Cuba isn't the Saudi idea of fun.

The Bahrainis experimented with a National Assembly to let off steam. There was so much steam that Saudi Arabia got the jitters. The fractious, mainly left-wing Assembly was dissolved in 1975. No one's running around organising ballot boxes for the next election.

Now there's talk of Saudi Arabia paying for a causeway to stride the watery divide. It's a connection viewed with concern by both sides. The Saudis worry that their strict Wahhabis will go across at weekends to make whoopee with air hostesses and alcohol. The last thing these balanced Bahrainis relish is to become the dumping ground for Saudi repressions. Behind the walls of their glorified housing estates, the rich Bahrainis have their own lives to lead.

The blonde in the desert

There are 8,000 certified alcoholics in Bahrain. It's typical of them to publish the figures. Ask Saudi officials how many alcoholics there are in the country and they say there aren't any because there isn't any alcohol. Bahrainis are too realistic to try the old-fashioned double-talk any more.

Even before the al-Khalifas, the island had accommodated whole waves of conquerors (Portuguese, Persians, Omanis, Saudi Wahhabis). When the slave trade was on, Bahraini sea captains were in on it too. Before the Japanese came up with their cultured junk, Bahraini divers brought up the best pearls (Catherine the Great sported some of them). When the oil came, they led the way in playboys and Cadillacs.

Now respectability is the order of the day. At least that's what it seems on the outside. And on the inside? There are the blue movies served as the last course at some select mixed dinner parties. Only I'm surprised; to the Bahrainis it's a nice way to round off an evening with friends. Happily married couples go away for the weekends; not always together. Each drives off through the traffic to the countryside (all of five miles away); the rich wife is going to her 'bustan' (garden house by the sea). The husband is off to his. He's having a stag party; rutting on the menu but not obligatory.

It's all discreetly handled in the same way that they neither parade nor deny their private family shoot-outs. Take Sheikha Dana, for example. On the day her husband was doing the honours at Bahrain Airport when Concorde flew in fifteen minutes ahead of schedule on its much-publicised inaugural trip, Sheikha Dana wasn't there handing out bouquets. Her husband, Sheikh Isa bin Abdullah al-Khalifa, might have the crucial job of Director of Civil Aviation, but Sheikha Dana was mucking out the horses as usual.

Sheikha Dana lives in the middle of nowhere, if there's room for nowhere on such a minute island. She's protected by salukis, six of them that greet a visitor with paws on the fence and a hell of a racket. The only other living things in sight are a bunch of sleek, leggy Arabs. The horses. Sheikha Dana wanders out to call off the dogs. She's wearing her customary jeans and shirt with a jaunty red gingham cowboy hat. She looks about forty; she has the tough sexy appeal of a woman who deserves flattery from men. When she takes off the hat, long blonde hair tumbles on to her shoulders. Sheikha Dana is the Scandinavian who landed a Bahraini oil sheikh when the al-Khalifa didn't go in for that sort of thing. They haven't changed.

The story is romantic enough. Dana's Swedish father worked in the Ukraine under the Tsarist regime. He married a Russian and they both took flight to Scandinavia after the Revolution. Their half-Russian, half-Swedish daughter hit the University of California in the late fifties: 'A Swedish girl in Hollywood in those days was really quite a sensation. They all thought I'd be modern and free.'

A fellow student, an Arab, asked Dana to teach him Russian.

'God knows why. He thought if he knew Arabic it would be easy to learn Russian.'

A year later they were engaged. After they married and Dana had her first child, Isa bin Abdullah went home 'to see what he could do about the family and all that'. Nothing.

Dana ended up in Beirut alone with her daughter; the al-Khalifa under the weasly eye of old Ruler Salman decided to make an example of Isa. 'They confiscated his lands' (a considerable forfeit. As the ruler's first cousin, Isa owned desirable slices of Bahrain). 'They confiscated his passport. They even confiscated his name; he was just left with Isa bin Abdullah, not even al-Khalifa.'

Isa tried cunning. Dana was living on nothing; he reckoned the only way to squeeze his family for money was by divorcing her. 'I got a page torn out of a school book through the post. It said "I divorce you," three times, signed with the al-Khalifa seal and a cheque for £900. Isa put in another letter telling me what he was doing.'

What was he doing? Marking time, hoping his family would come round. No way. He went back to Dana (annulling the divorce) and tried job-hunting around the Middle East. The al-Khalifa had got in before him; word went round that Isa bin Abdullah was an outcast. No one would give him a job. Finally an English headmaster in Beirut took pity on him and offered him a teaching post. 'Even before he had time to collect his first pay packet, he got a telegram from home welcoming him back and forgiving him. It was brilliant on their part; at first they thought he'd give up and come running home. When he didn't, they changed their tune.'

But did true love win out in the end? Not on your life. This is Bahrain, not bed-time stories. Dana and Isa moved to the east coast of Saudi Arabia and he commuted to work on the island (she wasn't included in the 'royal pardon'). Then, for everyone's peace of mind, she was settled somewhere further off, in Cairo. 'They were difficult years for me. On top of the problems of being alone with two children,' she's recounting this without a shred of self-pity in her deep, disturbing voice and periwinkle-blue eyes, 'there were all the complications of being a foreigner alone in Egypt in Nasser's day. One day a poor boy came to the door and asked me for some "baksheesh" for having put a tap on my telephone. What could I do? It was so funny, I just gave him the money.'

Her daughter's American passport caused additional trouble when the Egyptians started throwing out Yanks. 'One evening they came for her. There was a knock on the door; I opened it just a crack and suddenly there was this foot in the door. I didn't know just how large a foot could be. They took her out of bed. I followed them to the police station and only by some miracle managed to get her out.'

Finally, Isa bin Abdullah struck a bargain with his family. If he took an al-Khalifa second wife, Dana would be allowed to come to Bahrain. She arrived with the stallions she had been breeding in Cairo. Just as well. She arrived to find Isa off to London for a year's course taking his al-Khalifa wife along. 'I had a hard time, I tell you. The family were watching me like hawks, only waiting for me to put a foot wrong. But by the end of the year I had passed their test.'

Ruler Salman had died; his son, the new Ruler Isa was altogether different. His new Highness let Dana into his stables. (As well as the best pearls in the Gulf, Bahrain has also got the best horses.) 'There was chaos in the royal stables. Those that were kept under the eye of His Highness were too fat, and the rest, much of the finest Arab stock in the country, were being totally neglected. They were nothing but bags of bones.' She's dedicated to nurturing the pure Arabian stock and as a result Ruler Isa's Arabs are now the finest in the Gulf again.

She's tackling the salukis too. 'They're the only dogs officially permitted to Muslims. It's because they don't smell,' she says pushing furry coats into close sniffing distance. They don't.

What with improving the salukis and breeding the Arabs, she doesn't have time for much else.

'Isa lives with his Khalifa wife, and I suppose we've been effectively separated for about ten years. Although he comes to see me here every day, he lives there. But we get on so well now it's funny. We vaguely discussed the question of divorce once but it wouldn't work because he wouldn't be able to come to the house any more.'

Sheikha Dana's daughter is away at Wells College in the States, her son boards at Wellington College in England. She lives alone in a small bungalow covered in bougainvillaea and exuberant yellow flowers. Only her husband (and one or two of the other al-Khalifa who have made a point of keeping in touch) come and visit. The English vet can't set foot in the house when he pays his calls, even though it's in a deserted desert spot. The gardener would talk. Occasionally Dana and her husband entertain old European friends who pass through Bahrain. The friends, understandably, find it embarrassing when Isa proudly presents Dana, as if to say 'look how well she has survived'.

Occasional forays into the capital open her up to Bahraini directness. She once ventured into a flower shop and the Bahraini girl assistant asked who her husband was. 'Isa bin Abdullah.'

'An Arab, what's his surname?'

'Al-Khalifa.'

'So you're that Dana. You're not sleeping with your husband any more I hear. How do you manage?'

'Yes, I am that Dana,' came the proud answer. 'Yes my husband lives in a separate house. But whatever passes between us is, I hope, our own affair.'

In Sheikha Dana's bungalow there is a private show of photographs. There's an old family portrait of her father's Swedish family. There's a picture of the two children when they were young. And there's a photograph of a fragile blonde and a startlingly handsome Arab. It was taken just after Sheikh Isa bin Abdullah al-Khalifa had married Sheikha Dana. Radiant newlyweds.

'We're not rich, you know'

In Saudi Arabia, the al-Saud are all powerful, and they are richer than the richest of their subjects. For even the biggest merchants safety means conformity. That's why when you've met one Saudi-based multi-millionaire, you've met the lot, give or take a private jet or two. Not so Bahrain.

Half a dozen merchant families underpin the finances of the al-Khalifa. They're autocratic rulers, up to a point, and chummy with their local sugar daddies, up to a point. They need the merchants and the merchants need them. The al-Khalifa stand between them and socialism. This mutual support system gives the merchants the freedom to develop their own individuality. Living in such a small space makes them tolerant of one another. You can go too far, though. Even the Yatim family had a nasty moment when their son slipped away to England to marry an al-Khalifa girl. And the Yatims are at the top. Taking away a royal brood mare is much worse than taking in a Nordic blonde.

Are there any rich left in Bahrain? At least 6,000 Arabs in the peninsula spend a quarter of a million pounds every year on jewellery, and six of these come from Bahrain. They are the same families who underpin the al-Khalifa. Not that you'll see the rocks hanging round their necks; it's not done here. What they buy is probably locked away in safety vaults in foreign banks along with most of their money. There are still a few rich left; how much of their wealth is still on the island with them is something else again.

The Yatims are rich; the Kanoos possibly richer. 'It's only a matter of a few millions here or there, but for my money I'd take the Kanoos any day,' as one merchant banker put it, over one too many drinks. General Motors, Goodyear, Champion Sparking Plugs, English Electric, Kelvin Marine, Toyota, Wimpey . . . Not for nothing are the Kanoos the only Bahraini family al-Khalifa ladies regularly go to coffee mornings with.

Maryam Kanoo's home is a cut above most. It means that it's every man's idea of the dream holiday villa in Spain. The furnishing is Fry's Turkish Delight, toned down to Ideal Home proportions. Mrs Kanoo is tidy looking, like the country's roads. She's big, clean, wearing a nicely-made tangerine dress. There's a gabble of Kanoos present. They all have the same face, not unlike a friendly anteater's, with long dark hair.

The only way you can judge Kanoo wealth from their home is by noticing what's not here. It's more negative distinctions: no peeling wallpaper, no lifting tiles, no warping doors.

The al-Khalifa are here in force, including no less a personage than the ruler's wife, Sheikha Hasa, with her sister, daughter, and a spare daughter-in-law. To call it a coffee morning is a typically Bahraini understatement. The board is groaning with stuffed pancakes, meat balls, cheese cakes, tartlets, cinnamon squares, almond mounds, poppy seed bon-bons and it's only an hour or two till lunch.

Someone's dwarf tomato plants are doing well this year: 'Can my man bring you some over? And I wouldn't mind a couple of your rose cuttings, the ones by the door.'

'You know when I first got married I used to do all my gardening myself. But it's no good, the heat's too much for me. But at last I've found a Pakistani I can really trust.'

Who would expect to find horticultural freaks in a place like this? But here they are. It's another of those British legacies. If they're not swapping plants, they're chatting about the problems of foreign domestics. At least there's no language barrier. Bahrainis and Pakistanis both learned from the same British grammar books.

Talk of tea roses is gently but insistently interrupted by the latest visiting peddler. Marina Volochine, a Russian who got out by marrying a Greek diplomat, is trying to interest gardeners' corner in silver-covered, jewel-embedded Korans, 'a very special gift for your husband'. Her problem is not one of language either; one esoteric group she charms in Russian, the next in French, and she tries her luck in English on the row of al-Khalifas (they do tend to clump together). It's not that she doesn't know how to sell. She hits just the right note of threadbare breeding so familiar in Russian emigrés. She'll set them up, but she won't outshine; she's the wife of a diplomat after all. But the Korans aren't moving. Her work is too subdued; she's used silver where gold would do, and amethyst where an emerald would go so nicely.

The waiting game: everyone's waiting to see what everyone else thinks. It's an agonised moment for Marina. Everyone's delightful, polite – but non-committal. The moment breaks. Someone says that someone heard that Nevine was thinking of buying a Marina piece. And what's more, Nevine's mother had declared it to be 'charmant'. Ah, Nevine . . . that's all right. The Korans start moving.

Who is this paragon of taste? Nevine is a prize variety of Alireza. Yes, there's another clan of Alirezas in Bahrain. But unlike their Saudi cousins, these Alirezas are not in the island's first league – more of a reserve, one might say. The Alirezas in Jiddah have a hint of 'non-origin', as it's tactfully put, around their name. But they're too powerful and respected for that Iranian connection to matter. The Alirezas in Bahrain live on a knife-edge. Here Iran is a threat; hailing from Iran is a liability. People will forget it only if you marry a well-born Egyptian like Nevine Maghrabi, Abdullah Alireza's wife. They won't forget the taint of Iran if you revert and marry from the Iranian mainland, as elder brother Muhammad Alireza did.

What makes it worse is that Muhammad is the family honeypot; he's got the warmth, charm and spontaneous affection of the Jiddah clan. But watch the reaction at the mention of Alirezas. Frown. 'They're not typical. They speak Persian at home, you know. What do you want to spend time with them for?' I say that it's Nevine I'm going to see. 'Oh, you mean Nevine. That's all right, that's good.'

Nevine's front door is opened by the most spectacular man. He's massively tall, pitch black, majestic and big-bellied. This major-domo is dressed from head to foot in an emerald green kaftan trimmed with gold. His white head-dress completes the dazzling effect.

It is a very small house for such a big man. After all those hideous houses, I can hardly believe my eyes. French eighteenth-century panelling throughout, French eighteenth-century furniture of the finest quality, and just the right silver knick-knacks,

No fakes here. Nevine's mother understands that you don't put double cream on truffles.

Nevine's mother's a proper lady. She's here to supervise the forthcoming birth of her latest grandchild, just as she was here to supervise the birth of Nevine's house. 'When I got married,' says the heavily pregnant mistress of all this, 'I swore I was going to live in an entirely modern house. I longed to get away from all that French stuff I'd known from childhood. But after three weeks I telephoned Cairo in desperation: "Mama come."' Mama flew in with the panelling, furniture and all. Madame Maghrabi is the darling of Bahrain drawing rooms. ('Isn't she perfect?' the question asked by le tout Bahrain).

A bit too perfect for my taste, certainly a bit too overpowering. But Madame is what fixes Nevine's retiring husband, Abdullah, fine of form and face, on the right side of the Gulf. Nevine herself is sweet, distinguished-looking, but no pusher.

It's time for lunch. There are three cut-crystal glasses by each place at the table. When it's been established that I don't drink, the wine glasses (for red and for white) are taken away. The Alirezas don't drink either but they wouldn't like a guest to feel she couldn't. It's the only meal of such sophistication I'm served in Arabia. The vichyssoise ('Mama's recipe') is just right, and the chives are fresh. The presentation of the canard à l'orange (Nevine's speciality) is ritzy and restrained. The meal may be Europe; the conversation is Bahrain. Sitting opposite me is discontented Samira, Abdullah's niece. Samira, twenty-four, single, dumpy and aggressive, has been giving trouble. Nevine, in her sweet, winning way is trying to get through to her. Samira has come straight over from the boutique she runs, in the middle of Manama. She wears blue jeans, T-shirt, and a rebellious look. Running a boutique isn't the issue. It's the chic thing to do – Yatims do it, even al-Khalifas do it (though the royals don't serve).

Briefly, this is the situation: a girl from Samira's background can run a business, a car, serve in her own shop, but she has to be home by dark, isn't ever allowed out alone with a man, and is expected to stay in with the family. No one's suggesting that

Samira's dating. Unthinkable. But she's kicking. This takes the eccentric form of staying late at work to avoid going home. For several nights now she hasn't closed the shop until after seven. 'I mean it's not safe in Manama at night. Any man can just walk through the door,' explains Nevine gently. The meal is over, the family debate goes on. Samira doesn't look a jot convinced.

You might think that none of the great merchant families could be more different than the Kanoos and the Alirezas – that is until you meet the Fakhroos. They've done all the usual things; brought slaves from East Africa, shipped spice and wood from India, and changed at the right time to those money-spinning modern agencies. Ahmad Yusuf Fakhroo, one of the grand old men of Bahrain, is devoted to the ruler. 'He is one of the finest men in the world,' he says with tears in his eyes, shuffling his carpet slippers. He catches the glazed look and pulls himself up proudly. 'I can see you don't believe that. But of course you wouldn't know that I don't need to praise him. I am not dependent on him.' How true; it's the other way around.

But Ahmad Yusuf is the last of a line. Not one of his eleven children will go into the family business. They've gone professional: a teacher, civil servant, engineer, architect. This is what happens with time to the entrepreneurial empires. 'He is both proud and disapproving,' says his architect son, Abdul Rahman, 'He's like a father whose child is caught driving at the age of ten. It may be wrong, but it's clever.' Abdul Rahman, curly-headed, spilling over with indignation at the world, rails loudly against his country's inefficiency and the suppression of free speech. Free speech? He couldn't talk the way he does in Saudi Arabia.

The father may secretly be satisfied with his sons who refuse to run after money, but he makes no mention of the two Fakhroo cousins. They were last seen studying at university in Beirut. Later they joined the Dhofari rebels down the Gulf of Oman, the guerrillas supported by communist Yemen, and they haven't been seen since.

But for the time being, the top families tolerate their differences, overlook each other's failures and pull together doing business as they always have. They support the al-Khalifa financially and each other socially.

Nowhere else around here but Bahrain would you find the wives of the ruling family and merchant princes grouped around a bed in the maternity ward of the local hospital. Nevine has just had her baby. Everyone has sent flowers, and Nevine looks wonderful. There's another reason this scene couldn't happen anywhere else in the Gulf. Bahrainis actually trust their hospitals. Everyone else everywhere else who can afford it flies to Europe to deliver.

But can you bank on it?

There's a narrow, bumpy, unpaved street in the middle of Manama with a little corner store where old men sit on benches outside, talking parish-pump politics. Go up the street and on the right is a tall, white, blank-walled house with a rabbit-hole door. This is where the merchant bankers from the classier establishments in the City of London gather regularly to talk global money.

Light streams through the old stained-glass windows from the central courtyard. A Bach sonata (courtesy of Aramco's non-stop classical music station from Dhahran on the Saudi mainland) provides pianissimo background. Numbered lithographs hang on the white, rough-cast walls. The bankers aren't pondering how to get their hands on Bahrain's surplus funds; they have their eyes on pickings lower down the Gulf.

Bahrain was the first to have oil. It will be the first to run out of it. It's bidding to become off-shore banking centre of the seventies (more respectable, naturally, than the Bahamas or the Cayman Islands). To induce the bankers into luxury, streamlined offices in Manama the government takes a paltry licence fee of 10,000 dinars a year from each off-shore operation. It's attracting newcomers, despite rents that have doubled in six months. The bankers keep their books in Bahrain and do their deals elsewhere.

These Brits are having their usual grouch about the difficulty of explaining to newly-rich clients that 'medium term' investments don't mean three to six months. They mean three to six years. And as for long-term investments, that will be another education in itself. To boot, Arabs don't trust one basket to hold all their golden eggs. They have a distracting habit of spreading investments between banks, sometimes between as many as eight. On top of all this, there's competition from the Swiss, as devious and secretive as their Arab clients, and those highly aggressive Americans. They're all elbowing into this traditional British territory.

The City of London had a good moment last year. The Swiss ruled out any new deposit accounts in Swiss francs in Switzerland. Alas their resourceful financiers countered by opening branch offices in Luxembourg, which isn't subject to Swiss banking rules. The Arabs can hold their trusted francs there all right. The Swiss still have only ten per cent of the private Gulf money; the Americans have fifty per cent. These British bankers are making sure they can hold on to their share. One of them is celebrating a small coup. He has finally persuaded a particularly good client from Abu Dhabi to grant him 'a management agreement'. He won't have to waste time tracking down his elusive client in future to seek his approval for every money-move he makes on his behalf.

Lost down another bumpy back street is the one place the merchant bankers in residence go for an evening out. The migrant, minor businessmen stuck in the fluorescent junction of the Gulf Hotel won't find their way here. You have to ring the doorbell to get into Keith's. 'In' businessmen, bankers and a few Bahrainis come to eat and relax over a carafe of wine at rustic tables by the light of guttering candles. It's King's Road, late sixties.

Keith, a bronzed delight of indeterminate age, the medallion hanging on his polo-necked jersey catching the light, hovers round one of his regulars. Charlie Colchester's godfather arranged for him to come to the island to work for Gray, Mackenzie, a prestigious part of the Earl of Inchcape's group. Charlie came to sell liquor.

'After two years here I began to have qualms about selling alcohol in a Muslim country so I went into business on my own as an agent for foreign companies, things like that. I was absolutely shocked at the attitude of the Europeans who walked into my office. You wouldn't believe their arrogance. Their basic attitude is that these darkies are a bunch of wogs. It just escapes them that this is a dignified nation of people who have been trading for centuries and who are very shrewd indeed. Firms send such second-rate people if they send anyone at all. Lots of them think that a once-yearly whizz-through by a £3,000-a-year sales rep is all it takes. Don't think the Bahrainis don't notice; they're just too nice to let it show.'

He downs another glass of plonk, his earnest, young face getting longer and longer. 'Then you get the lot that come over here running down British business or moaning about the high rate of income tax back home. The Bahrainis rightly reckon they're just rip-off merchants out to fleece their joint. Not that the Americans are any better. They stroll in as if they're doing the Bahrainis a favour. They come in blind, and – what's worse – they go out blind. I get letters from presidents of large American corporations addressed to Manama, Bahrain, Saudi Arabia; to Manama, Bahrain, Oman. More often than not they add insult to injury by ending it off "The Persian Gulf". It does so much long-term harm, you can't imagine.'

Poor Charlie. But Collingwood's aren't like that. Collingwood, the old-established British jeweller, have taken him on with free rein to sell their goods in the tactful way that appeals to him. Jewellery might not be what the Arabs need most right now. But it's what they want. What they need are solid industries, to take over when the oil runs out.

It's not only a question of knowing when to develop but how to do it so that it works. Bahraini realism acknowledges its limitations but it also knows its strengths. Bahrain works as a 'service centre'. Communications are easy and there's an educated workforce to staff the offices. This unusual achievement (for the Middle East) can be traced back to a day in 1919 when a band of local merchants, mostly illiterate, put up money for a private school. The ruler appointed an al-Khalifa as Minister of Education to preside over the inevitable boardroom squabbles. Another first in the Gulf.

Today, that minister's grandson is in charge of education: Sheikh Abdul Aziz, graduate of the School of Oriental and African Studies, London University. In his schools, boys and girls have only two periods of Koranic instruction a week. 'Well, after all,' he says leaning back in his swivel chair sagely, 'it's no use teaching religion at the expense of physics.' (Tell that to the Saudis.)

An education system that has been going for fifty years has had time to throw up exceptional men, not ones hand-picked by the al-Khalifa but brainy boys who got on. The most outstanding is the only man who figures when you're talking about Bahrain's economic future. He's the star-turn at high-powered international planning conferences; he's the country's show-piece. Yusuf Shirawi, Minister of Development and Industry, is respected and heeded by all the merchant bankers and businessmen.

His mother died when he was young but he was groomed from the start by teachers who pushed him hard. He won a scholarship to university in Beirut. He followed that with a postgraduate award in chemical engineering at Glasgow University. Back home, he creamed his way up to the top to become Director General of Oil before independence. Now he's Bahrain's Mr Planning.

Even after this build-up, the physical presence of the man is stunning. It's not just his looks; the grizzled hair, the face of a Levantine shipowner, the second skin of his well-cut suit. It's the performance. It dazzles. What makes Bahrain different? Quick as a flash Shirawi produces from nowhere a big, old book. He leafs through it with a broad smile: 'Look at this. It's a message sent to a merchant on this island in 1996 BC, complaining about the bad ingots he'd delivered to Mesopotamia. That's what makes Bahrain different from its neighbours. Four thousand years ago we were quarrelling about the quality of ingots.'

Political trouble ahead? Another broad smile: 'There are two groups of people in the Arab world who are really impossible to govern: the Palestinians and the Bahrainis. They're both intelligent, educated, and they won't take no for an answer.'

Apart from exploiting Bahrain's tolerance of foreigners to create that 'service centre', he's carefully stoking Bahrain's economy to run on feasible post-oil projects: an aluminium smelting works, a dry-dock; whatever needs the skilled workforce that Bahrain can provide. His models are Japan and Switzerland; they too have educated people and no natural resources.

What's the other side of this success story? May Shirawi, his wife, is a Shia. Yusuf is Sunni. Shia and Sunni Muslim sects are to Bahrain as Catholic and Protestant were to Ulster before violence. They co-exist uneasily. The Shirawi Shia-Sunni marriage, another first, seemed to promise so much. May was brilliant, beautiful.

Today she sits at home, proud but left out of the Bahrain round. 'So you've met May?' a drawing room cow. 'I don't suppose you know about her first child? It was born without arms. It died at the age of five when it fell out of bed and suffocated on the floor. That's what happens when you mix Shia and Sunni blood.'

May's house is simple: an upright piano for the children, the World Encyclopaedia for her. From childhood she has worshipped Yusuf ('my headmistress always used to say "If you work as hard as Yusuf Shirawi …" '). Now she is married to him, and they are very close, when he can manage to get home.

On the wall of her sitting room, there hangs an embroidered sampler that reads: 'God grant me the serenity to accept those things that I cannot change, and the Wisdom to change those things that should be changed.'

The Shirawis are doing their best.

Jaded pieces I

At the top of the heap is the ruler: Sheikh Isa bin Salman al-Khalifa. (Actually he was promoted to emir on independence, but everyone still calls him The Ruler.) Sheikh Isa's salary is six million dinars a year. Not bad. He's always in debt. He's such a generous man, and he does like to have his old friend Captain Algernon 'Algy' Asprey in to do up his place from time to time.

Say Bahrain to anyone (anyone who's heard of the place, that is) and you'll hear about this Don Juan of Arabia who has a telescope in his palace trained on the airport runway. 'Be careful, he watches every plane that lands; he watches every pair of legs that come down the steps. He's on the look-out for new talent . . .' Does he indeed. With planes coming in from all over the place at all hours of the day and night, he'd be a busy man. And incidentally he can't see the airport from his palace – it's miles away in Rifaa.

'And all those wives . . .' they go on. That makes Sheikha Hasa laugh. Sheikha Hasa is the only wife Sheikh Isa has ever had; he's had her since she was sixteen and that was nine children ago. She's his first cousin, she puts up with an assortment of visiting European 'ladies'. But another wife? Oh, goodness me no.

Tuesday morning is Sheikha Hasa's At Home. There's a long walk past dozens of royal stables, through the archway, into the first courtyard. No sign of life. Emptiness. Silence. Down the cloistered walk, and . . . what's this? A heap of slippers outside a door. Inside a huge space hums with voices. After the sunshine, the darkness is blinding. It takes a while before you can make out the long, low, room, maybe twenty yards of it. It's flanked by sofas filled with women, women, women.

It's stepping back into the past, into another world. One by one the arriving guests file down the middle of the room, down the gaudy, patterned carpet towards the bale of saffron-yellow that is all you can see of your royal hostess at the end. A little closer, and her vivacious face takes shape. She doesn't look forty-six until you get very close. And she doesn't let you get very close for long enough to inspect much more than her thick black hair and shining young girl's eyes. She's having a jolly time. Which is just as well; she's probably the only woman in the room who is. Everyone else is on their guard; they're aware that Sheikha Hasa, for all her regal welcome, gets uppity if she feels that she's not getting her royal due. Behind her armchair is a mirrored wall. In it you can see the floor-to-ceiling photograph of Hasa's husband grinning at the other end. No wonder he's grinning. The room embraces an extraordinary collection of women. It seethes with Kanoos, ambassadresses, exhaustingly cheerful American oil wives, old al-Khalifas like wrinkled apples, young ones beautifully dressed, and peroxided English hags who have been around so long that they've got black-rimmed empty holes where they should have eyes. Heaven knows what they have seen. The ruler in his boisterous prime?

Among all this coming and going, upping and downing, shaking of hands and sipping of sickly, sticky juice, there's still time for a natter. No jewellers here, no talk of dwarf tomatoes. Everyone's talking about the latest movie. It's not *Jaws* (no one goes to the cinema in Bahrain; that's old hat). It's a sensational, amateur documentary (cinema vérité-style) of Bahrain's forty top ladies tripping round Morocco. It was another Sheikha Lulua special; it quite eclipsed her charabanc outing to the Windsor Safari Park last summer when they were all in London. Sheikha Lulua is the family organiser. Kanoo Travel, naturally, takes care of the details.

Sheikha Lulua has had a thorough grounding. She was married at twelve to Salman, a twenty-year-old cousin she had never seen. That was in the bad old days, but, luckily for her, Salman turned out to be a good thing. 'Right from the beginning I travelled a lot with him,' explains the jaunty grandmother. 'He made me learn English and then when we were abroad he would always tell me to go and get the information and buy the tickets. I was frightened at first and said "No, no, I can't," but he forced me to. He wanted me to develop. He always used to say "You must be your own person." ' Sheikh Salman is dead now, but his protegée travels on.

The affair of St Christopher's is being hotly discussed in the middle distance on the left. Some remark about the English school's standards going down since the Arab quota went up. A cross admirer denies it. Even so, one ultra sensitive woman confesses that she is thinking of taking her children away.

Visiting time is limited to fifteen minutes. You know when your time is up, when you have to make room for the second sitting. The cue is the censer of fragrant burning sandalwood borne round by another gauzy bundle. The women lean forward in turn to fumigate their hair or drapes. A second ample bundle follows, bringing ounces of Miss Dior to splash over their sugary fingers. On the way out, there's a last glimpse of the cardboard ruler with his Cheshire Cat grin. But where is the Cheshire Cat?

Jaded pieces II

The ruler is all over the place. He likes to be active. I drive to his palace to see him. From the outside it's another of those silent, monastic white-walled affairs like Sheikha Hasa's across the road. It's not difficult to get past the armed guards. I talk to them in English. They don't understand a word (that's puzzling); so to be obliging they let me in. Across the courtyard, there's a modern plate-glass, electronically-operated door into a plush suite of offices ('Algy' Asprey's been here all right).

I'm not too surprised to hear that Sheikh Isa isn't at his shiny, black desk, subtly curved with gilded Arab motifs. I'm just passing by. But on the way back into Manama, a white Mercedes is gliding out. A familiar face peers through the window. It's the ruler, bowing and beaming, waving his hand at all he passes. That's Sheikh Isa bin Salman's way. His friendliness is as legendary as his generosity.

He came as a relief to everyone when he succeeded his mean, conservative father, Sheikh Salman (let alone his meaner, even more conservative grandfather, Hamad). 'Sheikh Salman's death in 1961 was a longed-for relief to the family,' says one grateful al-Khalifa, 'Sheikh Isa allowed us to start travelling more, educating ourselves, living our own lives a bit.'

There are other differences. The father and grandfather inclined to boys; no one accuses Isa of that. Money problems Sheikh Isa may have, but with the National Assembly now 'subject to delay', he has come into his own again. He's flanked by one brother as prime minister, the family muscle man, and another as foreign minister, the family brain box. Isa's only al-Khalifa rival is the island's richest and meanest man, younger brother Muhammad. Muhammad has lost any chance of government power since his squabble with the ruler in 1968. The Bahrainis don't mind: they won't forget how he shone as chief of police and public security. (1965: riots, eight killed.)

Sheikh Muhammad broods in his white fortress of a palace and competes with Isa wherever he can. Isa runs a majlis for all the island's men to come for a moan and a prattle. Brother Muhammad must have one too. Isa takes delivery of a new model of Rolls-Royce (popular guess: about 200 cars), Muhammad (popular guess: about 2,000) doesn't waste a moment ordering his.

Muhammad sulks but he doesn't forget the call of business. A merchant, well placed to know, puts Muhammad's income at about 100,000 dinars a month. Add up just a few of his many interests: 12,000 dinars a month rent from the Delmon Hotel, 10,000 from the Jashanmal office block (home of Manama's biggest department store on the ground floors, the garish new dinner-dance spot, the Pearl on the top, and a crop of bankers' suites between – Kleinwort Benson, Union Bank of Switzerland, British Bank of the Middle East . . .). And don't forget 14,000 dinars a month rent for the National Bank of Bahrain building.

He's a rich sulk. Isa has never been a sulk. But he's happiest on Fridays; his weekend time-table is a fixture. He sits in the majlis early in the morning, goes to mosque and then to the sea-side. Not any old sea-side. The ruler has his own.

I'm scooting along in a Mini-Moke; there's a holiday feeling in the air. Twenty-three miles out of Manama (having got past the depressing view of the Awali American oil-town and the old ruler's palace rotting in the scrub) we come to a cross-roads. The Datsuns, Toyotas and Bahrainis turn left to the Bapco (Bahrain

Oil Company) beach. We turn right, down a mud path to a riot of green trees (at last) and the ruler's beach.

A soldier stops each car at the gate, to check in cameras. He hands out a cloakroom ticket and hangs up the camera on one of the hooks hammered into a nearby tree. It's already jammed with Pentax, Nikon, Leicaflex and Kodak Instamatics. This unusual cloakroom attendant stops the Mini-Moke, glares hard at me and then gruffly addresses the Englishman at the wheel. 'What nationality does it have?' This takes a while to sink in; he means me.

'It is British,' I answer indignantly. A long, thoughtful stare. 'Hmm. You look like Arab lady. No come in if Arab lady.' Only the sight of a British passport satisfies him. Then he's so embarrassed that he breaks 'gate rules' by having a chat. 'Me speak English well. Me one of few who can. That why I am gate job.' So that's it; the ruler has twenty-five soldier body guards brought in from North Yemen (the okay one, not the communist one). Why North Yemen? Because it's a long way away; they don't speak English, there's less chance of – well, whatever. The soldier even hands over his treasured rifle for inspection. It's cleaned, in working order – and loaded.

('They don't have bullets in those things,' says a regular watching the soldiers on their beach patrol, 'They're only for show.' Some show.)

Satisfied now that I'm no 'Arab lady', the guard waves us on. Only two Bahrainis (plus their secretaries, and servants) are allowed on to the ruler's beach. The ruler is one; his oldest son, Crown Prince Hamad, head of the army, is the other.

The ruler comes because he likes the view. The crown prince comes because he likes to see his father. Hamad doesn't come too often because he also likes to see his vivacious wife, Sapiqi. Hamad is trying hard to be his own man; he's even gone as far as revolting against the faithful 'Algy' Asprey in favour of finding his own decorator. Front runner: a blonde from London, one-time receptionist at a Bournemouth hairdressing salon.

Needless to say, Bahraini society hums with talk of terrible goings-on at this 'out of bounds' territory. There are rumours of taxis scouring Manama to take unattached European women to the beach (no fare charged). There's talk of Mrs Manchester's beach house. Mrs Manchester is the locals' nickname for a middle-aged wife of one of those limp-shouldered technicians. She, they say, is a particular favourite. Then there's all that old stuff about the closed circuit television in the ruler's beach palace with cameras trained on naked bodies sunbathing outside.

This scene of iniquity turns out to resemble nothing so much as Morecambe circa 1948. Small children build sandcastles and paddle. Reg and Bill discuss the price of beer and what it's like back in Liverpool. Elsie and Joan drop their knitting to sort out some intricate dress-making. The ruler's beach palace is nothing more than a green-tile roofed bungalow with candy-striped hammocks and chairs around it, facing the car park. Inside, is the sitting room snuggery with sofas and plastic tables.

It's true there are a mass of girls lying around listening to their transistor radios or munching sandwiches. Although they're all wearing bikinis, they have unappetising flabby thighs and they're hardly going out of their way to pose like something out of a sexy Bacardi rum advert.

About ten men ask if I'm an air hostess. By now this much-used Bahraini term is acquiring the same innuendo as the word 'model' in the sixties. But, it seems, there are 'air hostesses' and air hostesses. The first lot provide a good business for some people in Manama who are sent girl-scrubbing in Europe by various other people. The second brand are bona-fide cabin staff based here because Bahrain is the headquarters of Gulf Air. At any one time there are 400 of their girls in Manama, mostly with flight-staff boyfriends.

There is a lawn on one side of the ruler's bungalow. Here Elsie and Joan have gone back to their knitting, Reg and Bill are snoring slightly and their children play on the strip of beach. The beach runs beyond the bungalow, beyond the car park to open on to a broader sandy stretch. At the far end is Mrs Manchester's famous house. It's just a house. It's empty and it could belong to anyone.

Only the soldiers and the long new pier looking out to the

ruler's white tub (you can hardly call it a yacht, even if it is another of Algy's jobs) suggest that this is anything more than a two-star seaside spot. Of course, the waiters in snowy white uniforms aren't the usual ice-lolly vendors. At eleven in the morning and four in the afternoon they serve coffee and iced cakes on trays to anyone at a table under an umbrella by the sea shore. The cups and saucers are something of a jumble; earthenware flowered cup and gold-rimmed white china saucer, that sort of thing. But it's all free so who complains?

The white Mercedes sweeps into the car park. His Highness plonks himself down on a towel on a bench on a corner by the bungalow. The Mercedes departs and the ruler recovers from the strain of attending the Friday races. 'I'm worried about my horses. I don't think the jockeys are good to them; I won't let them race for a while and see if that helps.' His Highness is terribly pleased to see me. He's terribly pleased to see everyone. He enjoys sitting here watching the world go by. He's very, very short and very, very round but he's very, very charming.

He makes room on his towel for me, sends for an orange juice and offers a Benson and Hedges cigarette ('English, for you'). To my amazement, he's shy. He thinks I'm making a bid for him, enough girls do this afternoon.

I find a way in; I mention Sheikha Hasa. Now he relaxes. He's on home ground. I tell him how impressed I am by the way that building goes on day and night on the Sheikha Hasa office block in Manama (she's something of a property tycoon). He smiles proudly. He sends a servant to fetch something from the shuttered bungalow. It's a photograph of the Sandhurst and Mons-trained crown prince rising high over a fence on an Arab showjumper. He shows it to me; now he's bursting with pride.

'My son is a wonderful rider. He's wonderful. I have nine children, you know, they're all wonderful. Two are still at school in Switzerland. They write to me every week.' He confesses that he has had to stop telephoning them. Sheikha Hasa put her foot down because he fussed every time one of them complained about some minor school misery. He also has a mischievous sense of humour. He says that if I want anything more than a good gossip, he'll be only too delighted to discuss how bad British industry is on delivery dates. A big wink, a bigger beam.

He greets everyone going past. 'How nice to see you. I do hope you had a pleasant day,' this time to an elderly couple shuffling off. Everyone stops to thank him for a lovely day and he thanks them all for coming. He shakes hands with one blonde, aged four, and admires the older ones, who have now pulled themselves together for a good 'flaunt' past. 'I love sitting here,' another twinkle, 'but I do get a crick in my neck.'

After a long, crick-making time, he rises, shakes his tummy and calls for his red car. He's off to the high point of the Bahraini social week, he's looking forward to it enormously, he offers a lift.

Outside the gate where the Yemeni soldier is now awkwardly trying to keep his rifle in place while checking out the cameras, up to the main road. A stream of cars is zooming along. But this isn't the customary Bahraini thirty-five miles an hour. Something is up. Cadillacs, Chevrolets, an odd Lamborghini and hundreds of tin boxes are rushing into the distance. His Highness joins the current. A herd of camels look down on the procession. The cars are crowded with families, squads of girls, make-up flashing through dusty windscreens, young men, eyes flashing through even dustier windscreens. Every Friday afternoon in summer all Bahrain drives to Thompson's Beach. Every Friday afternoon in winter all Bahrain drives to the old, disused aerodrome.

At last we arrive at Thompson's. Through a storm of sand kicked up by thousands of wheels, the social zenith of Bahrain is realised. There are cars as far as the eye can see. Some are parked, others drive slowly round them. A few people, mostly families, get out and sit on the beach watching the huge red sunset. The teenagers stay put, drinking Pepsis, eating their picnic teas. This is the nearest 'decent' Bahrainis get to dating.

This is it; nothing else happens. The game is to find out who the girls are who are watching the boys who are watching the girls. Every now and again there's a slight nod here, a suspicion of a smile there. The atmosphere is tense with calf love. Many a marriage has started through two panes of glass, over a strip of tarmac in winter, a haze of sand in summer. The ruler's car joins the parade and then slowly nose-to-tail bumps back through the traffic jam to Sheikha Hasa. An hour later, as dusk falls, the Welwyn of the Gulf goes home after celebrating its day off in its usual style.

His Highness has had his idea of a good weekend. He does try, but he doesn't have a flair for more cultural occupations. His British ADC, Major Greene, recently thought that the time might be right to encourage him. There were empty niches in his newly-decorated majlis. Just right, said Greene, for a few choice pieces of jade. If he hoped to interest his royal master in the European pastime known as 'hunting out something rather special', he was wasting his time. 'Splendid,' said His Highness, 'go out and buy me a jade collection.'

That's Bahrain. 'We're not rich, but we're comfortable, thank you.'

Kuwait

Peering inside, afraid to look out

The men who came in from the cold

The Oil Arabs have a great game. It's called Bitching about the Other Oil Arabs. Westerners mustn't be tempted to join in, but it goes something like this: Bahrain, say the Saudis, is a dump. Kuwait, say the Saudis, is too full of itself. (King Faisal summed it up in a withering remark: 'There are three superpowers: Russia, America and Kuwait'.) The Saudis, say the Bahrainis, are fanatics. The Kuwaitis, say the Bahrainis, are horrid. ('What do you want to go there for, it's a dead city?') The Kuwaitis look down on everyone. They reserve a particular spite for Saudi Arabia. ('Who *really* killed King Faisal?' they ask in a loaded way.)

It's part of the contradiction that at the same time there's another standard game. It's called: We're All The Same Really. As they're fond of reminding you, the royal families of Saudi Arabia, Bahrain and Kuwait are connected. This means they were all hoofing around in the same desert a few hundred years ago. The al-Khalifa of Bahrain and the al-Sabah of Kuwait are even tribal cousins. But they have travelled far, in separate directions, in a short time.

In Bahrain you're always aware of the al-Khalifa. In Kuwait you could get by almost without hearing about the al-Sabah. They're the most inscrutable bunch of all. They keep their dirty linen to themselves. From behind the scenes, they run a different kind of set up.

The city's so large after Bahrain's suburban offerings. What's more, it works. Compared to Riyadh and Jiddah, it feels as if it's been here for ever. The broad roads are lit at night. Decent town planning from way back gives rise to directions as endearing as: 'off the sixth ring road'. And then there's the hot water: Kuwait has no fresh water of its own at all, but by spending a fortune it manages to make twice as much as it needs. Whoever's into desalination in Kuwait must be cleaning up a packet. I've just come from places where every tap was an adventure. Sometimes cow brown water came out. More often nothing. If I was lucky, clear water came out, cold. Occasionally, I had a Klondyke strike – warm and fast. Kuwait's reliable running hot water, taken as a matter of course, sums the city up perfectly.

And Kuwait State is a city, give or take a few thousand square miles of sand with more oil under it than anywhere but Saudi Arabia. Paradise? Take a look at a map. Kuwait's too close to too many people who don't like it. Those socialists in Iraq, over the border; if only they'd stay there. Iraq's invaded before now; it wants to again (what do you reckon Kuwait's 150 new Chieftain tanks at £200,000 a time are for? To fight Israel? Forget it). Then those Aryans across in Iran. Friends? The Iranian embassy in Kuwait counts as a 'hardship post'.

One way and another Kuwaitis are in a chronic state of paranoia. At least it's not the same paranoia as Saudi Arabia's. That makes a change: it's the result of being a minority group in your own country and refusing to face up to it.

There might be a million people in Kuwait (remember the golden rule: don't trust population figures here.) There might be 300,000 Kuwaitis, plumped up by bought-and-paid for Bedus.

Proper Kuwaitis, with a talent for sticking their heads in the sand and ignoring reality, lead a good life. They believe that you're closer to Allah in their country than anywhere else on earth. The most proper Kuwaitis (the al-Sabah and the eight or so families who arrived with them in 1766, the 'heritage' gang) know better. As they've got richer and richer, they've got cannier and cannier. They understand the full extent of their insecurities.

One of their greatest is that a quarter of the population is Palestinian. Before I started this journey, 'Palestinians' meant to me Arafat, guns and refugee camps. Here I am in a city where Palestinians are what make my life comfortable. They make things work. But their life; that's another question.

I'm in a nightclub, watching a young man of twenty-five, a qualified engineer. Even if I didn't know who he was his slick Western suit would mark him as an outsider. Only proper Kuwaitis wear national dress. As it happens, he's the son of a Palestinian who helped to create a key ministry in Kuwait twenty years ago. I can't name him. As a Palestinian, even though he was born here, he'll never be safe. He's as taut as a whippet. He's concentrating hard on a pretty, unusual-looking English girl. He's not out for a lay; it's not that kind of concentration.

When the crowd moves to the table, he gets to sit next to her. I listen as he homes-in on her: I can hardly believe it: 'The minute I set eyes on you, I knew I'd be able to talk to you. You look so wise; you're the first girl I've met since I got back from the States four years ago I feel can respond to me as a person.' The girl has a kind face but she hasn't said much to justify his conviction that a 'meaningful relationship' lies ahead over the giant Gulf shrimps. I'm just about to switch off when I sense an intense, low-pitched eruption. 'Do you think I'm odd. Do you like me? I'm not odd; I'm not drunk. I'm just tired, so tired. I get up at five-thirty every day. I stay in the office until late at night. I only go home to sleep. I'm killing myself with work. Why do you think I do it? Do you think I like work? Do you think I need the money? I've got all the money I need. But I can't stand going home. What else have I got? I've had to wait four years to find one girl I can talk to. Girls in Kuwait are all the same. They only care about money and clothes. Talking to them is like to talking to a bit of wood. I will never marry a girl from Kuwait.'

Anywhere else, this would sound like soap opera. But he's right; he won't marry a girl from Kuwait. No good Kuwaiti family would have him. No matter how much money they have, how trusted they are on high, Palestinians are second-class citizens. Every year the minister of the interior can, if he chooses, naturalise fifty people as a reward for long service to the country. This engineer's father gave such service. He's still Palestinian.

That young man's lucky; he's got brains, money, a future. What does this older Palestinian have? He drives for a civil servant, he works for the government. For sixteen years he has had the same job; he can't get another. He makes ninety-six dinars a month; a Kuwaiti would get 200. He pays thirty dinars a month for rooms in a squalid street. At least his children can go to school. The government offers free schooling now to non-Kuwaiti children – if they arrive here under the age of seven. The driver's five children were born in Kuwait so they go to school – with half a dinar a day pocket money. 'All other children have half dinar. Kuwait rich country.'

There's a note of whining desperation in his voice. It's as distinct as the smell of poverty. His life is made up of dreams. Dreams of the family orange grove he knew as a child in Palestine. Dreams of renting a small shop – non-Kuwaitis can't buy property. ('Then I will be my own man.') Dreams that his children will escape. When he gets home at night, he sits over them as they do their homework, reminding them it's the only way out. And mostly he dreams of spending more time with his wife. 'My wife no learn English like me, she no write. But she so good; she better than me.' He will see her in eighteen hours time; his usual working day. That's his future.

At last a Palestinian I can name. It's a big enough name. Khalid Abu Saud, director of investment at the Ministry of Finance. He moves four billion dollars a year around the world. It's the Kuwait government's investment abroad.

The Minstry of Finance has a lot of doormen; forty is the usual count. The Bedu on the door are Kuwaiti. Every Kuwaiti is entitled to a government desk or door to sit at. The building reeks of urine. It's a long smell up to Abu Saud on the top floor. His office has two naked light bulbs and a few tatty chairs. Khalid Abu Saud is round and grey with fatigue.

He's had this crucial job for eighteen years. He arrived from Palestine only two years after the old mud walls of Kuwait city were torn down. There was nothing much here but the start of an oil boom. The polish and education came later. He caught the eye of an al-Sabah who recognised the faithful nature of the man and the fast brilliance of his mind. He's risen to a position of fantastic financial importance. He was finally made Kuwaiti in

1974. But he's still not proper Kuwaiti. He can't vote; he doesn't wear national dress, that all important uniform.

To give you an idea of the complexity of his job, I must tell you a typical Kuwaiti financial arrangement. I've just met an American investment banker who knew that Iceland needed money and knew a Japanese bank who knew a Kuwaiti who knew which Kuwaiti had four million dinars he wanted to lend abroad. The Icelandic government has its loan.

Khalid Abu Saud will have heard about this. It's his job to know every money-move in Kuwait. Thirty telexes an hour drop on his desk. He holds up bundles of paper: 'I have the movement of every share all over the world here in my hand. We have our own offices and representatives everywhere. I've never given business to any banker who has walked through that door on his own initiative. But hundreds of them come every week and I know they can't go back empty-handed after coming all this way. At least they go back with a visiting card saying "Khalid Abu Saud".'

I'm surprised at his apologetic tone. I've heard the way bankers talk about him in the hotel lobby; they question each other closely like small boys waiting to know who the school head has chosen for some special honour: 'Have you seen Abu Saud? You've met him,' they say with envy at a peer who's pulled it off. But, of course, the accolades of the hotel lobby are meaningless to Abu Saud. He's been conditioned by the Kuwaitis, and to them he's still 'brilliant but Palestinian'. It was only a while ago that there was a public fuss about having a Palestinian in such a key position.

Other things hurt: he's laying down a pensioned future for a Kuwait without oil. Even so, some of his long term, feather-bedding designs ricochet. He masterminded the Kiawah Island property deal, buying up the only totally unspoilt resort coast along that stretch of South Carolina. He's calculated, probably correctly, that more and more Americans will be taking vacations at home. Miami? Another big city. If you're not in the Palm Beach bracket, the choice is pretty limited. Really carefully developed (and the Kuwaitis won't have to skimp on pennies;

they can afford to buy the best), Abu Saud reckons Kiawah could net a fortune long term. But long term hasn't yet entered the time-scale of any but the most sophisticated Kuwaitis so he's already being accused of buying a slice of nothing.

He was hurt most when he pushed through the £107 million takeover of the St Martin's Property Corporation (making Kuwait the landlords of New Scotland Yard). The Splash headline in a London newspaper screamed: 'The Arabs are coming'. Kuwait winced. Abu Saud gave up. How could he ever explain to the hostile British public that no less a patriot than the Governor of the Bank of England, Sir Gordon Richardson, had made a personal appeal to him over lunch to take some action that might stop the bottom falling out of the quivering London property market.

He learned. He's organising the purchase of five per cent and seven per cent block shares in big banks all over the world, particularly America. He's buying silently, protecting himself and Kuwait from unsavoury publicity.

It's late. It's the weekend; we're both tired of talking money. He asks me to lunch to meet his wife: 'My wife is an angel. She lives with a man who is diseased. What else am I? I have the disease of buying and selling and making transactions. My son came home from school the other day and asked whether he was Christian or Muslim. I'm ashamed that I've given so little time to my children that my son doesn't even know what being Muslim means.'

Somehow I know it'll be all right to mention Israel. (Normally I never mention it at all; if trapped I call it Palestine. If I didn't I might be in for a marathon lecture about being the brainwashed victim of Zionist propoganda.)

Abu Saud answers simply. 'Israel is a reality. I'm in a position to say that because I know at what price and my family have paid part of it. My father was killed in Jerusalem in the 1948 war. My brother was killed at the same time by Jews in our house. We had the misfortune to live near a mosque, you see. My mother is seventy-eight, she still lives in Jerusalem but she's too old to travel. She'll never see her grandchildren again.'

I leave him knowing that this gentle Palestinian, sorry I mean Kuwaiti, feels many things. Bitterness against Jews isn't one of them.

Singing the blues

Tiffany's travelling circus has already 'done' Saudi Arabia when it arrives to 'do' the Blue Room for the week. The troupe from Fifth Avenue hire a suite, seven single rooms and an overkill of security men who cause alarm by charging huge meals to the Tiffany account. The Sheraton Hotel's Blue Room is something of a world famous institution. The 1973 oil embargo was signed round a table here. So too was the Kuwaiti government's seventeen and a half million dollar purchase of the uninhabited Kiawah island. It's The Venue for visiting accessory salesmen.

Henry B. Platt ('Just call me Harry'), the great-great-grandson of founder Charles L. Tiffany, is handing out copies of 'The Tiffany Touch – the fabulous, fascinating story of the world's most famous jewellery store and its glittering clientèle'. He's also adding style to the swimming pool patio, browning his fiftyish bachelor body.

'We've waited a long, long time before coming here. We've waited to be sure that they were ready for us. You know I'm not just in the jewellery business, I'm really a student of international affairs. I always make a great point of finding out everything about a country before I go there; and they're always so impressed by that. We had a wonderful time in Saudi Arabia. I was in every royal palace. I met princesses. I went to so many parties. Not that this is an entirely new area for us of course. We've sold in New York to King Faisal and to his father King Saud who was ruler before him.'

Hard as it is to interrupt Harry's flow, I can't help feeling that this slight reconstruction of the family tree wouldn't go go down well in palaces where everyone remembers the bitter rivalry between the two brothers. 'Faisal's father Saud?' I query.

'Oh yes, his father. I know the families well you see.' His clean blue eyes sweep the patio for the pool boy. He needs a drink.

'We've had a great success here. Sheikha Badria, who is one of the royal family, graciously opened the exhibition for us. And she has even invited us to her palace for dinner. I do believe we're the first Europeans ever to go to dinner with her.'

'We've sold a lot here. Of course I can't tell you who to, because we're very discreet. I mean, I never mention names. When Christina Onassis, who's a very good friend of mine as it happens, used to come into Tiffany, or even Jackie, who's also a very good friend of mine, I would never dream of telling anyone. There's someone else I could mention who rings up all the papers every time Christina walks in.' Harry turns himself over with care; time to toast the other side.

'It's our policy in New York, of course, never to discount our prices. As a matter of fact it's one of the things we're known for. But I say "when in Rome do as the Romans do" so in very special cases we offer fifteen per cent discount here.'

The Blue Room is small and square; it's on the mezzanine floor opposite the hotel's mosque. After Harry's pool-side commentary, I wander up to see how business is doing. A chic, young sheikha is examining the wares. She decides on a few trinkets. She starts to haggle. Of course she does; this is Kuwait. She wouldn't do it in New York. When she hits the fifteen per cent ceiling, Bruce Cummings, clean-cut East Coaster, starts to fidget.

'We have a very special reputation,' he elucidates 'our quoted prices guarantee the same standard of top-class workmanship in all our designs, and the finest quality too.' At this point the Sheikha cuts him off and switches to Arabic. She opens negotiations with the smartly-dressed society woman 'borrowed' by Tiffany to get Sheikha Badria for the opening. Bruce Cummings is taken off for a quiet word. A price is agreed to everyone's satisfaction.

Just as well that Harry isn't at coffee next morning with three members of Kuwait's oldest trading family. One was at the Tiffany's opening:

'Tiffany's are just like the others. They all think they're bringing us something new. But Tiffany's don't even realise that they've been sending us their catalogue from New York for fifteen years. We've had Boucheron in our home, Bulgari of Rome three times and my husband has bought me collections of diamonds. In our safety deposit box, we have a priceless wedding necklace made in India for my grandmother studded with rubies and diamonds. So don't talk to me about "new". But the thing I really can't take is the way all Westerners treat us as a new "market".'

I return to find Harry back at the pool, his Palm Springs' tan coming along a treat in the Kuwaiti winter sun. 'When you think it over, Tiffany is the obvious choice for this place. It's exciting for them that we come from New York.' He lowers his voice confidentially. 'You know, Harry Winston is a Jew. That's all right in New York but I don't think it would be all right here.' (Didn't anyone ever mention to Harry B. Platt that King Faisal used to go to Harry Winston too? He even bought Queen Iffat's engagement ring from him. What was Platt doing at all these Saudi parties not to notice Winston jewellery all around him?) 'I won't go out of my way to tell anyone how successful this trip has been when I go home. It would hurt the feelings of the people here.' It wouldn't do him much good in New York either.

Over dinner at Sheikha Badria's after the departure of Tiffany's, someone did mention the sales figure in Kuwait; it was not impressive. It might have been wrong, but they do know about money in Kuwait. They have a very special reputation for it. They also have a very special reputation for liking to buy in secret. The Blue Room exhibition might not have netted any whoppers, but I would not put it past the Kuwaitis to nip on the next plane to New York and make straight for Tiffany. They would rather miss out on the discount in return for having Fifth Avenue privacy the way they like it.

Kuwaitis have an even more special reputation (throughout the Middle East) for being cold and reserved, with only a surface friendliness. It's hard to get past it, but you know when you have. It happened to me thanks to a countess. I came a cropper over her in the Blue Room.

A little background: in December 1974, Gainsborough's Countess Clanwilliam was packed up with a lot of other canvases and flown to Kuwait by Roy Miles, thirty-eight-year-old Belgravia art dealer. She went on show in the Blue Room with a £42,000 price tag, a Stubbs or two and a complete set of Pieter pastels (which used to hang in Lady Sassoon's country house). This show of Old Masters was reported back to London journalists from Miles as the social event of the season. He hinted at a big deal but there was no talk of a firm sale. The British press gave him a good splash.

A year later, I am sitting in a drawing room making small talk. My hostess, her eyes fixed somewhere above my head, is friendly but reserved. My eyes are glued to her expensive, soft leather boots. Is this really Kuwait? I cast around and drop Roy Miles's name. My hostess produces a cutting from a London newspaper. The punch-line comes in the last paragraph. She hands it to me and I read: 'One thing which really fascinates the Kuwaitis is the way the eighteenth-century subjects frequently posed adorned with pearls. Kuwait was traditionally a pearl exporter (before the oil, naturally) but, as the Arabs never wore them, they didn't know what they were used for.'

I snort; she smiles wryly. I suddenly recognise it; I should do. I wrote it. I break up. It all seemed so plausible a world ago in London. 'I know I should apologise,' cracking with laughter, 'But it's so funny. You must think I'm an idiot.'

The thaw sets in and six snooty Kuwaiti ladies laugh too. I know I've broken through. 'Ah. Another for the collection of Blue Room stories, a good one,' says my hostess, looking at me at last. 'But I can cap it. I was at the airport one day when a European dealer was clearing customs for a Blue Room exhibition. His embassy had sent someone to meet him so the stuff was cleared fast.

'But someone must have told the dealer in Europe that you can't get a thing done out here without a bribe. So out came his wallet with a wad of notes for the customs man. Imagine the confusion of the poor diplomat. There he was trying to make the dealer understand that the packages had been cleared long ago, but nothing would satisfy the man until he paid his bribe. The customs man thought he was mad. But he wasn't a fool. He took it.'

And yes, the story's true. Incredulous, I checked it with the embassy concerned.

The Sellers' market

At their worst, Kuwaitis are crashing snobs. They go on and on about their ambition to house the Bolshoi Ballet Company (much to Saudi disgust Kuwait has diplomatic relations with communists). So nothing less will do than having the best man over from London to advise them on building their own National Theatre. 'Something like the Paris Opera House is what we have in mind,' says the minister unpretentiously.

Then you find out that the same Kuwaitis oohing and aahing about hosting the Bolshoi never bother with ballet when they're abroad. So what's the point of all the fuss? It's easy; if the Bolshoi dance for London, they should for Kuwait. Kuwaitis can't stand being left out of anything chic.

Most of them have perfected the art of seeming to be arrogant; some of them are. They're also sarcastic and cutting. 'I suppose you could call us the English of the Arab world these days. We have the same kind of stand-offishness as you; only we're so much better at it.' Is that 15-love for a complete put down, or love-15 for sinking so low? It's neither really; it's a question for them of saving face, of seeming to be the best.

And in order to keep the chorus line of saved faces in neat order, there are definite rules about how proper Kuwaitis go about matters. It's increasingly 'the wrong thing' for instance, to fly in a designer to do over one's house. 'Further down the Gulf they're like the Americans in the early days – new rich and title hungry,' sniffs one Kuwaiti. 'They go to London and pick up any decorator with a fancy name – as if money can buy breeding.'

John Sellers is Kuwait's very own David Hicks. He's an al-Ghanim protegé (you don't come higher than that) whose job it is to coat some of the city's richest houses with Kuwait's newly-acquired sense of 'good taste'.

He's a thin-hipped, streaky blond cockney from the East End of London who landed on Kuwait in 1966 during his flower power days en route to Japan via India. His story involves Beirut, a New York ex-cop, an Italian-Swedish blonde hoping to make a killing (her only offer of employment was as a stripper) and finally a Lebanese architect who took to Sellers. He was impressed enough to rope him into his practice in Kuwait.

Four years later Sellers opened on his own. Now he has twenty designers working for him, a large brown and red office with leather-buttoned sofas and a caged parrot. He's the dearly beloved of the kind of Kuwaiti women who keep appointment books (a latest craze). 'I can spare you half an hour on Wednesday week,' they say to a friend on the phone after poring over their advance bookings. Then you find out they're free all day tomorrow. Sellers has to fit in doing their homes with those appointment books plus another of their current crazes – going to Kuwait university, chauffeur-driven naturally. They go to pass the time; not many get round to passing the exams.

Sellers has to find ways of doing their homes in near-furtive conditions. It goes without saying that his clients lie through their teeth that they did it all themselves. Face saving again. The fact that Kuwait's so small that everyone who's had a Sellers' job knows everyone else who's had a Sellers job is beside the point. Sellers is careful never to repeat himself in any two drawing rooms and that way the mistresses of each can coo at one another about how clever they both were to scheme it so well.

His discretion and taste don't come too expensive. He's too shrewd to price himself out of the market for those thrifty 'old money' Kuwaitis. He charges under £7,000 to design a room and stock it with everything.

'When I arrived here there was decor chaos,' Sellers, talking through his shaggy moustache, remembers to signal to the Indian tea boys brewing up on the other side of a glass wall. 'No one knew what they wanted and they were scared stiff of choosing. They didn't have the confidence to let me do anything new. One guy gave me carte blanche to do up his den so I designed a fantastic room in simple colours but with huge cushions covered in beautiful fabrics round it. It seemed so obvious; every time Kuwaiti men get together, they always end up slouched on the floor.

'The guy was horrified; he wanted "proper seats" and yet I knew he'd be sitting on them just the way he would on a cushion. He didn't have the self-confidence to try it. It's all different now. Now I can do pretty much the same sort of thing I'd be doing in England. Well, to be honest, a great deal better; they've more money to spend here.'

The tea arrives in a second. Sellers' operations are geared to instant delivery. 'When I was working in London, I used to hang around being artistic and temperamental. I'd have to wait until I was in "the right mood" to choose colours. But here, wham, you've got to have it all drawn out by tomorrow morning.' His clients want it now; they don't want to wait. After all, in a short while they'll be on the move again.

No kidding; one architect has watched a house he designed and carefully landscaped bulldozed five years later to build something better. Nothing unusual. At one stage, they didn't even have to be bulldozed. They simply fell down. Sellers is already drawing up plans of a new house for a family whose last house acquired his finishing touches only a few weeks ago. That's how fast Kuwait moves.

You can see their progress clearly laid out. Start off in the middle of Kuwait city and there's still a few old houses left over from the mud days not so long ago. Drive out to where the development started when the oil money came in. Here are the early, garish, rainbow-coloured houses complete with jutting-out balcony, copied unthinkingly from foreign magazines. What on earth's use is a balcony here? In summer no one can sit out on it for the heat. In winter the cold winds drive sand into feet-high heaps on anything as dumb as an exposed balcony.

Drive on to the more functional copies a few miles along: neo-Georgian mansions complete with columns. They look bloody stupid in a desert capital. Another minute's drive and you're into the Americana modern belt that went up a couple of years ago. Nice enough if this was California. It isn't.

Nor is it Spain – which didn't occur to the next lot of progressives who started getting an Arab nationalist itch in their house plans and put up Spanish–Moorish villas. But right out on the edge of the Kuwaiti suburbs, in the smartest residential area of all, Salamiyya (where Sellers has his office) you'll find the avant garde of today. Sellers' taste-hungry clients are now into designing homes on purified 'classical Arab lines'. Basically that means blank, fortress-like walls with slit windows and huge spaces inside. Purified? Hogwash. But beautiful, all the same.

And please don't run away with the idea that the whole of rich Kuwait is on the hunt for elegance. Near Sellers' office is Mobilia House, Decor and Furniture. They still do a brisk trade in casts of Venus de Milo and three-foot-high Botticelli's Birth of Venus (complete with shell). There's a ready market for their Lebanese carved, hand-painted, white, gold, and powder-blue bedroom suites with seven-foot double bed, twelve-foot wardrobe, two matching chests of drawers-cum-dressers with mirrors, twin triangular corner tables also with mirrors (only 1,500 dinars the package, says the salesman. Can he mean it?) And they sell plenty of those 'old gold' antiqued or cut-glass Syrian chandeliers (60 dinars each) to add a soft-romantic haze.

This is what Sellers calls the 'Louis de Lebanon' look. It's what he had to do before his clients could be persuaded that there was an alternative to plush velvets and tasselled brocade. What few Kuwaitis have discovered, it seems, is that there's an alternative to getting a decorator in and claiming to have done it yourself. It's called 'having the confidence to get down and do it yourself'. No they haven't got that far in Kuwait.

They have got far enough to have the most amazing dress shops. Salamiyya might not be the Faubourg St Honoré yet, but it's getting there. Lanvin and Chloe hang artistically in a boutique appropriately named 'Versailles'. Only the best from the Paris houses of Dior, Scherrer, Patou, Givenchy and Nina Ricci hang in nearby 'Ruban Blue'. There's Charles Jourdan in 'The Red Shoes', Carita of Paris runs a hairdressing and beauty parlour. And you can only be suitably impressed if you remember that bargain basement mess in the shops of Jiddah or Riyadh and the seedier end of Oxford Street that Bahrain's boutiques take after.

I overlook one characteristic Kuwaiti dig: 'Our Yves St Laurent is ravishing compared to yours in Bond Street.' I don't bother to point out it's the same clothes, the same displays – I'm resigned now to the fact that Kuwaiti has to be best.

At least I'm not the only target; they dig at each other the same way. One Kuwaiti was caught wearing the same YSL suit as another woman, who's telling me the story: ' "Where did you get yours?" she asked me. I told her Beirut. "Oh there," she said, "Yves St Laurent made mine specially for me." It's a lie, it has to be a lie. They were identical. But I'm sure she gave it to her Indian maid that night.' Incidentally, the woman telling me her story didn't get hers in Beirut; she bought it in Salamiyya.

They get their roles confused in Kuwait just as they do in Saudi. Except, of course, it's not the same roles they're confusing. Here they can't decide whether they want to be the smartest, most exclusive things on two legs wearing all the right labels, or the sharpest chicks who know how to buy cheap. They can't make up their minds which role is the more sophisticated. So at one moment an al-Sabah sheikha will say she doesn't go shopping with her cousins because she hates the way they spend more than a hundred dinars on a dress. The next she'll say that only Charles Jourdan boots will do because only their leather is soft enough for her. They're keen on boots, Kuwaitis. Leather boots here? They want to be like Europe you see. That's why none of those smart boutiques would take money if they hung out an Arabic name above their shop – Versailles, Ruban Blue, it gives away the whole game.

When you come down to it, the Kuwaiti women's arrogance isn't solid. It plates and protects a sense of deep insecurity. That's why I can forgive all those stabbing remarks. Underneath all the bullshit, they're loyal and they're kind. And who am I to poke fun? I can be a bitch and show-off of the worst order when I feel unsure of myself. And away from the shops and the beauty parlours, life isn't half so grand or secure for these rich Kuwaiti women.

The odd couples

'All Change Please' is the motto of Kuwaiti society. All those new houses; all those independent females. Kuwaiti women are legally the most advanced in the Gulf. They even got the vote in 1975. The country claims to have a world-renowned women's movement. In case you haven't heard of it, it has thirty members. As a status symbol it's fine. As anything more potent, it's a failure. Kuwaiti family life is often a desolate mockery of freedom and companionship. In its own way, it's more segregated and harsher on women than Saudi Arabia.

Most men in Kuwait spend their time with other men. There's homosexuality, but that's not the reason. There's a Kuwaiti institution: the diwania. It's a large room with a separate entrance tacked on to or under a house. Every evening most men from the inner circle of Kuwait (some 3,000 in all) go to each others' diwanias. They play cards, gossip, do business, watch television, and, occasionally, import belly dancers. It's respectable enough; it merely excludes wives.

Then there's adultery; rather a great deal of it. Among men that is. I don't know how men are supposed to commit adultery with women without women committing adultery too, but that's the marvellous paradox of the double standard at work again. Kuwaiti men are even less inhibited about their sexual activities than Saudis.

Their attitude to Western women in their country is equally less inhibited. I'll never be able to smell sandalwood again without being reminded of a conversation I have with one young Kuwaiti. It goes on for an hour or more. The jist: why am I so prejudiced against Arab men that I think all they're interested in is sex. I haven't even mentioned the subject; he's brought it up. And why, while we're about it, won't I sleep with him? And if I won't sleep with him why do I go round looking like the kind of girl who can cope with life and therefore with sleeping with him? That's the Western woman's Catch 22 in the Gulf. Either you're not tough enough to be able to cope in the country, or you're tough enough to cope and that's synonymous with being tough enough to sleep around. It's like being stuck on a roundabout.

You're also tough enough, it seems, to be beyond surprise.

This man is from a 'heritage' family. He's in his late thirties (he looks fifty). He's on public boards and corporations – the works. He plops himself down next to me and, without invitation, treats me to the saga of his private life. Since I'm fondling my notebook at the time and he knows perfectly well that I'm a journalist and he's perfectly sober, I wish I could name him. He's old enough and certainly big enough to know what he's doing. Alas, I can't.

He launches forth: 'At last I'm going to Cairo to see about my flat. Every week I book a flight, every week I'm so busy I cancel. I bought it some months ago and gave the decorator £1,500 to start work. But he's spent that and I have to go and arrange matters. Of course I buy it and I do everything. My wife wouldn't know how to make a house. Our house in Beirut, I did everything. Even my house in Kuwait, I made everything and then I called her in and said "There you are".

'My wife is very busy. My mistake was in making five children, one nine or ten months after the other. My wife holds so much to them, I come home at nights and find our children in our bed. I tell her very often "I do not like to sleep with children, I like to sleep with you." Finally I say, "All right, you go and sleep with your children. I'll sleep in my bed."

'Now it's not so bad. I feel sorry for my wife; she loves me too much. I can't help it but I don't like to be with her so much. Last summer in London I said to her one Sunday, "Today I will be with you. I will take you for a walk in the park." She loved it, but me, I didn't like it. If I go with my friends for a walk I say "There's a pretty girl." I can't say that to her so we have nothing to discuss.

'I'm very hot and strong. I must have a woman every day or I can't sleep. But my wife she only wants three times a week. So I have four girl friends in Kuwait, two in London and one in Cairo. Every morning I leave my house at eight o'clock and I go and take one of my girl friends to my private flat and we enjoy ourselves for say one and a half hours and then I go to the office.

'Today I make my wife at one-thirty, I make one girl friend at three and then I go to diwania until twelve and then I make another girl and then I go home to my wife. Today after lunch my wife in bed she made five times and I made one. All my girl friends are the same. I wait and then I say "Is that enough?" and then they sigh and say "oh yes" and then I roll on top and that's that. My French girl friend in London say she has never had a man like me in her life.

'I don't know if my wife knows or if she doesn't. I say to her many times, "If you don't like me, you can go away." But she loves me. What can she do? My wife wouldn't want another man. What would I do if I found out she had one? I would push her out straight away with her children and tell her to go back to her home. Of course it's different for me. I'm very hot man.'

I'm too stunned to react. What can you say to such a man? I ask him if he thinks his wife is happy and what she does every night when he goes to diwania. 'Happy? She has me. She loves me so much that we have four servants but she washes all my clothes herself; she would kiss my feet. What does she do? I don't know. She stays inside our home, she talks to her children, watches TV and is on the telephone very much.'

He is incapable of recognising his wife as a person. No wonder she spends so much time on the telephone. All over Kuwait, there is a network of telephoning. Women telephoning women, women telephoning strange men. It's a fantasy life.

The most sorry story of all was told to me by a young girl from a good family. She had a 'love affair'. It was pure fantasy, until she got hurt. Then it was real enough. She is twenty-five, dark, pretty, thin – too thin. 'One day I was so bored that I picked up a telephone and dialled a number. Just any number. A man answered the telephone and we ended up having a conversation. He pleaded with me to give him my number, and that's how we started having a romance. It was all on the telephone. It went on for six months and we hadn't even seen each other. We were dying to, so I arranged to meet him in a supermarket by such and such a counter. I said I'd wear a pink shirt. I took a girl friend and he took a boy friend.

'We were just able to see each other and talk for a few moments. He was wonderful looking. After that we used to arrange to take drives at the same time just to be able to wave and smile. This went on for five years. But then my family found out about it, so he said it was time for him to be formally introduced to me.

'He met my brother and it was obvious there was going to be a proposal. One friend even gave me a betrothal present. I was happy, you understand?'

I understand. Marriages are still arranged, mostly they have to be. There's a limited circle from which a girl of a certain family can take a husband. To find one for herself would be happiness indeed.

'Then it started. First I got threatening calls from his mother and sister warning me off. His mother said he had been promised to another girl from birth. The man said he didn't care. The summer came and his mother went away taking him with her. He went for a week. After one and a half months I still hadn't heard a word. Then someone told me he was back; still no word. At last I worked up enough courage to telephone. His mother put it down on me.

'One day he telephoned. He didn't even say "hello". He just asked me a question: "Listen, do you hear that noise?" I listened and I could hear a faint swishing. "That's my wife. Sweeping." That's all he said.'

At least her family stuck by her, even though she had broken every law of their society. Everyone in that limited circle from which she could marry knows about it. Not much hope of a husband now.

Ways and means

Not all Kuwaiti women allow themselves to be drawn into loneliness. They don't all remain passive. There are single girls who work, who lead an independent social life of sorts. Sometimes mothers push brothers and fathers into cutting down these girls' freedom. They want them back in the family prison. It's a question of jealousy. Older women resent having missed the opportunities. 'Imagine, all those hundreds of years of purdah and the veil,' said one educated woman, 'and I had to miss freedom by twenty years.'

More forceful girls marry an acceptable man and then bully their way into getting what they want—freedom to go out to work, public places, restaurants, Europe. The more fortunate find a man who doesn't want just 'diwania and separate existences', and knows how and when to compromise.

Hind al-Naqib had an uncertain, disturbed childhood. She was born in Iraq but the family moved to Kuwait soon after the revolution there. They got instant Kuwaiti citizenship, for they were cousins of the Iraqi royal family and that counts for something here. Her family were received as proper Kuwaitis. Unfortunately for Hind later, her father goofed by moving off to Beirut – it was easier to make money in the Lebanon in those days; he wanted education for his children. That the Kuwaitis didn't forgive.

Hind's an aristocrat and she's married to one, a 'heritage' Kuwaiti. She's nearly thirty, has been a mother for most of her twenties, was a headmistress and is now a university teacher. She's one of the rare Kuwaiti women who entertains for her husband, Abdul Rahman, a government minister. She's one of an ever rarer breed of Kuwaiti women; she has insight into herself.

'I was a very spoilt child and very precocious. I behaved like a child when I went to university in Beirut. I never did a stroke of work, I don't know how I passed the exams. I always tried to live up to my reputation for behaving badly – it gave me a kind of distinct identity.'

'But at home we lived like Kuwaitis. I was never allowed out in the evenings so I used to rage and scream at my father, "Let me, let me go out like everyone else!" And then, straight after I graduated, I got married. It was arranged for us. Afterwards I used to get terribly angry whenever my husband admitted it. I was so embarrassed about it that I used to go round saying that we had fallen in love.

'Those first two years back in Kuwait were awful. It wasn't Kuwait; I was used to a sheltered life in Beirut. Getting used to each other was difficult. The trouble with us Kuwaiti girls is that we're spoilt. We get married young and go on treating our husbands exactly like our fathers – "want, want, want!"

'I was bored to tears shut up in the house all day and I used to lie in wait for Abdul Rahman and nag him with questions, wanting to know every single little movement he'd made since he left the house. I just wanted attention; he was normally unaffectionate. I got so bored that I spent every moment of my life when he wasn't home on the telephone.

'That was when Abdul Rahman pulled me up short. He told me that I would be appalling in ten years time and that I had to do something useful. He sent me out to teach. Everyone got their knives in then. "Poor girl," they said, "he can't even make enough money to keep his wife."

'He was a good deal wiser than his years, Abdul Rahman; he didn't care. It did the trick. All that energy I had been turning in on myself suddenly had an outlet. I started getting friends of my own. It was good for my confidence. Abdul Rahman does go out quite a lot in the evening with his friends. But now the women take it in turn to entertain. We can't go to a public restaurant, not our kind of women, so one lot invite the men one evening and the other lot the women. It works. But the one thing that has made my marriage easier is that I can truly say I never fell in love and I don't believe in it. I'm very grateful for that.'

Less grateful women resort to cunning. If they're single, they weave a refined mesh of cover-ups – involving girl friends, sisters, drivers, nannies. All this to go to occasional mixed tea parties or dinners. 'Wherever I am, I always say I'm with my best friend and my best friend always knows to back that up when my mother rings to check,' this from an al-Sabah. 'And it's not as if this is the high life. It's so innocent – what's wrong with a little dinner party once a week and maybe a drink? Fortunately my driver is very loyal. My mother once tried to trip him up, saying she knew I'd been to a house with a mixed party and Europeans. He wouldn't give me away.'

Other girls get out of the country altogether. They go to university abroad and regard Kuwait as an obligation. They come back for a few months, do nothing, grow fat, and can't wait to get away again. But that has its drawbacks when the inevitable time comes for marriage. There's the all-important matter of virginity. Before the troubles, everyone used to go to Beirut for their trousseau. Some girls threw in a quick bit of hymen-stitching too. One Kuwaiti girl asked a gynaecologist why he went in for (her words) this barbarous practice. 'I was outraged when I came back from the West and was asked to perform such an operation,' he replied. 'But what can I do? I know the girls haven't done anything wrong. It's their society and the men that are at fault. I can perform a simple formal ritual that will make it possible for them to go on with their lives. Yes, its disgusting and it's barbarous. I can't change society but I can protect the girls. And after all, I'm an Arab too. I understand.'

I'm sitting around with a few Kuwaiti girls. We're having the same old rap I know from Hampstead and Greenwich Village – consciousness-raising, alienation and ecology. But it's not Greenwich Village: one of them mentions that she is by no means certain that one of her relations wouldn't kill her if she was found not to be a virgin. 'Everyone says "I'll kill my wife." or "I'll kill my sister if . . ." You never know who means it literally. I had a girl friend whose father took her out to the desert when he found her with a man. We never saw her again. Whenever we went over to tea we'd ask after her. Eventually we stopped asking. How do any of us know what would happen to us?' Her friends nod.

'What men want when they get married is blood and pain. Unless they get blood on their wedding night, they might send back the goods. And don't tell us that not all girls bleed, or about horse-riding and sport. Tell the men. It's an obsession with some of them. In the old days women who were worried used to go to a 'wise woman' before the wedding and she'd give them a sheep's bladder with blood in it. They'd stuff that inside on the wedding night and that did the trick.

'Some men might not mind if you're not a virgin, or if your hymen is already broken. Some would understand. But how do you know when you get married which type you're getting? You've only seen him a few times. I wouldn't take the risk.'

Some wives, when they get lonely enough, take an even graver risk for Kuwait. They resort to cunning and boy friends; drivers or stray foreigners. This one, who looks unassailable, regularly books into a beauty salon for a day's massage and facial. She turns up all right; then she tips the receptionist heavily for silence and slips out to see her German boy friend. When he told me I didn't believe him. I figured him for a big mouthed boaster (I still do). When she told me I thought she was crazy.

Can it be worth it? There's a woman in Kuwait who was caught talking on the telephone to a man. Her husband shot her in the neck and called her brother: 'If you want to see your sister alive again, you'd better come round at once.' Her brother got her to hospital secretly. Next morning all Kuwait knew about it.

She now leads a quiet life and everyone agrees that it's forgotten. The end of an ugly scar juts below the scarf round her neck.

No exit

Kuwaiti women can seem so together on the surface that some-times I long to ask them why they don't wake up and fight back. Why do they have to be victims, underhand and afraid? 'The way out is through the door,' as the saying goes. Then I realise how futile and out-of-place my conditioning is here. And anyway, can I be so sure that I'd be any different had I been born to this life? Not after Najat Sultan, certainly.

Najat Sultan has woken up; she's working for change. 'In 1972 I tried to get a group of women to work together. I con-tacted some thirty-five of the 230 women graduates there were in Kuwait then to come to a meeting. No one turned up. I tried the same thing in the traditional way – arranging a tea party. No one came. And then I realised it was the wrong approach, that I had to work more gradually, talking to individuals and concentrating on women who were already working or were in important positions to give a lead.'

What is she trying to accomplish? Her aims are so modest as to seem prudish. 'I just want to make women aware of themselves and of their position.' Just. In Kuwait, that's like asking Palestinian commandos home to tea.

People talk of Najat as articulate, cold and tough. She sounds rather alarming. She works at the government's Planning Board during the day and every evening sits in the art gallery she and her brother Fawaz started together. Here Najat Sultan holds her salon; here she's at her most slick and buoyant.

The 'slick' Najat is a beautiful girl with a cloud of fluffy, dark hair down to her waist. She has a small, neat-featured face with huge, rather anxious deep brown eyes, not so certain of themselves after all. She's unusually dressed for Kuwait: dark trousers, loose Peruvian-style jacket over a white shirt and loads of necklaces. Bedu jewellery and some she made herself.

It's very NW1. The prints on the walls of the white, deliberately austere gallery may be by Kuwaitis and other Arab artists but they were all trained at Western art schools. The sophisticated, slightly Bohemian girls around Najat talk intensely, and with a certain contempt, about other Kuwaiti women. Some of Najat's own phrases are good if obviously well-rehearsed and well-aired. 'In Kuwait we suffer from double apartheid: class and sex. Kuwaitis and non-Kuwaitis, men and women. They are separate societies within one society.' It's impressive and I've heard other patter like it in Kuwait.

But there are other Najats; the simpler, warmer, gentler creature that's Najat at home with her mother and 'Baby', her sister. She's more honest. 'I've clipped my wings a lot recently and I'm much less sociable. I've had to; my brothers and cousins objected to my seeing so many people.' The way she talks about other women changes too. She shows more understanding, more compassion. 'Husbands complain about their wives' extravagance. But how can you possibly blame the women? Things are all they have to fill the vacuum.'

And then there's the unself-confident Najat. European friends invited her to a party; she came, slightly out of control through fear and uncertainty. Her defence was to turn up in an outrageous fancy dress costume, Edwardian, with a big, floppy hat. 'That was when I first felt affection for Najat,' says a friend, 'The moment I could see how much it cost her to come into that room, she sudenly became vulnerable.'

But there are people in London who'd laugh at such a story. They remember her when she spent years there at Byam Shaw, the posh art school, doing a jewellery course. She knocked everyone sideways: beautiful, cool, very together and right on top of London's social scene. She never talks of those years now; she's buried them completely. The Kuwaiti social scene has defeated her since then.

What's ahead for her? Not much. She may look twenty-four but she must be in her mid-thirties. No Kuwaiti man would take her on and there's no question of her marrying a foreigner, not now. She's from far too good a Kuwaiti family; those brothers and cousins (guardians of her and, therefore, their honour) wouldn't complain. They'd behave as though she were dead.

She enjoys her work but it's not much fun living in a society that sees you as a joke, if not a freak. What woke her up? Maybe it was seeing her aunt's life. Her aunt married a good-looking man who left her after two years. He left her with two children, never divorced her and she had to stay with his parents. Maybe it was seeing her own parents who were much happier – during the sixteen years they spent living in India, away from Kuwait. Najat went to boarding school in Cairo, so she's been cut off from her family once. That was enough. She came back to Kuwait in 1959, hardly able to speak Kuwaiti Arabic. She doesn't fit in and she doesn't want to get out; once of that was enough too.

The most daring thing she can ever do is to go out for dinner to a restaurant alone with a man. But she has to mind enough to run the risk of being seen. Najat's far too honest to resort to scheming and cover-ups. 'If it's important enough to me, yes, I'll go and take the consequences. But I won't go just for fun.'

If I lived in a society where going out for one lousy dinner might turn me into a social outcast, I reckon my self-confidence and independence might cave in too. Najat's certainly have.

She went to London for a holiday recently. She was given Germaine Greer's number and lots of other trendy introductions. She didn't use a single one. Kuwait has undermined Najat Sultan. There's only one thing to be in Kuwait – and that, I'm afraid, is a man.

Crows and peacocks

It's only in Kuwait, where national dress means more than any amount of gold braid on a soldier's uniform, that I start to focus properly on what superiority this dress gives a man. In Saudi, I couldn't tell one thobe from another. Here (where the dress is the same, only the name's been changed – it's called a deshdasha), I begin to notice small but significant variations.

National dress does have a language that gives something away after all. Is the material rough or fine? Higher collars make an important man keep his head up; the downtrodden sink into their lower-cut collars. If a man doesn't do much, he'll fasten the collar with studs – he has the time to fiddle with them. If he does something, he'll probably make do with buttons. If he's very conscious of his position, he'll go to the trouble of having his dress made with hidden fastenings. It's more elegant.

Lowlier mortals have short hems with heavy-duty shoes poking out inches below. Higher ones have long hems (they don't have to bother about dirtying their clothes. What are a few extra laundry bills?) and you don't even notice their shoes.

Above all, there's the head-dress which can say more about a man than his best friend would. Chic variation number one is to throw up the sides of the head-dress. This takes a certain style and can only be done by a man with good ears and a firm jawline. The movement can be seductive – at least in Saudi Arabia, where every square inch of revealed skin is charged with meaning.

There are, therefore, dozens of ways of wearing a head-dress without any style at all. Too much left hanging over a man's forehead makes him look like a half-wit. If the rope (originally used for hobbling his camel) is jammed too far down on his head, he looks like a neatly tied parcel.

And here's another interesting difference between Kuwaiti men and Saudis. In Saudi their attitude to national dress is an extension of their attitude to their country – a bundle of contradictions and complexities. For them, national dress is a strait-jacket. It's another of those insidious ways in which the free play of their individuality is stifled and suppressed. They pine to break out, get abroad and change into a Western suit. In Kuwait, their attitude is that national dress is a mark of rank. Only Kuwaiti Kuwaitis wear it. They'll make noises about how inconvenient it is with the same convincing tone as a much-decorated statesmen groaning at having to put on yet more badges, sashes and medals.

Throughout Arabia you can tell a man who spends most of his time abroad. He's the one who's forever scratching his head. That table-cloth makes him itch. He's one of the few that probably looks better in Western clothes. All Arab men look better in national dress unless they've the total confidence and know-how to find a tailor to cut a suit to their mould (most of them rush into a store and buy ready-made; they don't like to have to 'design' their orders and they haven't the patience to wait for fittings) and then have the wherewithal to carry it off.

In national dress the tall and slim look like film stars, the ascetic like saints. Figures paunchy and stooping, gutted by years of outrageous living, become venerable vessels of wisdom. Then you see in London the figures you last met in Jiddah, Kuwait or Abu Dhabi. It's an appalling shock, better avoided. The film star has turned into a waiter, the saint into a beggar, the wiseman into a carpet vendor.

Regardless of what it does for their figures, national dress confers an advantage on an Arab over everyone else he talks to who doesn't wear it – and that means women, Westerners and foreign Arabs. It also enables him to get up to all those tricks that become possible when you're wearing long drapes – it turns the crow into a peacock.

Sitting down becomes a whole performance; the vain man won't crease his apparel. Then there's the question of pockets.

A man's role is circumscribed by the fact that he can't carry anything but the odd minute gold lighter around with him. The thin cotton reveals the contents of his pockets to all the world – he couldn't be disfigured that way. So the oil-rich Arab can't play the role of the Useful Man who's always equipped with string, cigars, spare handkerchiefs, pens and other white rabbits ready to whip out in an emergency. It renders him 'helpless', in need of an entourage.

Worrying about all these problems means that on top of feeling he's running the world, an Arab man has to be all those things women have long been accused of – excessively preoccupied with details, obsessed with self and therefore doomed to look at other people, and the world, through a delicious haze of subjectivity.

Oh yes, their women might spend a fortune dressing up like the rich usually do everywhere else – but that's the whole point. No matter how much they spend, how well they dress, how much they go for chic or exclusivity, rich Arab women now look like any other rich women throughout the world. And the Western world isn't agog to know what's in the minds next of those all-powerful oil sheikhas. They're only interested in the all-powerful oil sheikhs. It's the modern way of setting their women physically apart.

And the men are going to keep it that way. Don't listen to any Saudi or Kuwaiti man who tells you he wears national dress because it's more practical. It might be in summer but he won't often be here in summer. He wears it because it stamps him as a superior being. It's written all over him in black (his cloak) and white (his dress) that he's the thing to be right now – Arab, from an oil state and a man.

The thoroughly modern Sabah

The best thing of all to be, of course, is an al-Sabah man. The al-Sabah sheikhs are the epitome of all that's well-bred, well-dressed and thoroughly modern. At least that's the picture they present. The emir (not ruler) is hardly seen, except in his photograph that hangs everywhere in Kuwait, and no one publicises his idea of a holiday treat in London. He enjoys riding around on the underground, the Circle Line for choice.

Handsome, educated al-Sabahs go out to important embassies. Oxford-educated charmer, Sheikh Salim (now a government minister), polished his ambassadorial posts in London and Washington until they gleamed. His brother-in-law, Sheikh Saud, is another in the Omar Sharif mould. He brings to his new ambassador's office suite in London the sleek showmanship of a barrister-at-law (called at Gray's Inn in 1968).

The fact that at the moment there's inter-family strife of a somewhat awkward nature going on is kept strictly behind Kuwaiti palace walls. When the al-Sabah have sorted out the jobs among themselves, Kuwait will get to hear the results. Meanwhile all that most people care about their ruling family is that they keep the state steady and don't hog all the jobs. In the sixteen-man cabinet there are now eleven commoners, albeit 'heritage' men from top families. Few early risers get excited when they catch a glimpse of a good-looking, keen-eyed man wandering around the fish and meat markets at five in the morning. It's only the conscientious Crown Prince-cum-Prime Minister checking on food prices again.

No one talks any more about how Emir Mubarak 'The Great' bumped off two brothers in his anxiety to get to the top job in 1896. The mid-fifties antics of the present emir's older brother, Sheikh Fahd, are all in the past. Sheikh Fahd went in for an imaginative life-style, they say, but that wasn't the problem. More distressing was his failure to distinguish between his personal income and the national cash register during his time as head of the public works' department (among others). Eventually the family put their heads together in private and arranged for him to leave office. Shortly afterwards he died: officially of a heart attack on a pilgrimage to Mecca. Intelligence sources favour the version that he died somehow on his yacht.

The al-Sabah have always been good at putting their heads together at an important moment. That's how they got to rule the place. After a shocking drought in the desert in 1710 some of the most aristocratic Bedu went down to the Gulf for a sight of water. They wandered around until they settled on a convenient spot, Kuwait. Someone had the bright idea of sending one of their clever young men off to see the nearest Turkish governor to get permission to stay put, on condition that they kept quiet. His mission was a success. He was an al-Sabah. His family has been top dogs ever since; everyone else who was around at the time is 'heritage'.

At first I'm impressed by the mere sight of all those god-like, highly educated al-Sabahs with their faultless Western dress in Europe and tightly-hugging jeans off-duty in Kuwait. Then I start to admire the family's desert-conditioned sense of timing. There are the little touches: the latest stand of Ambassador Sheikh Saud and his wife, Awatif (known as the Princess Anne of Kuwait). They have desegregated his diwania; husbands and wives are both invited now. Too bad this bold couple have been posted to London; no one else has yet had the courage to follow their example.

There are the bigger flourishes: the lively National Assembly, admittedly packed as far as decent with al-Sabah supporters – all those highly vocal backwoods Bedu. The emir himself, sick or not, knows that the al-Sabah have to keep one jump ahead of getting the boot.

But the al-Sabah have always had trouble with their women. No sooner had they settled down in the 1760s than a grisly tribe attacked them, dying to carry off a particularly beautiful al-Sabah daughter, Mariam. The al-Sabah band fought well; Mariam's honour was saved.

They still haven't mastered that weak spot. Not that one likes to bring it up but there was that small bother over Sheikh Saad's daughter a while ago. It was a sheikha who brought it to my notice; other Kuwaitis are too tactful. Sheikh Saad, Hendon Police College trained, is minister of defence and security. His daughter made the mistake of falling for a Muslim Lebanese when she was at university in Beirut. They eloped to Cyprus.

No question of the daughter being forced to come home; she

was too old to be treated as a 'minor'. Much to the family's horror, Interpol nearly got involved with this errant daughter: someone alleged that she had stolen pieces of her mother's jewellery. It was all a terrible misunderstanding. The unfortunate sheikha now works in Australia. No one knows how to undo the bitterness but certain female cousins secretly send her money. 'It's disgraceful. After all, she married an Arab, what more did her father want?' says one prominent sheikha after I tactlessly mention that another sheikha has mentioned it to me. 'I feel sorry for the girl, I really do. But that's not what matters. It's that incidents like this ruin everything the rest of us are doing to live down the old days.' The al-Sabah are thoroughly modern about everything, except their women.

It's Monday lunch time. Sheikh Nasir and I are bowling along in his silver sports car (complete with statutory Japanese LM-Im Mobile car-phone with push-button dialling). We're off to the races. Sheikh Nasir's cheery; news from the track has it that the going's soft. Good for his horses; Nasir keeps forty at his Amneaf Stable outside Kuwait. He's in keen competition with Uncle Khalid who keeps seventy at his stable, Al Salam.

The horses are already in the paddock for the two o'clock. Nasir goes off for a quick word with his Egyptian jockey, Hisham, walking his three year old maiden, Hakima. The sheikh has a feeling that his quartered green and red racing colours will show to advantage this afternoon.

Sheikh Nasir bin Sabah al-Sabah is the son of Kuwait's foreign minister, and son-in-law of the emir. At twenty-eight he's chairman of United Fisheries and director of Gulf International. More significantly he's director of Lonrho, the British public company whose front-page boardroom rows, involving tax-free payments in the Cayman Islands and so on, led Edward Heath to coin that bon mot 'the unacceptable face of capitalism!' The press coverage of Sheikh Nasir's first attendance at the annual Lonhro share-holder's meeting after several million shares passed expensively into his hands wasn't flattering. The usual Arabs-are-coming Western paranoia; Kuwait winced again.

Nasir takes me up to the members' stand where a large party

of his relations are already installed. Uncle Khalid, a correct man, as befits the president of the emir's diwan (court), sits stiffly in his front-row armchair behind his telephone and two Venetian vases of yellow plastic flowers.

Here is the result of past generations' greed for wives, from white to ebony. Half of the al-Sabah royal family present are black. Khalid's half-brother, Misha'al, the son of a slave, keeps up a non-stop flow of jokes, shouts and anecdotes while he cracks, and scatters, nuts everywhere. He stamps on the stand boards to hurry along the servant below, who scurries up and down all afternoon with trays full of tea cups. Ahmad, the crown prince's son, a slimmer version of his father, slips in and hardly opens his mouth. He's the only one to keep quiet. It's a gang of the lads having a tremendous outing. The powdery sand-track is indeed soft. There's much peering through binoculars, learned race-talk and cruel slashing of whips by eager jockeys.

It takes a while to absorb the sight (and sounds) of all these sheikhs, normally so dignified, rushing around like a bunch of loonies. But it's not long before I notice that I'm the only woman, apart from Myra Davies. Myra's a blunt, Welsh, outdoor type who has somehow got into the way of looking after Khalid's horses. Except for Khalid, everyone thinks it's a hoot having women here. It's obviously a novelty. Myra's always here because Khalid worries about how his horses are doing on their new Indian barley feed. Every racing afternoon involves at least one lengthy discussion about the quality of his beasts' diet. Anyway, Myra doesn't count as a woman. With her hair tied back from her face, her absent husband off doing a day's work for the Kuwait Oil Company, she's almost one of the lads.

Don't the sheikhas ever come? Myra laughs: 'With rare exceptions, being married to a Sabah,' she explains patiently, as if to a child, 'isn't like being a wife as we understand it. It's like being a stud mare.' Mares at stud in al-Sabah palaces don't go to the races.

Sheikh Nasir is one of the exceptions, explains the all-knowing Myra. Not that his wife, Hasa, would be here either. 'It's just that they're, well, different in other ways.' In any case, Hasa is under doctor's care in Paris. She's resting in her apartment, trying not to have her third miscarriage in a row.

Nasir is having a smashing time. He strides to and fro in his two-inch platform shoes (he's very short, for an al-Sabah, and wishes he wasn't). He stuffs his hands into the pockets of his long brown national dress and digs into the betting. Highest stake, after much angry haggling: ten dinars. They're off for the first race: 1,000 metres, entry fee three dinars, first prize eighty. Nasir's Hakima starts well but finishes third. His big face (it is big enough for a man wearing twelve-inch platform shoes) registers thunder. It soon passes.

Jockey Hisham walks by on Hakima. He looks apologetically at Nasir. But Nasir's already involved with ribbing Khalid and any number of his cousins. They're generous to each other over winners. When Major General Adbul Latif al-Thuwaini, under secretary at the Ministry of the Interior, leads in his winners in the second race and then the third, they're pleased for him. Misha'al and Nasir do point out, though, how keen the general is to rush down and be photographed with his horses. At last, a winner for Nasir – Mashalla in the fifth race. He almost falls down the steps in his hurry to get in front of the camera.

It's an afternoon of laughter, teasing, sand driven into my eyes. Whenever he remembers, Nasir is the perfect host. When he forgets, the rest of his family do the honours – even Uncle Khalid comes round offering an occasional nod. It's about as formal as a donkey derby.

Now I understand why Arabs, even royal Arabs, don't like to keep their horseflesh in Europe where it could gallop round more fashionably in the Arc de Triomphe or St Leger. Where would the fun be for these exuberant owners stuck with the champagne and shooting-stick crowd?

Nasir's servant comes to give him a nudge. Has he forgotten that he's flying to Cairo in an hour's time? Nasir's expressive face registers panic. Then he looks me straight in the eye: 'Would you like to come to Cairo tonight? I'll send you back on my plane tomorrow.' The back of Uncle Khalid's head freezes. I don't hesitate. 'I've always wanted to see the pyramids.'

It's seven o'clock in the VIP lounge at Kuwait airport. Sheikh Nasir is impatient. Officials stand around, edgy to anticipate his every wish. His only wish is to get off the ground. Unfortunately he forgot to tell his air crew about going to Cairo. At last the English captain arrives to announce that the crew's all present and correct, but there's another problem: fuel. The Falcon is carrying too much luggage to fly without refuelling. Luxor is out of gas, so is Syria. Would Sheikh Nasir mind cutting across to Jiddah first?

The crowd in the lounge swells by the minute. Sheikh Nasir is royal here, it means too much bowing and scraping for his taste At this point, the captain learns that he won't be flying back until tomorrow. 'Can someone telephone my wife?' he asks with the resignation of a man who left for a day trip to Khartoum last time and came back a fortnight later. I don't have a visa for Egypt. Nasir waves that aside. I don't have a visa to re-enter Kuwait, another wave.

Time to board. Sheikh Nasir marches across the tarmac followed by a large troop of well-wishers and a small troop of passengers. We're off; alas with the plane so full, there's no room to watch a film on the videotape, so it's stereo Shirley Bassey.

Two hours later the Falcon approaches Jiddah. I'm up in the cockpit with Captain Jim trying to put me at my ease: ('don't feel uncomfortable, we've had plenty of girls aboard before'). Jim was enjoying a quiet afternoon with his wife and co-pilot Rudi was fishing eight kilometres out to sea, when someone was sent to find them. Adrian, the blonde, delicate-looking steward, was playing with his new dune buggy on the beach ('I borrowed the money for it from Sheikh Nasir; I'm counting on him not to ask for it back').

The generator has failed. The windscreen is iced up. 'Where's my chamy,' mutters Jim, 'I can't see a bloody thing.' What a life; he had only just got the Kuwaiti ground staff used to servicing the old HS 125 when Nasir bought this second-hand Falcon from 'Tiny' Rowlands of Lonhro. To cap it he's now talking about ordering a long-range Gulfstream GU2.

Jim moans all the way to landing point but somehow brings her down smoothly. It's the last smooth moment for hours.

Of course Jiddah doesn't have fuel. It's the middle of the Hajj. The place is littered with planes. What a contrast to the crisp cold of Kuwait as the hot, humid air of Jiddah hits me. I never thought to be back, at least not this soon. Nasir wishes he had never agreed to come. Take off will be ten-thirty, then eleven-thirty. He stomps between the lounge and the plane, helpless but angry. Everyone is surprised at the predicament: 'I don't understand this country. How can Saudi Arabia of all places run out of oil?'

At midnight the Falcon takes off and Nasir creeps into the back with me to dine on Adrian's sensitively cooked chicken. His exuberance has been crushed. 'It makes me feel terrible. All this waiting. I'm so scared at what you must think of me that I don't know how to talk to you.' Nasir is an unusual al-Sabah; he's upsettable. He feels responsible for the inconvenience in Jiddah because I'm his honoured guest.

Nasir is an extremely attractive man. He may be short but he has a well-built body. His face is too big for it; but he has huge brown eyes with long lashes. He's also very rich. It's not just the usual al-Sabah rich. Gulf International, the company started by his father with a Sudanese vet, is growing vast.

The Falcon comes in to land at Cairo at three am. The cockpit window on Jim's side is so iced up that Rudi is bringing her down. This is always a nerve-racking hop. One captain (I'm not surprised to learn that Jim's the third in a year) tried cutting corners over Luxor and the next thing he knew, there were five military jets screaming around. The plane was heading directly towards a missile site. The jets didn't shoot down the Falcon because a SAM missile was waiting for the honour a few minutes on. There was a rapid change of course in the nick of time. We cut no corners this morning but not being able to see makes Rudi jumpy.

Wheels are down, flaps are down when Jim remarks in a tight British voice: 'I say, Rudi, you're landing on the road actually. The runway's over there.' A quick swerve and we make it.

The embassy official is dutifully waiting – he expected us six hours ago – with more Sheikh Nasir this and Sheikh Nasir that. My passport has him mesmerised. What, no visa? Nasir grabs his briefcase and my arm and drags me out of the VIP lounge into Cairo. It's three-thirty in the morning and an al-Sabah is marching along a deserted road with a strange woman in dirty jeans. The funny side hits us: it's hardly jet set but it's fun. We find a taxi to take us to the Meridian Hotel. This glossy tower boasts a view of the Nile, fourteen floors, swimming pool, a nightclub with the best belly-dancer in Cairo and a receptionist night manager with a wonderful way of lifting a surprised eyebrow.

Nasir's long brown dress looks plain silly in this marble lobby. Yes, the manager's found the suite booking, but could he please have, pause, the lady's name. Nasir remembers 'Linda'. He sticks. I don't help him out. There's a long, long, silence before I add demurely 'Blandford'. The eyebrow is working overtime and Nasir's glaring to kill.

It is four o'clock when we walk into suite 727. Disaster. It has a sitting room with kidney-shaped sofa but only one bedroom. Nasir refuses to take the bedroom and leave me on the sofa. I point out that he's too fat for the sofa. Impasse. We break so that I can take a much-needed bath. The only suggestion he never makes is that we share the one bedroom.

We compromise, order a nice cup of tea and sit on the balcony overlooking the Nile. It's the kind of night Hollywood makes films about – only the dialogue is wrong. By now I understand enough of the Arab fear of losing face to appreciate Nasir. He admits that he flunked his law degree at Kuwait University (some achievement for an al-Sabah). 'I was twenty-one and I didn't know what to do. So I went to my cousin Hasa and asked her to marry me. I told her that I couldn't think of anything else to do. It was very hard for me because Hasa was the clever one of the family and I'd always hated her for being intelligent.'

'Hasa said she'd think about it. She said "yes" and that gave me the confidence to go to London to do a two-year course in business studies. We had a small flat and it meant that I had the chance to get to know her. We didn't have friends in London so we were together all the time. If we had stayed in Kuwait, it wouldn't have been possible.' So that's what the Welsh woman meant about Nasir's marriage being, well, different.

He's leaning on the balcony looking across at President Sadat's guest house. His father often stays there. The President has invited him too – Nasir's company has the fishing rights for the Aswan Dam and he's putting up a 400-bedroom hotel. He rocks backwards and forwards on those strange platform shoes. 'People say I'm a big international businessman now – it doesn't make sense to me. I'm running a company my father started. I have to prove myself. It will take years before people stop saying I'm just bringing my family's money to Gulf International while others do all the thinking.'

He feels he's running a race against his deficiencies. 'Do you think I have an inferiority complex?' Of course I do, why ask? 'Sometimes I wonder if I should see a psychiatrist. Maybe if I know more about what's wrong with me, I'll be more clever and confident. Hasa says failing my exams was the best thing to happen to me. It made me work to prove myself. But I feel so stupid. I love to meet new people, but what can I talk to them about? Someone in London promised to organise a dinner party for me and invite some society people, but I'm too scared. I could talk to them about Islamic art but who wants to hear about Islamic art?'

It's nearly dawn. Nasir remembers that the crew will be turning up after the airport's red tape, and that his father has a house – a five-acre estate near the pyramids. He accepts that I won't take the bedroom, and that I won't stay in the suite alone while he goes to the villa. (Alone in a Cairo hotel with no visa? He's crazy.) 'You're being stupid, but let's go,' he says.

The reception manager puts his own interpretation on our reappearance. It isn't easy to walk out of a hotel with wet feet (the cleaners are dousing the lobby) and dignity. We camp on the kerb until the crew turns up and then pile into taxis to head for the villa. Nasir hasn't stayed there for ten years, nor has his father. Somehow he finds the way and then has to go round the garden shouting out in the hope that there are still some servants. They come running out, and as dawn breaks we all get to bed: Jim and Rudi take one room (Jim's moaning at the musty smell

Adrian is on his own downstairs (shuddering at the bathroom's rusty taps), I get the master's bedroom. Nasir sleeps in the garden house.

At ten, the sheikh and I are having breakfast. The servants have hurriedly unwrapped and polished a fleet of cars. A refrigerated truck has turned up; Nasir's younger brother, Hamad, has got back unexpectedly from a hunting trip in Libya. He's off somewhere in Cairo, but he's sent over his record catch of 500 bustards. ('I bet we get stuck with those disgusting things on the flight back.' Adrian flinches.)

In Kuwait, I wanted to see the pyramids. 'Right,' says Nasir. He's super to be with. We do the Sphinx, ride camels, but he sees through my disappointment at the grubby, tourist-infested sites: 'I know they're not what you expected; please don't put on an act.'

Driving to lunch another side of Nasir slips out. The radio is on softly. A lush orchestra changes tune. 'It's Beethoven's Fidelio,' exclaims 'the stupid one' with delight, turning it up. We park at the restaurant and eat under the trees. He talks knowledgeably of music and literature; of paintings he's been buying through agents at Christie's.

His new home in Kuwait is a major topic. He's persuaded a French professor from the Sorbonne, an expert in oriental architecture, to design it for them. His talking of 'their' home is rare, too. Hasa weaves in and out of the conversation. She's had two miscarriages and he's terrified of her having a third. Then he takes a photograph out of his wallet and shows it to me. It's a snap of a delightful little girl. 'It's our daughter, isn't she lovely?' Now, wait a minute ... Another shock. They gave the baby to his mother; she was the firstborn.

At first he pretends that it was only because his mother had lost her youngest child in a car crash when the girl was born. 'My mother was very depressed, you understand, and we felt it would help her.' Finally he admits that in the thoroughly modern al-Sabah family, the paternal grandmother still has the right to the firstborn child. Sheikha Awatif, his sister-in-law, wife of the Kuwaiti ambassador to London, gave her eldest son to her husband's mother. Ambassador Sheikh Saud was himself brought up by his grandmother. Nasir just won't discuss it.

Sheikha Awatif is much more forthcoming when I ask her how it feels to give away your first child after carrying for nine months. I don't mind asking her; she's easily the nicest, most sincere woman I meet in Kuwait. She's not evasive (it's not her nature) but she fears I might not understand. Too right. 'It's not so hard as you may think because you know it will happen. I see my son every day when I'm in Kuwait, just as Nasir and Hasa see their daughter. But I accept that my son loves his grandmother more than he loves me, just as my husband loves his more than he does his own mother. It's natural that that happens.'

Nasir won't talk about it at all. Perhaps he can't accept the apparent contradiction between the modern image his family's trying to project and the way they stick to this practice that many might find archaic if not a little strange.

No, he's not simple nor stupid. He directs the talk away from treacherous personal ground to international politics. I direct it to Israel. He looks hard at me (watch an Arab watching you if he's trying to weigh you up. He'll stare straight into your eyes It's unnerving.) 'My lawyer in America is a Jew. Does that answer the question you were really asking?' Bullseye.

Lunch lasts for hours, chewing on roasted pigeons while their unknowing relations perch in the trees cooing above us. It's finally time to make for the airport. Nasir insists on driving me there; It's not only because I'm his guest. He wants me to see something. He drives the Mercedes into the centre of Cairo and makes me look, look hard the Arab way.

The street stinks; stick-thin children sit in what would be gutters if this was a road. Women, eyes hollowed by poverty, crouch against grubby walls, selling sticks of sugar cane. Egypt has nearly forty million people. This street is rich living compared to the life most of the others know. 'Now go back to Kuwait and remember your sight of the Pyramids.' I take the point; Nasir drives the car on.

The Falcon flies home non-stop. I'm the only passenger – along with Hamad's bloodied bustards from Libya. Adrian wasn't wrong; those birds got on board. Nevertheless, he's in a confidential mood. There was that bag of diamonds ('as big as nuts, they were') Nasir took to Paris last time he went to see Hasa. There's that solid silver Rolls-Royce stuck in Bombay that Nasir can't get out of the country. And what happened on Nasir's nine-day trip to Acapulco, well . . .

'Still Sheikh Nasir works hard. I'll say that for him.' I'd say a lot more. So too did all of Kuwait next day.

The thoroughly exceptional Sabah

All of Kuwait says rather a lot about everybody. They don't say very much about Sheikha Badria. They mention her frequently enough, all right, but it's in passing. They take her for granted. She's exceptional; what else is there to say?

A lot, frankly. It's something I keep coming across, time and again, in Arabia. There's that handful of women whose personalities soared above their society's limitations at a time when women were literally boxed in, bundled up and blotted out (as far as the outside world was concerned, anyway). In Saudi Arabia, for instance, there was Princess Hassa, the strong, forceful mother of the crown prince and his six full brothers. In Kuwait, there's Sheikha Badria.

At the Hilton Hotel, the top women of Kuwait are gathering for a luncheon in honour of Audrey Callaghan, doing a grand Arabian tour with her husband James (in his capacity as Foreign Secretary). If you haven't heard of Sheikha Badria and meet her here for the first time, you might not think anything of her at all. You might not even notice her. She's a plump, middle-aged woman who's quiet. Unlike most Kuwaitis, she's listening rather than talking. Perhaps she doesn't understand a lot of the jabbering going on in English around her?

Then slowly you might become uncomfortable under the scrutiny of a pair of extremely active eyes, Sheikha Badria's. Of course, she understands every word. She's renowned for the way she slightly unnerves people with her quietness, making them talk more than they expected to. She's summing them up.

Maybe when you were searching out the state of the pound in this morning's paper, you noticed the name above an announcement of today's foreign currency prices – The United Trading Company. That's Sheikha Badria's outfit. She owns one of Kuwait's two largest moneychanging and financial institutions outside the banks. She has real estate valued by a conservative local at fifty million dinars and she not only makes decisions about her company's long-term strategy and day-to-day dealings – she makes all of the decisions.

Take another look at that face; it gives no clue what's on her mind but it's tough and canny. At home, she's different. And then again she's not. She's welcoming and warm, unusually so for Kuwait. But there's still no clue what's on her mind. You won't get one, either, from chatting to her. You will if you watch her drawing her Palestinian manager to one corner after dinner and talking business. In a moment, she changes: leaning forward, she delivers a low, rapid, decisive burst of words while her eyes continue to scrutinise the room as if she's looking for a mouse. Then she listens intently to her manager, nodding briefly.

She rejoins her guests; she's smiling and retiring again. Take a closer look at that face: the bones show, it alternates between looking gracious, imperious and maternal, almost without moving a muscle. She's great company but you won't learn anything about her from Sheikha Badria herself. You will from looking to her background, her home and her daughters.

'Ah yes, Sheikha Badria,' say Kuwaitis, 'Of course she's different. She was the creation of her husband.' At first I go along with that view. At seventeen she married Sheikh Fahd, a first cousin, twenty years older, who was the first al-Sabah to be college-educated abroad (the American University of Beirut). He went on to run substantial portions of Kuwait's government before his death in 1959. Yes, Sheikha Badria is the widow of that Sheikh Fahd. She's also the granddaughter of one of those two brothers murdered by a third, Emir Mubarak 'The Great'. Her family were exiled so she grew up in Iraq, away from the al-Sabah conforming influence – that made her different for a start.

When Sheikh Fahd asked for her hand, Badria's mother (who had black blood) was opposed to the marriage. He was poor and he was black too. 'Ethiopian blood, they tell me,' says Badria's daughter, Lulua, whose long neck, straight features and tiny bones speak the remark anyway. Badria married her cousin regardless and in the early years they travelled abroad together a great deal. Another difference.

In the early fifties, Fahd started taking over government responsibilities. He asked Badria to work with him. He was serious; he wanted her to do things, not just carry the titles. History has not been kind to Sheikh Fahd, but he had some fine qualities; intelligence was one of them. At first Badria refused: 'I lacked the self-confidence and experience.'

Then came a trip to the States in 54; she spent a few months looking round hospitals, improving her English and acquiring enough confidence to go without the veil when she returned to Kuwait and to accept the post of director of hospitals. It was the start of the country's health service (which, incidentally, is a good one. Kuwaitis don't need to fly to London for every twinge. They choose to.)

Sheikh Fahd hadn't made a mistake; Badria showed her mettle. She hired good people (good Palestinians) while remembering that medicine's about patients too: 'People used to ring me up at all times of the day and night and ask me to accompany their mother to hospital or sit through an operation on their wife, because the doctor was a man and that frightened a woman.' She didn't refuse. 'It was tiring, I'll admit.'

She was also busy having several children and earning a reputation that stuck among foreign diplomats as 'the Sabah wife who entertains'. Now if she was purely Fahd's creation, her career would surely have lost momentum after his death. The reverse has happened; today she's the first al-Sabah visiting foreigners approach to open their exhibitions. 'They all need sponsors. None of them are frightened to come to me. How can I refuse?'

Of course they're not frightened. She may be guarded with you but she treats you immediately as a friend, an equal. (This need I remind you in Kuwait, not Jiddah.) And the United Trading Company which she started in the sixties? 'My mother was a born businesswoman from way back,' says one of her daughters with a huge smile. 'While other women were always given jewels by their husbands, my mother turned them down. She always asked my father to give her property instead.'

So that's Sheikha Badria's background. Now for her house – correction, palace. Picture a flying saucer, wildly extravagant and all curves. That's Sheikha Badria's home. Next to it nestles a very normal old house with straight lines. That's her old home; the hermit crab's discarded shell. Her daughters live in that now.

Badria's domed living room (really domed: it has the silhouette of a perfect blancmange) is magnificent, grand, enormous – any words you can think of to describe a pale fawn marbled floor with every item on it rare and carefully chosen.

Sofas follow the curve of the room; there's an Arab urn in its centre, Chagall lithographs on the walls, a French eighteenth-century dresser, fine art nouveau glass. On a low table is a chess set, made of gold and enamel, inset with turquoises. Plants, tapestries, stained glass panels; it's a Parthenon for a princess, with a touch of the Assyrian tarbrush in style. Yes, it's truly magnificent. It copies nothing; it's restrained and yet studded with colour. Badria never learned this from Fahd.

Then look at her daughters: Amina, stunning, with her American accent, she could be a wealthy black from the States, only there's something wilder, freer about her. Maybe it's those Grecian curls bubbling over her head; maybe it's her mouth which always looks as if it's about to fill with laughter. Why the American accent? The Scots-American, Mrs Stevens (Sheikha Badria was the first to introduce a foreign nanny to Kuwait). Later she sent her daughters to school in the States: one to a Methodist school, another to a Quaker one. It means that English is their first language and their Arabic is poor. 'I can't speak Kuwaiti,' says Fatma 'and that's awfully important. I can manage as long as we're talking about nothing in particular, but as soon as there's an interesting conversation, about politics or philosophy, I simply can't follow what they're saying.' Okay; they can't speak Kuwaiti Arabic but Fatma's interest in politics and philosophy is no pose. That's one bonus. The daughters' sense of humour is another.

Take Amina, for instance. Her cult figures are Prince Charles and Barbara Cartland, she says. Everybody laughs and jokes about it for a while and then she slips in again with an innocent look on her face. She enquires whether, if she were to marry the Prince of Wales, the British newspapers would carry the headline: 'Oil queen flies in'. That's when you know Sheikha Badria's high-spirited daughters are more aware than they seem; Amina, in the nicest possible way, is having a dig at the Western media.

Who teaches them now? Who's grounded them to become what they are all along? Their mother, of course. When Sheikha Badria's said goodbye to the last of her Lebanese and Palestinian guests ('Mama is always most at home with foreigners . . .'), she draws two of her daughters into a small antechamber. She sits down like an Arab man in national dress, legs apart, hands on her knees and briefs them – on business, current affairs, familiy politics. It's the only moment in the evening when they stop larking about and become quite quiet.

As long as they keep the rules (ie, to the palace, under their mother's eye, when they're not abroad studying) Badria's daughters get the protection of this astonishing woman.

She's content to have the protection of being an al-Sabah; she enjoys its perks. 'We once travelled to Morocco with mother on holiday. We went with some friends by car for three weeks and no one knew who we were. Then one day we were booked in a hotel and mother had to stand in a queue for an hour to change some travellers' cheques. That cured her of wanting to travel incognito again.' Roars of laughter all round as her daughter tells the tale.

And what made Sheikha Badria so different? I still don't know. Why does one superb actress become a star while another equally superb actress merely stays in work? It's an indefinable quality. Every now and again, Arabia throws up the odd 'star'

– Sheikha Badria is one. And even *her* daughters admit that the best kind of al-Sabah to be is a man. It's a far easier, far safer station in life to be called to.

Nights and knights

The next best thing to being an al-Sabah in Kuwait is being an al-Ghanim. It says it all: glamour, heritage, money, power. His Excellency Abdullah al-Ghanim is minister of water and electricity, and a jolly good job he makes of it too, (not that his department has to scrimp to make ends meet). Until he went into government, Abdullah, a small, lively man with a booming deep voice, was in business – contractors, pharmaceutical chains, importer of engineering equipment, toys and gifts, manufacturer of sanitary towels. His wife, Lulua, runs all that now.

Lulua is the Lauren Bacall of Kuwait; she has the face of a Dior mannequin; it's there to show off clothes. But she's a brainy clothes-horse. Everyone says that Lulua has two husbands – Abdullah, thirty-seven, and his younger brother, bachelor Dirar, thirty-one. She cherishes him. She sends her chauffeur over to his house of an evening with a full scale dinner – on the off chance that he's in. And in return Dirar adores Lulua just as he adores Abdullah. That's lucky. He doesn't fall over himself with enthusiasm about his father, who lives conveniently far away – in 'Panorama', a well-situated Berkshire seat. Dirar is the Jet Set of Kuwait, says one diplomat admiringly.

A high-powered speedboat sets off one Friday for a weekend picnic on a nearby island. Dirar al-Ghanim has finally stirred his air hostess girl friend, Vicky. She flew in from London late last night. She flies out to Bombay tomorrow.

At first she's rather cross and sleepy. Slowly she wakes up as the fresh sea air rushes past the boat. Vicky, Moroccan-born with Egyptian nationality, is a sultry piece with sensuous lips and fluid hips. These show to advantage later when she treats the party to a display of belly-dancing. Her act is all hips and tiny footwork

– spoiled somewhat, when Dirar joins in wearing a couture beach suit that doesn't conceal his friendly paunch. He waves it around like a sexy schoolboy.

Dirar apologises profusely for the whisky and gin bottles littering the island's beach. 'When will these people learn that there's more to life than spirits,' he sighs. He has organised champagne on ice. He left the food to his houseboy. That's obvious. The picnic hamper contains some fruit and a few measly sandwiches.

It's a hot, relaxing day. Dirar steams about in the boat trying to locate brother Abdullah, out fishing with some friends on the family yacht 'Bibi'. Lulua is at home with her two daughters; she doesn't like the sea, she says. 'Bibi' doesn't want to be raised so Dirar goes back to making a fuss of the enticing Vicky.

She has her own flat in Kuwait. 'No of course I didn't get it for her,' he says later, crossly. 'She wouldn't want me to and anyway I'd never respect a woman who let me keep her. Mind you, I didn't feel right dating Vicky at first. She works for Kuwait Airways and my accountancy firm audits their books. It almost seemed unethical.' He has 350 people working for him in eighteen offices. It's the only private professional firm to span the Middle East. He's in partnership with Price, Waterhouse and a Palestinian, Talal abu Ghazaleh. He's touchy enough about trading on the al-Ghanim name so he runs the company in his Palestinian partner's name. Don't underestimate the significance of that.

There's no excuse for his not being a success as a playboy too: his late brother-in-law was that legendary Badr Mullah, founding member of Annabel's. His closest international playmates are Princes Bandar and Turqi bin Faisal from Saudi Arabia. Sure enough, he goes in for the right kind of night life in the right kind of places.

'The Bahamas, Nice, Rome, London and all that are fun. But it's artificial and all the same. I just go for a few days. The first night I'll be out until the morning looking round every discotheque, every club. Then finished. It's always a group of Arabs. Not many other men can afford the time or money for our way of life when we play.' At home in Kuwait, he organises parties that have people who go in for that kind of thing scrambling for an invite.

Next evening, Dirar and I are lounging around his sloppy sitting room in his sea-shore bungalow. For once there's no one else here. He sent his driver to collect me. Not for my sake, oh no. 'I'm an al-Ghanim. I can't be seen in the Sheraton.' If that makes him sound like a self-important playboy, then picture Dirar sitting on the floor in his national dress, eating Lulua's nightly offering, playing his favourite tape. It was recorded in a working men's club in Scotland. It's a totally incomprehensible comic turn. The Glaswegian accent is so broad that it takes me a while to work out that it's the English language I'm listening to. Dirar's roaring his head off. He knows the tape backwards.

'If you ask me where I've made the most friends, I'll tell you it was Glasgow. I understand the Scots. They're a tribal people like us and they accepted me.' After Millfield public school, he spent seven years in Glasgow articled to a firm of accountants. He somehow crossed the line between his basement flat with evenings in the local pub, and the county set – hunt balls and debs' dances. 'I did it on my own. The name al-Ghanim meant nothing there.' Having grown up in the West, this Kuwaiti easily accepts me as a friend. There's no feeling of strain.

He tries his Glaswegian accent on me. I don't understand a word but I can recognise that it's perfect. He breaks into English to tell me there was a girl in Glasgow. She was the only girl he has ever wanted to marry. Something held him back. The same logic that would stop him marrying any European or any foreign Arab like Vicky. 'Lulua and Abdullah would accept her for my sake and they'd force our friends to accept her. But what kind of life would she have? Even if she was an Arab she'd spent her life fighting against being an outsider. Kuwaiti women have their own dialect. That's how tight the circle is here.'

Kuwait means as much to him now as his work. He has a habit of rushing off for a few days without warning. But it's to look for new clients, not girls. 'I have plenty of women; I don't pay for them but I don't have time to play romantic games either. I was in Morocco recently and an American girl came up to me and started talking so I took her out for dinner. Afterwards we went back to my room but it was getting late so I told her straight: "I've got a business meeting at seven-thirty in the morning. Are you coming to bed or not?" She went through a performance about how it was only our first date.

'I explained to her, "I'm here for three days. If you think it's more correct for us to wait until the last night, fine. But while you're making up your mind, there are three alternatives. I can take you home now because I'm tired; you can sleep on the sofa or you can get into bed with me." ' He can't remember which she picked. (That's one way the callous Arab playboy myth takes shape.)

Dirar has two heroes: brother Abdullah and Abdalatif al-Hamad. Al-Hamad, thirty-nine, born with a silver spoon and Harvard-educated to a golden touch, plays King Arthur in a fair and beautiful castle (by the same architects as New York's Seagram Building) in Kuwait's Camelot – the Kuwait Fund for Arab Economic Development. He has at his command 1,000 million dinars to buy goodwill in the Arab world with selective aid-giving. The fund was set up in 1961, soon after independence and the inconvenience of buying off Iraqi intervention with thirty million dinars. Whatever the motivation behind it, King Arthur himself has become the world's model of how to run an aid-giving agency.

I've seen Abdalatif at work in his ivory tower. He's impressive. Dirar and I are having tea with the al-Hamads at home. Abdalatif has a sheaf of papers to put away for tomorrow: progress reports on an irrigation scheme in Yemen, (the communist one, not the other one this time), a thermal power project in socialist Syria and an appeal from a Western television producer in London for another kind of project – a prestigious historical drama series. That one will get a firm but polite 'no'.

Fattda and Abdalatif puzzle Kuwaitis, who sarcastically nick-name them 'the lovebirds'. Despite her attendance at the inevitable university course, Fattda is less like a Kuwaiti than a Mother Earth: she's soft, flowing with silk and feminine. There's a draw-back to being married to a knight; he spends months off in foreign parts. 'I'm no different from my mother. My father was a captain of a ship like most men were then. He sailed to India and Africa and once he was away for a whole year. My mother spent her life waiting for his ship.'

Dirar chips in to remind me of an old Kuwaiti proverb: 'Those who go to the sea are lost; those who come back are born.' It's his way of saying that even the richest, oldest 'heritage' families have known loss and hardship.

Kuwait might not understand the al-Hamads' ideal of being together whenever they can, but Dirar admires it just as he admires Abdalatif's intellectual lustre. Their home is serene, expensive (an al-Hamad doesn't have to stint) and it has some of the loveliest old pictures, calligraphy and furniture collected from Islamic lands everywhere. It's a long, long way from Louis de Lebanon.

As Dirar and I drive off to another of Lulua's pre-packed feasts, he talks of Abdalatif and Fattda with awe. He shies away from any mention of his own marriage; there aren't many girls fit for an al-Ghanim and, secretly, he's afraid of being tempted outside the circle as he nearly was in Glasgow. 'I haven't time for marriage,' he puts his foot down hard on the accelerator. 'And, anyway as you've heard, Lulua al-Ghanim has two husbands – Abdullah and Dirar.'

Gatherings at the country club

Kuwait has a unique institution for this part of Arabia. It's an everyday version of the Royal Enclosure at Ascot. It's just as overdressed, has twenty founders (five royals, the rest 'heritage') and only they can put up new members.

The Hunting and Equestrian Club is miles from anywhere. As you draw up, it looks like a military base. It's fenced in, walled at the front and its gates shut firmly on outsiders. Inside the Elysian Fields – compared to Kuwait's dust bowl of desert and concrete – it's green. Those generous donations mentioned in the club report have built stabling for forty-seven horses, a nine-hole golf course, a skeet-shooting range.

But Kuwait comes less for the sport than for the pièce de résis-
tance – an American-style country club house. You'll find everyone
on the daily-sprinkled green lawn, neatly hedged and bordered,
sitting at tables in mixed and family groups. This is the Brookline
Country Club all over again – Boston brought to Arabia in 1974.

Mustafa Behbehani has just come from work – at the emir's
diwan. The blue sky over his head makes a change from the ninety-
one English turn-of-the-century pictures of busty women in
various stages of undress that decorate the ceiling of his office in
the palace. A couple of ravishing American-educated al-Sabah
girls compliment him on his new season's stock. Behbehani owns
a boutique in Salamiyya. The role of shopkeeper seems an odd one
for this court official from an old family. 'Why did I open it?
Because it's the only thing my father's never done in business,' he
explains bashfully. Knowing the size of his father's empire, I can
believe it.

There's a roar as one of the emir's grandsons makes his entrance
in his steel silver, red and black decorated Trans-Am with Trac
Action 60 Big Boss tyres. He's come for a ride on a horse. The
sheikh is sixteen. There's a flurry of Kuwait youth as he opens his
car door and puts out a chubby, jodhpured thigh. This is the
city's one legitimate flirting ground.

Khalid al-Rodan is too old for that kind of thing. He's Dirar
al-Ghanim's greatest pal after all. That isn't the only position he
has to maintain. He's another shopkeeper. Sportsman, the Lilly-
white of Kuwait, opened in Salamiyya a few months ago. It's a
chrome and carpeted exercise wonderland of rowing machines,
saddles, tennis and squash equipment – marred only by a window
of grotesque silver trophies, made in Japan for Kuwaiti football
clubs.

In the cool of the New England club-house lounge the colour
television is on. No one's watching; there's too much to talk
about. 'Bassima darling,' one woman spots a friend flicking
through some comics, 'You're looking marvellous. I can't take
my eyes off you.' Nasty moment, as I wonder, not for the first
time, who dresses for whom around here.

One young mother in a clinging jersey tea gown (whom I see

here nearly every day) has one scrap of talk to cover her presence: 'I'm determined to learn to ride. I'm taking my first lesson to-morrow.' She shrinks into her club chair as none other than Lulua al-Ghanim strides in with a file of supporters. She's come to see how the arrangements are going for the al-fresco Malaysian social on Saturday night. Lulua's here in her capacity as head of the club's social committee, considered a landmark by the women's movement.

Outside there seems to be some rival excitement. The careless watchman had forgotten to close the gate after the last sheikh. A grubby, family jalopy trundled in. Out spilled delighted children who made a beeline for the swings in Kiddies' Corner.

The faded, grey figure of Mrs Cullinan, wife of the club manager, hovers in horror. She collects herself in time to go for Mr Cullinan, who walks over to the newcomers, tugging the club's guard dog behind him to make his point. The dog sits down and falls asleep. The family tumble obediently back into jalopy as fast as they can, and trundle out again. They were a Bedu family who took 'Kuwait for the Kuwaitis' too seriously.

In between the black-haired, spirited al-Sabah and their friends, all with perfectly elocuted English, I spot a few Europeans. It's a real honour for them to be invited in here. They won't be invited any further into the circle. At one table, waiting for her children to come back from their ride, is a blond, pretty English-woman. She's Primrose Arnander, wife of Christopher. This merchant banking meteor, double first in Greats at Oxford, came out two years ago to a big Kuwaiti job. He's now doing another big Kuwaiti job. They are as far into the inner circle as any resident Europeans. They've been invited to two Kuwaiti homes to dinner in as many years.

At every Kuwaiti table, a story does the rounds. My favourite today concerns the farce of a 'heritage' off-spring who became so incensed at Kuwait's 'hypocrisy over drinking' that he decided to martyr himself. He had had enough. The country is officially 'dry', the rich all have bootleggers and the poor get stuck with 'Flash', a local brew, mostly made from distilled perfume. It blinds and maims.

The would-be martyr packed his suitcase full of whisky bottles, flew into Kuwait and presented himself at customs. He hoped to be brought to trial, to become a cause célèbre. To his chagrin, he was outwitted. They confiscated the scotch, sent him home and ignored the affair. All Kuwait knows about it, but all Kuwait also knows that the authorities can't be caught out as easily as that.

It's been another lovely afternoon at the club. Some might complain that the Malaysian tent is blocking the view of the sunset and that the sprinklers are dowsing the tea set. Everyone complains about the flies. They're everywhere; a continual headache for Mr Cullinan. The club's backers have put aside enough money to build a swimming pool with cabanas, another one and a quarter million dinars to knock down the present club house and erect something more fanciful. No one will cough up the money for Mr Cullinan to do something about the horse manure. The members hate the flies but the flies love the shit.

The loner

Every Thursday afternoon and some time on Friday, an unobtrusive car drives into the Hunting and Equestrian Club. A dignified man with a shock of white hair and an impassive, quizzical look gets out. There is something about him. You know he doesn't belong, but all the sheikhs, ministers and excellencies around make a point of going up to him.

He acknowledges them, smiles, chats and then goes off to the stables where Jamida, 'the crazy one' as he calls her, is waiting with her Texan saddle. She's one of the rare horses to come out from Bahrain. The ruler chose her himself for Sheikh Khalid, Kuwait's top horseowner. Sheikh Khalid, president of the emir's diwan, presented her to this man. He mounts Jamida and rides off by himself. He's a loner; that much is clear.

Where does he come from? He holds Kuwaiti, Syrian, Algerian, Jordanian and, most recently, Saudi Arabian passports. It's the last that gives the key. He was the man who had the idea that became OPEC. He was the first Arab to talk of nationalisation, the first to say 'Arab oil for the Arabs'. Abdullah al-Tariki was the first Saudi Arabian minister of petroleum and mineral resources.

The story of oil in the Middle East is the story of his life, except that he would never compromise and he was an honest man. Al-Tariki can't be bothered to tell that story. He looks to the future, the past doesn't matter to him. But eventually he unlocks it for me.

His father had a caravan between Riyadh and Kuwait. When Abdullah was born in 1919, in what is now Saudi Arabia, there were no countries or borders. His father took him to Kuwait slung over the side of his camel in a sack ('I was only six and he expected me to stay on the back of a camel all night. I kept losing my head-dress or my stick.') He was to stay with a half-brother and go to school. 'In the morning I'd get up and clean the house and in the evenings I'd collect the goats out in the desert. It's all villas there now.'

His apprenticeship started at eleven. He was sent alone on a steamship to Bombay to work for an illiterate merchant. Abdullah could read and write; he became his secretary and book-keeper. The next trader he worked for felt that this quick-witted urchin should be given a chance. He sent him back from India to Arabia with a letter of introduction to the Saudi minister of finance. Abdullah had to ride a camel from Kuwait across to Mecca to present it. He was chosen for schooling in Cairo.

To this day he boasts of being the school's swimming champion ('breast stroke'), of making it as a King's Scout ('only the fifth in Egypt'). Mostly he studied. 'I wanted to be an engineer even though I was very dumb in chemistry. An Egyptian officer told me that when God created people, he created their wealth with them but it was up to them to find it. He told me that when he served in Turkey he saw geologists running up and down the mountains looking for minerals, looking for wealth. That sounded like a good idea.'

Next came a scholarship to Cairo University and after that a masters' degree in geology and petroleum engineering in Texas.

He was to become the first Saudi oil technocrat. 'In Cairo the Americans were something new to us. They meant a lot of gold watches, gold rings, a lot of chewing gum. I just got the idea that I would like America very much.'

He hated it. New York? 'I got a guidebook, looked up hotels and walked into the Waldorf Astoria. I slept on a mattress on a floor behind Times Square.' Texas? 'They thought I was just a skinny Mexican.' He was lonely. 'I met an American, a blonde, who wanted to get married and she liked me.' Enough to go back to Saudi Arabia with him.

The Saudis forced him on Aramco in Dharan. He was the only qualified Arab in an American joint and Aramco didn't like it. They wanted to house him in the Arab workers' barracks. He stuck out for an American-executive apartment. That solved nothing; his wife was ostracised for marrying a native. 'It wasn't a happy time.' A typical Abdullah remark.

In 1958 King Saud moved him to Jiddah to be the country's number one in oil. In 1960 he was made minister (Yamani was nothing then). Abdullah was a power. He had a house by the Creek full of people, laughter, gazelles, dogs – King Saud's cast-offs: 'King Saud brought five greyhounds from England because he felt like racing them. When he got tired of the idea, I took on the dogs. They were males and females so I ended up with seventeen.' He turns everything to a joke.

The oil company men hated Tariki. He found some weak points in their book-keeping. He forced Aramco to pay back 145 million dollars. 'My one aim was to break our fifty-fifty participation agreement with them. I spent a year negotiating with a Japanese company to give us fifty-six–forty-four. Then I found out that Faisal's brother-in-law, Kamal Adham, was their agent. They'd already given him one million dollars commission but on top of that they had a secret agreement to pay him two per cent of their profit. I got mad,' one of his favourite phrases, 'I forced the Japanese to cancel the two per cent commission to Adham. I think Faisal never forgave me for that.'

When King Saud got the push in 1963, Tariki resigned too. 'I couldn't stay in the country without working and it was obvious that Aramco wanted my head. I wasn't bitter about it. I can't hate.'

The Algerian and Kuwaiti governments immediately took him on as their oil adviser, posts he still holds. He lived happily in Beirut with his second wife (the American had left years ago) until 1970. One day the Lebanese kicked him out without warning or explanation. The long arm of Faisal's unrelenting spite had reached Beirut.

He tried working from Cairo, but who can with a telephone system that takes two days per call? The Kuwaitis were delighted to have him when he moved here: 'He's come home,' they say.

For the last ten years he has been an oil consultant to many governments (just look at that list of passports). He also publishes a magazine: 'The Oil of Arabs'. When Faisal died, Tariki flew to Saudi Arabia to make peace with an old friend, now King Khalid. He got his passport back but he can't understand why I should find it surprising that soon afterwards he published an article in his magazine headed: 'Remove the parasites from around the crown'. It attacks everyone around King Khalid. 'Khalid is my hope but he's surrounded by parasites. I've always said what I believe. Why stop now?'

We talk in many places; his office, the club, his car. One day he invites me to dinner. He wants me to see his son. In his office in the Kuwait Airways' 'skyscraper', he's a commanding figure. At the club, he's a respected figure. I walk into an apartment where the television is almost bigger than the sitting room. The food is ample and his hospitality warm, but the flat is too small to be anything but simple. He doesn't mind. I don't mind. His son, Zakhr, does.

Zakhr is tall, slender and as good-looking as Abdullah must have been at his age – he's twenty-four. What strikes me is the contradiction of his outer shyness and inner anger. He doesn't know who it's directed at. He hardly knows his father; he remembers a big powerful bear living in splendour from his childhood in Jiddah. Now he's stuck with an ageing man in a small flat and he can only talk to him through a servant who has been with Tariki for years. He doesn't know what to say.

What is he supposed to have in common with Abdullah? Zakhr is the son of the divorced American wife. He grew up to hate his absent father; he still won't see his Lebanese step-mother and six-year-old half-sister (fortunately, for the moment, they live in Cairo. Abdullah goes there for a week every month.)

Why is Zakhr here at all? Because he's not an American although he sounds like one. He was brought up in Beirut and the States. He's graduated from Yale University and he needs a job. He needs his father to help him get one in the only country where he's legally supposed to belong – Saudi Arabia.

'Am I an Arab? I don't know what I am. But I've come to live here anyway. The outward things are easiest. I can put on the head-dress' (he's wearing jeans and a red jersey) 'and it's like a wall around my eyes, my security blanket if you like. The inner things, those are what I can't work out.'

Zakhr went to Jiddah recently. The Juffali merchant family, powerful enough I would think to make their own appointments, promised him a job. There's been nothing since but silence.

(Later in London I find out that word probably went to the Juffalis that Tariki was all right again but not all right enough for them to hire his son. Zakhr may be a twenty-four year-old, much-needed, Yale graduate and Saudi, but in traditional Arabia he's the son of the father first. No one claims that Tariki was dishonest or subversive. The way it was put to me in London by a man close enough to the throne to know was: 'He was ahead of his time. Nationalisation wasn't in fashion then; it was a word Tariki should never have used.')

Tariki is going back to Saudi Arabia. Partly for his son's sake. Partly for his own. He's going to buy a ranch and raise trouble. 'You have to be in a place where you can be effective. I could go and attack the corruption from Europe. But if they reached me in Beirut, they could reach me in Europe. Look at them, everyone of them is corrupt, it's disgusting. No one is secure in that country. No wonder they just want to make their money fast and get out. I'm fifty-six. I shall go back to Saudi Arabia and I shall go on saying what I believe. And if a truck "accidentally" runs me over or I suffer "a premature heart-attack", better that way. I would rather finish it all like that than learn to be afraid.'

'Once I thought revolution might be an answer. Now I see what the military have done in other countries – they change the old bad ways for new bad ways. I feel, I hope, that all it needs is time. Just enough years and the people, even the royal families, will learn enough to make change from the inside. It's safer that way.'

One day we are driving by the sea and he falls silent (unlike him by now). He thinks for a while and then says with deep feeling:

'It's useless to be a Kuwaiti or a Saudi. It's a piece of a thing, it's not a thing in itself. This is what oil has done. This change is not normal. Rags to riches can happen to individuals, not to nations. These artificial creations like Kuwait, drawn on a map by other powers, they will never accomplish anything. They will always spend, never produce. We just open the tap, let out the oil and change it into dollars. They talk about oil-producing countries. That's a joke.

'What we have is a torrent of rain and no dams. We are so stupid. I remember once when St John Philby told King Ibn Saud that he shouldn't touch the people, that he shouldn't let the oil touch their lives. At the time we thought he was a colonialist, an imperialist stooge. I remember laughing at him myself. Now I wonder if he wasn't right after all.'

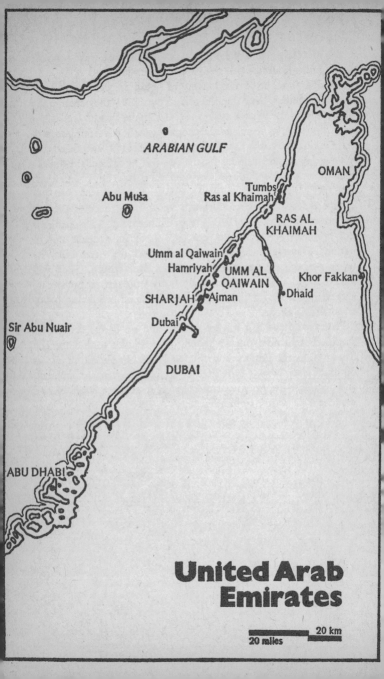

Qatar
Abu Dhabi
Dubai
Sharjah

'pieces of things . . .'

Nutty present, dotty past

'When I was oil minister, I went to Qatar for the day to see the emir. He gave me two suitcases jammed with Rolex watches and silk clothes.' Abdullah al-Tariki is briefing me on the Lower Gulf in the cushioned atmosphere of Kuwait. 'After I had to leave Saudi Arabia, I went to see the same emir. He wouldn't give me five minutes, he was so afraid. And now every statesman and leader in the world is flying in to see the head of that tiny place. Isn't it a joke?'

Al-Tariki is appalled by the news that Léopold Senghor, President of Senegal and international prize-winning poet, has rearranged a whole tour to suit the convenience of Qatar's emir, His Highness Sheikh Khalifa bin Hamad al-Thani. President Idi Amin arrives waving his begging bowl with less finesse. He evidently hopes for more than £1.7 million which is all the emir thinks he deserves. Emir Khalifa aspires to be a leader of global dimensions (which an adviser prefers to translate as: 'He's aware of his place in history'). The emir was a wild success at the Elysée Palace when President Giscard d'Estaing laid on a formal 'do' in his honour. Now he has his eye on fame in America. He went to all the trouble of flying over a private English tutor, who hung around the palace for a while before being sent home. The emir kept skipping lessons. He's made progress, though, on his personal set of Linguaphone records.

This Napoleon rules over a sandpit slightly smaller than Kuwait with less than a tenth of its population. He had a miserable, misunderstood adolescence. Despite the handicap of his chronic sinusitis and lack of formal education, he keeps himself busy from six-thirty in the morning until late at night, unstimulated by alcohol, cigarettes or skirt-chasing. He turns up unexpectedly on building sites to make sure the cement is of the right consistency. He watches carefully the productivity estimates of the Qatar Flour Mills. He doesn't neglect the West Bay Land Reclamation Project where he (and his detachment of security guards) frequently check out how dredging is getting along. And if programmes on the new television station aren't up to scratch, he's on the phone right away. You should have heard him going on about the low standard of entertainment during the long Ramadan evenings. Fortunately he missed the studio run-through of a recent documentary on Qatar's history. It took a visiting businessman to point out discreetly that there was something amiss with the background music. It was the theme music from *Exodus*.

It's clear that he means it when he says with one of those smiles intended to disarm: 'My first and last hobby is to devote all my time and power to serve my nation. When I see all these industrial and constructive projects, I feel the happiest man in the world.'

Not happy enough to dispense with the bodyguards, even for a short promenade in Hyde Park on his annual summer holiday in London. This manic, aggressive, chubby-cheeked emir suffers from an insecurity complex. Can you wonder? His grandfather had always promised him the throne but it accidentally ended up in the hands of his greedy first cousin, Ahmad. Khalifa pottered on as minister of finance and petroleum until 1972 when Emir Ahmad's son took to making a 'death list' with Khalifa figuring prominently at the top. There was one of those autocratic family councils and Ahmad was packed off to exile. His son lives across the Gulf; he's hospitalised in Iran as a morphine addict. (It would have been too embarrassing to have him as a patient anywhere in the Arab world and the Iranians, for reasons that become plain further down the Gulf, decided to oblige.)

Sheikh Khalifa nobly took over the throne and gathered a posse of his own al-Thani fans around him. These don't necessarily include such notables as his brother, the foreign minister – he's competition. No, more dependent, dependable fans. He's taken his first new wife for fifteen years, an educated, young cousin. Unfortunately, he's been too busy to let Qatar know whether or not she has 'publicly appeared'. Society women tactfully carry on visiting his last wife. He's hauled his oldest son, and crown prince, back from Sandhurst Military Academy to head the army. He's plucked younger son, Abdul Aziz, from his American university and handed him the Ministry of Finance. These sons don't matter much in power terms. The only man who makes a decision in Qatar is Napoleon himself from his office palace in the capital of Doha.

His office is easy to see. I can't miss it. It's a landmark. I walk in; there are two floors around an open courtyard. Every door opens on to an empty, unfurnished room. There's space for 500: forty people work here ('I think it's forty, we've never counted'), mostly dapper, harrassed-looking Palestinians. His Highness's stylish suite, decorated by David Hicks, is right up in the corner on the second floor. Lots of empty space before I get there.

Then there's the rest of the city. Doha reminds me of a dress store on the last day of the sales. Where there should be full shelves and rails, there's just a background jumble you don't notice for the extravaganza in size 18, the one purple organdie number that won't move and a few other outsize atrocities. I hardly notice the background of the small, low, tidy streets and houses in Doha (it's one hell of a contrast to Kuwait, that's for sure). Doha is dominated by a handful of the city's equivalent of those size 18's: the al-Thani palace, the Wall Street monolith that's the new Ministry of Finance, and the dazzling white museum that's the display piece of Qatar and the personal pride of Sheikh Khalifa. It was all his own idea.

I learn a lot about the differences between these countries by the way each wears the past and by getting to know the people involved with it.

In Saudi Arabia, a twenty-six-year-old Chicago-trained archaeologist has a budget of 800 million to freeze history while everyone else is busy destroying it. The Saudi director of antiquities, Abdullah Hassan Masri, PhD, was born in Mecca, youngest of ten children from a poor family. He's black; like many Saudis he has African slave blood somewhere in his not too distant ancestral past.

While studying in America, he lived through what he describes with cool academic interest as 'those days of rage', the height of student rioting. Abdullah had digs in Chicago near the pitch of the extreme Black Stone Rangers. He was there for the Weathermen, the Chicago Seven, the blooding of America. Today he sits in Riyadh in his unsullied white thobe, demolition noises outside deafening us and remarks after deliberation: 'No, I didn't feel involved in any way, why should I have? No one did *me* any harm, although someone did scratch the paintwork of my car. But how could the students and their anger affect me? I was always too conscious that their T-shirts and ragged jeans cost as much as a conventional middle-class wardrobe, and that the clothing manufacturers were having a field day.'

This superior supergrad has summoned the finest architects, archaeologists and designers to compete for a museum to glorify the splendid heritage of his country. By the time that 800 million riyals has gone, the heritage may have gone too.

Now how about Bahrain? There's a museum. The government driver has been designated to take me to it. The journey goes from camera shop (don't ask me why), to Government House, to a slipway by the marina, to the airport customs house. It isn't that he thinks the museum is hidden in any of these unlikely places. He doesn't know what a museum is, nor do any of the people we ask. I never reach the official museum but I find the country's real treasure-trove in the house of Sheikha Hayya al-Khalifa. Yes, a female member of the royal family wraps a turban round her head, puts on a pair of trousers and goes out to dig for the past. "Look, he has painted fingers, he must be a woman," I heard a workman say once.'

This plump, passionate enthusiast had to leave school at fifteen to marry her first cousin. She did a degree course by correspondence after having five children and Bahrain's past is now piled on the tables of her house. 'My interest started in 1960 when a bulldozer came into our garden. When it started tearing up the ground everywhere, I rushed in and grabbed everything I could lay my hands on.' She points to a Hellenistic bronze sculpture. 'But I'm afraid the bulldozer did dent that a bit.'

Now I'm in Doha. There's hardly anyone on the streets and the papers are full of some new industrial project. It's nuts. The place is an empty toy town, all it has is oil and every day they firm up deals that would make sense in a city like Cardiff with a proper labour force. How do you like the idea of 300,000 tons of steel a year being spewed out in Qatar? That's the aim of one £150 million plus project that Sheikh Khalifa has signed up with the Japanese. Who's going to work on the shop floor? Imported Japanese? And if you want to hear about Sheikh Khalifa's pharmaceutical plant or the ten million egg-laying-capacity battery farm, I could go on for ever . . .

If the future sounds ludicrous, the past is beyond belief. In the centre of this nowhere stands a white fortress sparkling like gnashers in a toothpaste advertisement. The Qatar National Museum on 'the Corniche' (where is this: Monte Carlo?) is centred around Sheikh Khalifa's old home. It's a shrine to his childhood and to the dead father whose memory he worships.

It was the very first thing he decided to build when he got the throne. On the night it opened, he decided to marry his young cousin as a way of celebrating. Who do I find masterminding this place? A sacerdotal, safari-suited public relations man, opera buff and self-taught archaeologist from the smarter end of Sloane Street in London, Michael Rice.

Rice is an old friend; he's been around this area for many years, though he doesn't speak Arabic. I've never seen him ruffled. He's the kind of Englishman Arabs dream about. Sheikh Khalifa patently did. He entrusted him with his favourite jewel in the development crown – the £2 million museum.

Some people might wonder why the emir didn't go for a big archaeological name? In this part of the world, they don't come bigger than Michael Rice's. He doesn't have any fancy paper qualifications, or any paper qualifications at all for that matter, but he designs superb museums and, what's more, he's a wizard with the Arabs, who can be a trifle irritating. You'd never guess from *him* that Michael Rice's Qatari venture was anything but a smooth, enjoyable experience.

Nor would any of the visiting heads of state suggest that a trip round the museum isn't exactly what they most wanted. They'd be fools if they did; it's obligatory before money flows from the Qatari piggy bank. I had the luck, at least, to go round it with Michael Rice. His concept and its realisation are magnificent.

No matter that a few rooms are locked because the guards didn't feel like staying around all through opening hours. No matter that they've displaced his lighting system so that I miss the exhilarating view of the room where the young Sheikh Khalifa touched his Koran. No matter that above the stunning first floor showing antiquities and films of Bedouin life – everything you wanted to know about this country and didn't know who to ask – there's a whole floor dedicated to Sheikh Khalifa. It's fitting. Downstairs movie pictures of life in the tent, and at the top show walls of photographs of the Emir of Qatar with an array of world leaders. Shaking hands, having a confidential word over a coffee table, but always upstaging his co-stars.

There's only one Qatari that comes into the (well-guarded) open and that's His Highness The Emir Sheikh Khalifa bin Hamad al-Thani.

Boredom by the sea

Anyone who has ever painted pictures by numbers knows that moment when blobs that were 8, 13, 21 and 40 start to make a pattern. It's sky. Other blobs shape into trees. I've been in Arabia long enough now to recognise some patterns. The silences and the spaces mean something.

This thumb of sand that's an 'independent nation' juts out from Saudi Arabia. Qatar caught Wahhabism from its huge next door neighbour when the zeal was in the air in the eighteenth century. But because it's tiny and was never locked away like Saudi (the

British were here too, remember) it's not quite as unrealistic. Women drive and work. Itinerant businessmen who've been tipped off make their way to Room 501 in the Gulf Hotel. This is a dry country, but Room 501 is the hotel's bar. The penthouse restaurant has a reasonably good wine list; as long as you know to ask the hotel manager (discreetly) for a pass to get in and can find the concealed express lift to get up.

But these are nuances: compared to Kuwait or Bahrain, Doha's a model Islamic town. To boot, Sheikh Khalifa has embarked on that moral rearmament campaign. In the past the al-Thanis, and their richer subjects, lived it up with the best of them. Sheikh Khalifa's ideal of the moral straight and narrow isn't something you pay lip service to.

There's literally no social life to be had in Doha for the Qataris. The sophistication of the Jiddah group or even the diwania male japes of Kuwait are jet sets away. Even Westerners have to be careful. Those who are caught offering Qataris alcohol can be, and are, chucked out. The government won't stoop to handling liquor permits for residential Christian foreigners, so they've made an unofficial licensing authority of a European embassy (which has to be nameless for the sake of those stranded non-Muslims). Nothing is allowed the Qataris but hard work and boredom.

In London these people are known for one thing: if you sell a property, if you let a flat, if you rent a hotel room, Qataris will leave it in squalor. (Actually, many complaining landlords and other know-alls suffer from geographical imprecision. They get everybody mixed up and the Qataris have somehow been handed the monopoly on the uncouth image.)

There aren't many people in Qatar, so there aren't many millionaires. Sultan Saif al-Isa is one of them. He lives in an anonymous, walled-in background affair that you wouldn't look at twice. I'm having coffee with Sharifa, his wife. She has at last solved the mystery of the disappearing furniture. On her annual summer visit to London she bought up a large section of Waring & Gillow's eighteenth-century English repro department. It never arrived. Someone's just told her that Waring & Gillow is on the boycott list. The furniture will never arrive. She'll have to make do with the present gloomy mahogany dining-room. She isn't bothered; they never eat there anyway.

Sultan, Sharifa, their seven children and two of their spouses stick to the long trestle table in the family 'canteen' upstairs. Sultan looks like Charlie Chaplin and talks like Edward G. Robinson. Sharifa, minute, lumpy, overrides his grumpy silences with a non-stop flow of affectionate chattering. I'm back in a scaled-down model of the all-embracing Saudi household.

Sharifa never wears the famous 'burqa', the mask. Many women here do; some cover nearly the whole face; those are worn by old women. This is the last generation that will see 'the mask' in the Lower Gulf. Sharifa's next door neighbour, a daring little creature, has just finished her latest creation – the briefest of masks fringed with fat Gulf pearls. She's playing with the idea of giving it up altogether. The unmasked Sharifa does wear a black cloak outside the house. Her daughters don't even do that.

Imagine sitting in this old-fashioned house, spotlessly clean but as unpretentious as a genteel boarding house with sales-room bargains and stuffed chairs from dead aunts. That's Sharifa's home. And through the door walks a schools inspector, second daughter Johara, aged twenty-one. She's wearing a mini-skirt that would stop the traffic in Piccadilly Circus. My eyes pop. The skirts that follow are better and better: there's Johaina's; she's doing her PhD in Cairo. She's twenty-seven, unmarried, beautiful, sexy with long scarlet nails and high platform shoes from Carnaby Street. I don't get time to catch breath until fifteen-year-old Harla, another beauty, walks in – at least she's wearing her navy floor-length school uniform. That soon goes. Sharifa finds my surprise amusing and teases: 'It's a new generation. You and I are out of date.'

The intriguing Sharifa was born in Bombay, went to university in Beirut and has family scattered everywhere across Saudi Arabia, Kuwait and Bahrain. She's generous to a fault, with a habit of stuffing too much food down her children and friends: 'Downstairs is for guests and you can eat what you like. Up here we're family and you must eat more.'

After dinner we always move on to the first floor landing – it's the family den. There's a heap of garish shoes discarded at the top of the stairs. One pair protrude: the Gucci moccasins of twenty-four-year-old Muhammad. He's being groomed to take over Sultan's business (Rolls-Royce diesel concession, machine shop, construction company and so on) and taking his part in it seriously. There's not much talk. What is there to say when the same eleven people meet every night? 'Pass another Seven Up.' 'Are you washing your hair tonight, Johaina?' 'How about a game of backgammon?' A game of whist is played out with concentration. Sharifa prattles on in her friendly way throughout. The patriach slumps as usual in front of the television. He has one laugh at least: some cowpokes stroll into a saloon and order whiskies. He translates the Arabic subtitles for me: 'May I have an orange squash?'

Johara sits apart tearing her nails to the quick. She's the only one who hasn't been able to put a thermostat on her emotions. She wants to get married or to get out. She wants an outlet. So did her older sister, Wafika. She married a penniless Egyptian. Sultan bought them a house but they're always over here. Johara envies Wafika. She envies Muhammad's wife who has just had her first baby. She envies Noor who leaves next week to start at Cairo university. Johara has done Cairo and there isn't much in the way of husbands for an educated girl in Doha.

All over the city, it's the same scene. Families gather every day because there is nothing, absolutely nothing else for them to do. I'm not surprised to run across the inevitable refrain: 'Why do you spend time with the Sultan Saifs? They're not proper Qataris; they're not typical?' Who is? The al-Thanis who came from Saudi Arabia for the pearling banks? The al-Thanis are too busy playing copy-cat to Emir Khalifa to seem real these days. The Darwish millionaires? They're pushed at me as 'proper Qataris'. Their origins are as Bahraini as Sultan Saif's.

This place was a deserted wilderness until recent years. Now it has schools, hospitals, an ultra-modern television station. And it's as dull as ditchwater, but clearer. This is the country that sends out the Qataris to earn that reputation for messy living in London.

It's worth spinning forwards a couple of months. I'm home and the phone rings. Sharifa and Sultan are in town. I must come round. Number 5, Green Street is about the most exclusive address you can have. It's one of those perfect Georgian town houses that fewer and fewer English can afford these days. The Saifs' two-floor flat has fine plaster-work on high ceilings, scalloped niches and an Adam fireplace. It's not pretentious but it's spotlessly clean.

Sharifa has a full time-table. They have flown in from Bombay (holiday for her, business for him) and she has to make time for Harley Street: with her dentist for toothache, and her doctor for rheumatism. In between she's negotiating with a decorator and Waring & Gillow – again. The family is on the move to a larger establishment in Portman square. Fitting eleven beds into a four-bedroomed Mayfair flat is no longer on. The new place is larger and more suitable. Sharifa is slightly horrified at the old tenants. 'Though they did leave the place nice and clean, they didn't have a bidet anywhere.' More loos and many bidets are on order.

By the time the family swoop down again in May, the new Japanese silk wallpaper will have had time to dry out and the Waring & Gillow repro will have been delivered safely this time. It's only to Portman Square.

Sharifa's expensive, tailored outfit is what I expect. It's the change in Sultan that amazes me. This is where Muhammad learned about wearing the right shoes. Sultan's suit is Savile Row best, his shirt is hand made, he looks as if he has just come home from a St James' club. No trace of grouchiness here. He's relaxed, warm and alive; he's out of Qatar. Sultan Saif al-Isa is too educated, too sharp not to be worn down by the strains of living in toy town.

Sultan's foxed, too, by the Qatari reputation in London. 'I can't think of anyone who comes here who would deserve it – and I know practically everyone. Doha is so small.'

Down towards the pirate coast

THE STORY SO FAR: The United Arab Emirates was founded when Britain formally withdrew in 1971. It's a federation of seven small sheikhdoms. Bahrain didn't join for a variety of reasons; Qatar didn't join because it has never trusted Abu Dhabi. And the President of the UAE is that well-known British property owner, His Highness Sheikh Zayid bin Sultan al-Nahiyan, ruler of Abu Dhabi.

Sheikh Zayid's father, Sultan, came to power in 1922 by inviting his ruler brother home to dinner and shooting him in the back. Sultan was later chopped down. The next brother got the job – he was duly murdered in 1928. It's that kind of family. Enter handsome, twenty-five-year-old Sheikh Shakhbut, elder brother of Zayid. He took over and became the legendary sheikh who kept his oil revenues in paper notes at home where the rats got at it (untrue) and who didn't want to ruin his people by development (true).

Time for Shakhbut to go, thought the British in 66. Fortunately Shakhbut's mother had made all her sons promise not to do one another in. Shakhbut was eased into gentle abdication. Brother Zayid ('The Desert Falcon') came to power. He's been spending money like crazy ever since. NOW READ ON:

I am determined to enjoy Abu Dhabi. After Doha, how can I fail? I've read about the Kentucky Fried Chicken houses, the wall-to-wall carpeted mosque lit by a hundred chandeliers, the oil income that makes it the richest state in the world per capita (not many capita, perhaps 25,000, more like 15,000). I reckon I am prepared.

But nothing prepares you for the weird atmosphere. The foreigners don't plan to be around long enough to bother about being nice to one another let alone the Abu Dhabians. 'In business we all behave like people who aren't going to have to live side by side for very long. We're out for what we can get and fast, no matter how. We rent a house and fix it so that we can take everything out at a moment's notice. That's how unstable we feel.' This from a bulky sheikh's pet builder.

Nothing prepares you for the sight of Zayid's lunatic, cost-crazy, concrete fly-over in the middle of a desert, while his simultaneous 'cheapest is best' policy in town ensures that new buildings are always falling down. Sheikh Zayid is moving into his seventh palace in Abu Dhabi. It's not because he's bored with the old ones. They keep collapsing around him. 'Sheikh Zayid? He's not living here any more. He moved last week; the ceiling fell down.'

Foreigners end up working seven days a week. They may take a day off. A few Brits go out to examine the desert flora and fauna. Others go down to the sea in boats. The Lebanese, and they're here aplenty, tend to get stoned in the morning and go into the office in the afternoon when the high wears off and there's nothing else to do.

Only the sheikhs have the power to do anything they like. And they like. I'm in a hotel dining room and an elderly sheikh is making up his mind whether or not he has taken a fancy to a girl at another table. She hides in the room of a friend, just in case. If a royal wants something, even a foreign girl, he can bring in the police if he so pleases to help him get it.

What else did I expect? All the British cared about in the old days was keeping the lower Gulf quiet. They stopped the local slave trading as unseemly, and the piracy as troublesome. They didn't bother to start anything. And once India had gone and East of Suez had been debunked, only a few Foreign Office Arabists minded about what happened here. To everyone else it was a quaint 26,000 square miles with oil coming in where only a few years ago nomads and pearl divers were wretched with poverty.

The British left Zayid in charge because they reckoned he was a co-operative chap who wouldn't let the country slip into the wrong hands. They didn't leave behind one school or one decent road in Abu Dhabi. Zayid's been trying – he's built schools and roads all over the Federation. His pride and joy is the highway between Abu Dhabi town and Al-Ain (formerly Buraimi), two hours' drive inland. Sheikh Zayid first won his colours as governor of this oasis; he still keeps a few wives here, not to mention his deposed brother, Shakhbut.

What the Qatar National Museum is to Sheikh Khalifa, the Hilton Hotel in Al Ain is to Sheikh Zayid – a personally chosen monument to his past. No one much stays in it but it makes him feel good. As for his present, to hear the toadies talk of Zayid in Abu Dhabi is to hear of a character that combines the wisdom of Socrates with the leadership of Frederick the Great. No one minds that he spends millions buying property in Britain. Everyone needs a place in London . . . and Sussex . . . even Scotland. And who begrudges him a palace or two in a very scenic area of Pakistan? He hunts there for two months a year. 'It's not fit to repeat the sort of things that are happening around here,' reports my pukka Pakistani correspondent, (none too pleased to find his estate close to Sheikh Zayid's.) But he has to have somewhere to stay with his million dollars' worth of new falcons. Anyway, the generous sheikh gives to his own people too.

He's given them time. That surprised the diplomats who didn't reckon the Federation could survive more than six months. For that alone he deserves the grateful admiration of the oil-thirsty outside world. And he has pipped the Emir of Qatar to international top billing on the world stage. He runs his embassies abroad on a suitably lavish scale. So lavish that one of them is known locally as the PhD (prostitution and hashish department). Of course Sheikh Zayid can't know that.

Nor can word of it have reached the one commoner whom Zayid really trusts – there's only one at any time and now it's Foreign Minister Ahmad Suweidi. Beside Zayid only Suweidi has the power to decide anything in Abu Dhabi so there's the constant clamour of diplomats, bankers and businessmen, all wanting decisions. Every 'yes' is going to mean money for some sheikh or other, so it's a delicate business working out whose bid to accept. No wonder this busy minister has to relax sometimes.

Sheikha Osheh may be in her late thirties. It's hard to tell. She never takes off her burqa. 'But it has shrunk, you see,' she says in a muffled voice through her abbreviated helmet.

Sheikha Osheh is one of Shakhbut's daughters and married to Sheikh Mubarak, perhaps the most powerful royal besides Zayid. She's graceful and gentle, in a high-necked, long-sleeved, full length dress with strings of pearls lying lightly on her bodice. Above this is the frightening mask. It fades as her personality comes through.

She lives in a protected nest, heavily scented, where time and space intrude only through other people. If only 'harem' wasn't such an emotive and misleading word, this is what I would call Sheikha Osheh's brightly coloured, velveted box. Women drift in and out, servants, daughter, grandchildren, English language teacher; and all the while Sheikha Osheh entertains her guests.

She's fascinating about falconing. She takes down a stuffed bustard from the wall and starts to explain the way it's downed; how you have to cover the dead bird in sand to hoax the falcon into believing it's lost its prey. Otherwise it won't let go. And how you mustn't let it have more than one peck at the bustard's brains or it'll lose its appetite and won't hunt any more. She describes it minutely; she has the zest of a devotee. Sheikha Osheh has never been hunting. Her husband once took her out in a car – to watch. But when he comes home he sits with her for hours bringing alive a world she never sees.

She doesn't know the town of Abu Dhabi at all. She never goes out in it. But she has one extension to this room that few other women like her share. Every morning after dawn prayers, her husband drives her out to the desert. They sit and drink coffee together before he brings her home and goes off to his Ministry.

Sheikha Osheh is the adored and only wife of Sheikh Mubarak. Polygamy still thrives, but people are becoming sensitive about it. 'It's tiring for the man and very hard for the women,' admitted one sheikha, herself not an only wife. It'll take time for most men to catch up with their closeted sheikhas and stop equating quantity with quality. No Abu Dhabi man thanks you for opening up the old sore about Sheikh Zayid's wives – he's on number eleven, intimates say fourteen.

A little girl brings in a huge Thermos flask of cardomum coffee. Ever since I first saw a burqad woman in the Gulf, I've wondered how these masked enigmas manage the simple task of drinking.

Sheikha Osheh lifts up her burqa like a car bonnet, takes the egg-sized cup and awkwardly tips in the coffee. Women take off their masks for prayers and husband. Going to the doctor is a trauma. One English female physician still hasn't found a way of coaxing her patients out of their burqas in her surgery. 'When they come to see me the first thing they do is throw off their clothes without my even asking them. They're completely uninhibited about their bodies. But they won't take off their masks. Their face is for them what our private parts are for us. You put on a burqa for the first time when you menstruate. The connection is obvious.'

An Afghani lady balloonist in a Chanel suit arrives to say hello. She has brought some photographs with her. Sheikha Osheh has never seen a hot-air balloon before. She studies intently the snaps of the blue and white contraption and asks the question to which I have always longed to know the answer: 'Hm. I understand how it goes up. But how do you get it down again?' Satisfied that this obstacle can be overcome, she earnestly presses the balloonist to come along to next year's National Day Parade. It would add colour. Sheikha Osheh knows; she watches the parade on television.

Women like Sheikha Osheh are the most rewarding part of Abu Dhabi. It sounds strange. I don't believe in shutting women away. But even without comparing them to the men with their smack of corruption and the stamp of spoiled children, these women are entrancing. They are open, preserved from double-think by the thick walls around them and they understand the essentials of a world they are never allowed to see.

What about London? Can't they kick their heels up there? A sheikha gets into a flying metal tube, transfers to a black limousine and is shut away into another room. It may be in the Carlton Tower or in a private flat. But it's Abu Dhabi again. Those black bundles I've seen all summer in Harrods aren't these women. They are their Bedu servants. Maybe they're the ones who earn the reputation for messing up pristine rooms and apartments. It's certainly not these sheikhas.

Sheikha Fatima has often been to Britain. She has stayed in 10 The Boltons, and at Buxted Park but even the First Lady of Abu Dhabi doesn't go out. Sheikha Fatima is the fifth and favourite wife of Sheikh Zayid, the only one he keeps in Abu Dhabi (the rest are in Al-Ain), the only one he takes abroad. You have to work hard to stay the favourite wife of Sheikh Zayid for fifteen years and Sheikha Fatima is a clever lady. They say she was ravishing as a teenage bride. She's had nine children since then and under the burqa, who can tell? Compared to tender Sheikha Osheh, Sheikha Fatima's the tough career wife of Abu Dhabi. She's the talk of the town.

She comes in for some criticism from traditionalists who say that she doesn't do her stuff for the Bedu any more but that's because she's cultivating the foreign Arabs. She makes it seem as if she's merely fulfilling her First Lady entertaining role. In fact she's culling everything they have to offer that she wants to learn – current affairs, news of international personalities, a whole picture of the world she wants to master. It's working; she has just returned from her first official visit abroad – to Mrs Sadat in Cairo.

This week Sheikha Fatima is setting yet another precedent. She's presiding over a special event at the new Women's Club, the only place sheikhas can go. Four avant-garde female Western artists conducted by a 'French Princess' are having an exhibition. It's opening night: there's the friendly buzz of masked and veiled women who rarely have a chance to meet. The unveiled young are radiant. Expectancy is in the air. Sheikha Fatima finally arrives and heads the fleet that sails into the exhibition room. They're the kind of pictures that a self-conscious Western critic might call 'a deeply significant comment on our troubled times'. Abstracts. Psychedelia. A field day for the Freudians.

There is a nonplussed lull as the ladies sweep round. One

black back starts to shake with laughter. 'Uterus,' she says pointing at one canvas. 'Ovaries,' at the next. It takes women like these
to see through the second-rateness of it all. Game, set and match
to the Abu Dhabi ladies.

Royal flush

There's one thing worse than being in London and seeing Sheikh
Zayid in black and white all over the British newspapers looking
like a Hollywood gangster. It's being in Abu Dhabi and seeing
His Highness moving and in colour on television, at intolerable
length, night after night, on the world's news. All those outdoor
shots with the wind catching his black cloak, enhancing that aura
which 'appears to combine a breadth of vision and political
acumen'. All those close-ups to show 'the generous and expansive
personality of the ruler'. That's the way the British write-ups go.
He certainly has a breadth of vision and he is generous, but he's
so heroic that he's a pain in the neck.

His Abu Dhabi defenders might do better to let his people see a
few snaps of Sheikh Zayid when he's off the stage. Why not get
some of those tireless photographers into the breakfast room at
Keir, the Scottish baronial estate where Sheikh Zayid often goes
to stalk deer and shoot grouse?

Across the table from his host, friend and business confidant,
Colonel 'Bill' Stirling, Zayid still looks like Sean Connery; but
when Bond is off-screen, minus his toupée. Zayid, balding, in his
cosy buttoned cardigan, with a woolly scarf around his heroic
throat is an altogether more appealing personality. He banters over
the long-stemmed glass goblets of orange juice, the plates of
kippers, kidneys, kedgeree and other squirarchical fare. And
although he doesn't speak English, he's made himself a regular
favourite with the factor and beaters.

They've got so much in common to grunt about – the nasty nip
in the air, the outdoor life, the passion for the hunt. Zayid,

always aloof in Abu Dhabi gatherings, is what's called a jolly good guest: the kind of man who puts an arm round children and makes them laugh. Hunting in Pakistan may be an even greater delight, but he can't let up in quite the same way. There's the power-play with fellow sheikhs manœuvring around him. To head the Al-Nahiyan clan is not a rest cure.

For a start all those wives have created a succession problem. Crown Prince Khalifa may have seen the error of his ways and been working hard to atone, but Sheikha Fatima has her own young coming along. She's steely ambitious for Sheikh Muhammad, her eldest.

Zayid also has to carry around the big bag of family skeletons. There was his favourite, Sheikh Sayid, who was Ruler Shakhbut's son and married to Zayid's daughter. Sheikh Sayid shot his sister and her pimp and died of diabetes in exile abroad. He was such a blue-eyed boy that Zayid couldn't risk flying home his body in case it became a political bone.

There was his other nephew who used to bury people up to their necks in the sand and leave them there all day – for fun. He died of drink.

Then there's Sheikh Shakhbut himself, the brother and ruler whom Zayid deposed. He makes do on £500,000 a year, living the peaceful life of a manic-depressive in Al-Ain. Zayid keeps in touch with him on the phone but he still feels the responsibility for the past.

Shakhbut's palace courtyard is deathly quiet: a cricket sings. An emaciated figure, apparently anchored to the ground by his heavy black shoes and socks, stands in the doorway. Sheikh Shakhbut likes visitors. Meeting him is a peculiar experience. He asks questions through an interpreter: 'How many students are there at Cambridge?' 'When was electricity first used in Europe?' 'Do bananas grow in Canada?' Once his idiosyncratic test has been passed, he relaxes and talks of his three months in London this summer, staying at the Grosvenor House, going to the Wellington Hospital for treatment: 'It was so cold that I never went out at all. I had to keep warm by walking round the hotel.' He is the only Arab I meet who doesn't complain that London boiled all summer. It's hard to put together a jigsaw that includes this old man and the statesmanlike Zayid whom I see in Abu Dhabi.

There's Zayid's other brother, the one you never hear about. He is also strange, and, by the by, owns half of Abu Dhabi. Sheikh Shakhbut was reputed to keep his money in old tin boxes. Sheikh Khalid actually did until the day he was burgled in a London hotel. A man walked into the room carrying a bucket telling the servant in her burqa that he had come to clean the windows. He walked out with a bucketful of jewels. She identified every man the police paraded in front of her. 'That's him!' she kept crying. But of course: all Europeans looked the same to her.

Fancy trying to cope with a family like this and govern a country like this when all your palaces are tumbling down and your court is, to put it politely, in disarray. Trotting round Zayid's offices is an exhausting business. Everyone you talk to claims to be doing everything and you know perfectly well that only the ruler and the foreign minister do do anything. There's no organisation or routine but Sheikh Zayid's personal office is always on the verge of beating the problem: 'We're reorganising ourselves on the lines of a mini White House,' says HH's PA. 'It should be ready any month now.'

When The White House of the Gulf gets itself together, when Sheikh Zayid has planted enough trees to turn his sheikhdom into the Black Forest of the United Arab Emirates, one cast-off in Al-Ain hopes he'll be remembered. Colonel Sir Hugh Boustead has survived service in the Sudan, Yemen, Oman and six years as Sheikh Shakhbut's political agent. He retired to England only to be flown out again at the invitation of Sheikh Zayid to run his stables. That was shortly before Zayid developed green fingers and forgot his other hobby horses.

Whatever time of day you arrive at the royal ranch, it's bound to be feeding time for the fifty-six horses flown in from all over the world, munching hay flown in from Iran, barley flown in from Karachi, served up by fourteen Pathan stable boys flown in from Pakistan. And the sun-pickled figure of Sir Hugh, in his two-gallon trilby, will be overseeing it all in the absence of Sheikh

Zayid, who might, or might not, one day regain his former passion for these beasts.

In the meantime, Sir Hugh plays medicine man, dosing the Bedu ('they come in in heaps') with eyedrops and remedies for dysentery. It's an unusual way for a politico to end his days, but then this is Abu Dhabi. 'By the way, if you need a bed for the night,' throws out Sir Hugh over the sore Bedu foot in his face, 'you're welcome. Archdeacons and brigadiers have slept right here.'

The day disaster struck

Dubai is the second largest sheikhdom in the Federation (1,500 square miles small). It seems to be a place with a sense of humour: its contribution to the National Day Parade procession this year is a float disguised as a dhow. It features dozens of blacks being foully whipped by an Arab slavemaster. I am looking forward to a place that has the gall to pull off that one before some horrified African ambassadors on the VIP stand.

My trip starts well. I choose to drive across the desert highway from Abu Dhabi. There's a tourist delight of sand and camels with no road sense spoiled by the view of Pakistanis road-building in the scorching winter sun. They're always telling you in Abu Dhabi that Baluchis from Pakistan are the only people who can stand the mid-day summer heat. A Pakistani millionaire in Dubai hooted at that one: 'I suppose the British POWs didn't notice the heat when they were building the Burma railway for the Japanese.' At least they're not prisoners of war. They're prisoners of money. The Pakistani road-builders get 900 dirhams a month working seven days a week. For 300 they can share a hut for four with no facilities.

The Pakistani businessmen in Dubai make a fortune, but they're scared stiff. They and the Indians own a good slab of Dubai, known as the Venice of the Middle East (more aptly, the Shanghai). But as foreigners they have no legal right to own property. What am I talking about – they have no legal rights at all. They haven't forgotten what happened to 600 fellow-countrymen working at the docks. They met to discuss the shortage of water taps on site. His Highness Sheikh Rashid bin Sayid al-Makhtum, ruler of Dubai, locked the gates and shipped them all back home. Bad precedent, he said.

With all these pleasant thoughts going through my mind, I miss the vital clue to what makes Dubai tick. It's the sculptured concrete clock tower at the entrance to town. All four faces tell a different time.

I roll up to the Intercontinental Hotel, resplendent with hanging plants and creeping businessmen. 'Yes,' says the girl at reception 'the Ministry of Information asked for a room for you. But the problem with the Ministry is that they think they only have to ask for something and they get it. Well, there isn't one. Come back later.'

I'm feeling a trifle queasy – sunstroke probably. Two hours across the desert in winter is a long, hot haul and I'm not Baluchi. The telephone seems a good idea. I clasp in hope to the name of Muhammad Zayid Bejaseem, director of information in Dubai. The office recognise his name immediately. He sounds very welcoming. 'Come and see me. Come straight away.' Promising start. But I have another number to call: it's the ruler's office. There, I have been told, Oscar Mandody is a great power in the land.

Mr Mandody sounds very welcoming too. 'Come and see me. Come straight away.' Going there first makes sense; the director of information will be delighted by my initiative. I call him back and explain the dilemma of the room (which he says he will sort out) and that I'm on my way to the ruler's office. He gives me his home telephone number, wishes me luck and urges me to call in case of trouble.

That is how it all begins. Bear with me, this tale is Dubai in miniature.

Oscar Mandody is Indian. This doesn't surprise me. Dubai for long enjoyed a special relationship with India and Pakistan: spice trading, the pearl business, gold smuggling, that sort of thing. Oscar Mandody is very sleek indeed. He sits behind his desk manipulating a roomful of people through half-closed eyes in a carefully measured voice. He's a snappy dresser; pink kipper tie, almost shiny blue mohair suit, long, oiled locks. He's quite a sight among all the Bedu elders who burst in wielding sticks and promises they've just extracted from Sheikh Rashid. I can't help liking Mandody. In all this chaos, I think he's one sharp operator who I'll be able to talk to. He's the trusted number two of Mahdi al-Tajir, businessman, fixer, UAE ambassador to Britain, and France, described by an admiring merchant banker as 'a cross between the Devil and the Grand Vizier'.

In the ambassador's absence, Oscar supervises the Department of Petroleum in Dubai, is managing director of al-Tajir's businesses, and always has day and night access to Sheikh Rashid. Oh, yes, he's the man to get things done.

He's toying with some Australian city planners who have just flown in with model underpasses. While I watch him beguile and confuse, I make a tally of what I know of his boss's wealth. Let's just say Al-Tajir doesn't sue when people call him 'the richest man in the world'. But only nineteen years ago al-Tajir arrived from Bahrain as a lowly customs officer. Somewhere along the line he and wily Sheikh Rashid got together. Tajir's a fast earner.

I cast my mind back to September: the UN in New York. I met al-Tajir's nephew, a diplomat with the UAE mission. I was having bother in London with a visa: 'My uncle is the only man who can help,' said Muhammad, bushy eye-browed, the image of his uncle. He wrote down his address on a piece of paper and shoved it across the table. He ordered another drink and added: 'In Dubai, we're businessmen. Come to my apartment at six-thirty this evening and afterwards you'll meet my uncle.' It's all coming back to me now. After I threw a frosty British fit, he caused such a scene that an Egyptian First Secretary came up later to apologise: 'Those Gulf Arabs. We can't do a thing with them and they're all too big for their boots.'

Now I have a nasty fit of shivering. If it's not sunstroke, perhaps it's an omen. I stay with Oscar until two-thirty. 'Trouble with a room, my dear Linda, we must see to that.' One telephone call to the general manager of the Intercontinental and the room is fixed. 'Come to my house later this afternoon for tea. You can meet my girl friend and we will talk.'

At the Intercontinental, the room is indeed fixed. The general manager sends fruit and champagne. Oscar's at work. I telephone the director of information at home to tell him the good news. An Englishwoman, his wife I think, answers and I leave a message that I have a room and I'm grateful.

Oscar practically lives in a zoo. There are goats, birds, dogs and people. I'm parked on the porch while he finishes a business meeting. At last I'm allowed in to meet Monica. Monica is Swedish, blonde, given to throwing herself around. She bristles at me at the first instant and hands Oscar his newest kitten: 'Go to Daddy, darling.' She makes tea and accidentally forgets to give me some. Oscar strokes the pussy as he goes through the drinks bills. It seems that Monica is extravagant on his behalf.

'Poor Oscar,' confides Monica in a woman-to-woman way, when he's out of the room, 'his wife gave him such a dreadful time, and he was so unhappy until he met me. Now we're very much in love but there are people who talk about us behind our backs.' I believe the last line. 'I met Oscar when I came out from London and he fell for me at first sight and begged me to stay here and live with him. It's worth it. I don't care what they say.'

Oscar returns and announces that Asprey are having a Christmas exhibition at the Intercontinental. We'll all go together. Monica and I have tacitly agreed that we're not going to be bosom chums. Asprey have everything laid out to tempt Dubai. Monica and Oscar end up somewhere near the diamond watch case. 'I'll lay you ten dirhams that she'll get one out of him,' says Oscar's friendly brother. It's a bet I don't take. Monica gets a watch and buys him a little something too, a very little something. 'Call me; Linda, will you?' purrs Oscar as I take my leave.

By now I'm feeling dizzy. I go up to the room and work out that it's not sunstroke, it's not the weird atmosphere – I am ill. The housekeeper obliges with a thermometer. It registers way, way over normal. I have Gulf flu. My voice is going, my body is aching, I feel sorry for myself. At nine o'clock the telephone goes.

'Linda, this is Zayid. Why did you do that to me? You have no right to telephone people's wives and tell them what you did.' It's not only flu. I'm evidently going mad. Zayid? It takes ten minutes to work out that the screaming maniac on the end of the phone is Muhammad Zayid Bejaseem, Director of the UAE's Information Office in Dubai.

By now I've got some sort of grip on myself. I manage to explain that I telephoned to say that the hotel problem was sorted out and that I was grateful. That does it.

'Why didn't you come and see me this morning? I waited in the office for you until three o'clock.' Liar.

'I was with Oscar Mandody in the ruler's office,' I explain patiently. Another explosion.

'How dare you go to see a filthy foreigner before you come to see me, an Arab? I am from Dubai. How dare you insult me like this?'

'But Mr Muhammad . . .'

'My name is Zayid, Zayid . . .'

'But Mr Muhammad Zayid, Mr Mandody is an adviser to the ruler, Sheikh Rashid. I didn't think I could be doing anything wrong by seeing him.'

'I know. You hate Arabs. You think we're scum who don't work. Well I've been to Cambridge,' at a language school as it later turns out, not the university, 'and I'm a man you should respect. And if you don't show respect I'll have you thrown out of the country as soon as I feel like it.'

At nine twenty-five I interrupt the threats and outbursts, put down the phone, lie on the bed and burst into tears of frustration and misery.

From bad to worse

Day two dawns in wonderful, downtown Dubai. The sun is rising and so is my temperature. I ring reception. There's a hotel doctor; he'll be up to see me. The telephone goes. It's that bad dream from the Ministry of Information. But what's this? A sweet gentle voice on the other end of the line. 'Linda, why don't you come to my office to see me, I know we have had a small misunderstanding but my wife misunderstood you.' Oh no, it wasn't a dream.

'I have flu and I can't get out of bed.'

'I'll send you a doctor.'

'Thank you, Mr Muhammad Zayid . . .'

'Just Zayid . . .'

'. . . but the hotel has arranged one already. I'll call you as soon as I'm better and we'll pretend nothing happened.'

'You're in bed ill? That's terrible. I'll come round to see you myself this afternoon.'

'Thank you but that isn't necessary . . .'

'I'll be there at four-thirty.' Click.

I quickly ring Aftab, a Pakistani businessman whom I know through a reputable contact in London. I explain that the last thing I want is to be alone with this apparent maniac in my room. Will he please come over for the afternoon? Of course.

The hotel doctor comes, diagnoses bad flu and leaves me dosed with promises of recovery and antibiotics. I trust neither. The Pakistani arrives in the afternoon, settles down to a stack of newspapers. We wait.

At five o'clock there's a knock on the door. Aftab opens it to admit Muhammad Zayid in national dress bearing one red rose. He has innocent big black eyes; he looks as if butter wouldn't melt in his mouth. He mistakes Aftab for the doctor at first so he treats him with a certain caution.

Zayid (it's as catching as the flu) climbs on my bed to stroke my face. Aftab tactfully brings forward a chair. 'My neck aches,' I whisper hoarsely, 'perhaps you would be kind enough to sit over there where I can see you.' Zayid stays for half an hour. All is peaceful in the sick room – until he asks where the doctor came from. I know what he's getting at but I play for time. 'From the hotel.'

'What's his name?'

'Dr Nimr.'

'Didn't you know he's a Palestinian?'

'I didn't ask him.'

'Dr Nimr, a Palestinian. What do you want with foreigners. Why is it always foreigners? What's wrong with Arabs?'

I squirm for Aftab. Aftab, a big noise in soap powder from Lahore, is too worldly to be annoyed. He somehow dusts Zayid out of the room still muttering with anger. Aftab gives me two aspirin for a Zayid-induced headache, orders hot chocolate and leaves.

Day three is no better. Behold, yet another side of the director of information. 'Linda, it's Zayid.'

'Zayid, it's eleven-thirty at night.'

'Yes, but you're staying in a room booked by the Ministry of Information. I am director in Dubai; you're staying in my room. I want to come over.'

'Zayid that is not a good idea. I will come to see you in your office when I am better to sort things out. And please remember I'm the guest of Ali Shammo, the Ministry's Under Secretary.' Mistake.

'Him, he's a Sudanese, he can do nothing. I'm an Arab. I'm the one who counts. You'll want a car won't you? Well, you won't have one. You won't go anywhere or see anyone in Dubai unless I drive you there.' He sticks to his word; I stick to taxis. Once I totter out of bed, Zayid's telephone calls become a part of everyday life. 'Linda, it's Zayid. I won't pay for your room unless you let me come over to see you. I've spoken to Sheikh Rashid and he won't see you.' Relief. I've seen Sheikh Rashid once and the last thing I want is to see anyone else in Dubai. Enough is enough. I'm heading for Sharjah, a few miles up the road.

'I've spoken to Sheikh Sultan, the Ruler of Sharjah and he's too busy to receive you. But if you let me come over, I'll find a way to make Sheikh Sultan see you.' I slam down the phone.

One day the telephone rings and it's not Zayid. It's none other than that power in the land, Oscar Mandody.

'I hear you have been having a spot of bother. Why didn't you call me?' Word travels fast. 'Never mind, pack your suitcase and come over and stay here with us.' I notice that he doesn't say he'll do anything about the director. (Nobody can, it would take the combined might of the UAE Cabinet to censure or remove him. He's a local Arab.)

I phone Monica to tell her what time I'll arrive. Her tone suggests I'm the last thing she wants in the house. I can't face more hassles, not on top of Zayid and après-flu. I stay put.

At seven-thirty on the morning I'm leaving, Oscar phones again and invites himself over for coffee. He walks into the room and makes it clear that he's hurt. 'You knew I liked you the moment you walked into my office. You should have called me. I admire you Linda, you have something pure about you.' Oh no, not that. Mandody starts on another tack: 'I don't believe in people any more. Everyone is rotten, everyone is selfish, everyone is cruel. You may be wondering why I have worked so hard?' The last thing on my mind.

'I wanted to prove that I could do something without the magical name of Mandody.' What? Oh yes, his father is a local doctor.

'I had nothing when I came here and you may not believe this but for the first ten years I worked for Sheikh Rashid and the ambassador, I never took advantage of my position. Now this place is too small for me. I'd like to retire to lead a simpler life.' He laps his coffee and elucidates.

'I'll buy a place in India, a place in the country in England, perhaps a flat in London and a place in Europe, the South of France, maybe and I'll need a house in the States. I've seen what money does to people. I admire the ambassador more than any other man on earth but I'm thirty-four now and I'm bitter.'

The confessional at this time of the morning is too much. 'And I feel I can be cruel to people I love but I can't help it. I'm sorry about Monica, she can be a nuisance. But I'm an extremely sensitive person. I wanted you to know how much I admire you.'

He leaves me – bewildered. I have no clue whether he's trying to pump, compromise, flatter or even threaten me. I can't wait to hit the runway back to London.

Suddenly, it strikes me. I think I know what he came for. While recuperating from flu, I've spent time in the neighbouring sheikhdom of Sharjah. Dubai and Sharjah aren't the greatest of friends.

What gave Oscar away was a line that I almost missed. 'By the way, Linda,' he asked casually, 'How did you get to see the Ruler of Sharjah?'

All that Dubai and Sharjah have in common is oil and membership of the UAE.

Something old, something new

There's no holier-than-thou aura about His Highness Sheikh Rashid, Ruler of Dubai. He's declared himself as a businessman. I see him sitting in his majlis, lean, sparking still, in his seventies and a rogue. He's an absolutely splendid man with a sense of humour to match. He wouldn't be in the least offended if it got round that one of his favourite wags is to pull up his long dress. He then waits to see which of his stiff courtiers will be the first to whisper tactfully that His Highness's balls are showing. He'd be the first to laugh. Sheikh Rashid doesn't stand on his dignity; he doesn't need to.

He's champing at the bit, eager to be off to Pakistan for a month's hunting. He packs his private 707 with his retinue and any spare Bedu around at the time. One of his officials is pre-occupied at present trying to hire a private train for him in Karachi. It's going to be a whale of an outing.

The women are not all delicate hot house plants either. One energetic sheikha, according to a British man on the spot, had an endearing habit of 'pointing a pistol at the breast of the biggest and strongest servant and asking him to oblige.'

Nor is Sheikha Hasana anything too unusual. At nine she saw her father slaughtered by his desert rival; her family's eyes were gouged out by swords. At thirteen she was forced to marry the brother of that rival. So who would be surprised that this sister-in-law of Sheikh Rashid took umbrage, a gun and wounded her husband's charming young fourth wife not so long ago?

Sheikh Rashid doesn't go in for polygamy. Apart from anything else, he's far too artful. He has stuck to one strong, influential wife so as not to have a brood of half-brothers squabbling for power. Crown Prince Makhtoum is a nice, fat, lean-living guy, popular in Dubai, especially among the younger set. He's made it clear, they reckon, that there won't be room for Mehdi al Tajir's individual style of operations once he's in charge. Time will tell.

Al-Tajir is the Mr Fixit for the UAE. He's full of bright ideas for Dubai's expansion: the dry dock, the aluminium works, etc. His collection of priceless Persian rugs, pearls and attractive women acquaintances is much publicised too. He can be very kind and cooperative to journalists. But he never seems to be in Dubai unless Sheikh Rashid's there. Still it's such a small country that it doesn't surprise me at all to learn that al-Tajir's going global. He wouldn't be leaving anything behind in Dubai; that fabled villa doesn't add up to much when you finally see it. It's a right come down compared with his Mereworth Palladian ideal in the English countryside with its eighty feet long gallery-cum-drawing room with magnificent frescos and a painted ceiling of utmost splendour by Francesco Sleter, (as featured in *House and Garden*). Al-Tajir's worked hard and he's done well for himself.

But his isn't the only success story in Dubai. It's the place that got rich on gold-smuggling to India; it's something people are almost proud of. There's so much less savoury 're-exportation' going on ('pharmaceuticals' for instance) that they're glad to divert attention to anything as glamorous as gold. Dubai's bursting with the character that Abu Dhabi lacks. It's the place to be if it's buccaneers you're after.

There's a funny thing though: even Mehdi al-Tajir has never set foot in the sheikhdom of Sharjah. Oscar Mandody hasn't been there either: 'I've been too busy.' Sharjah is five minutes' drive from Dubai – seven depending on which border you go for. The UAE borders are invisible and a mess. You might not believe this, but Sharjah is divided into four bits stuck all over the UAE. It shares half a patch of desert with the sheikhdom of Fujirah, half a village with Oman and half an island with Iran. When you're driving along the coast from Sharjah town to the fishing village of Hamriyah, there's a bend in the road. It straightens out after a few miles. You've just missed the sheikhdom of Ajman.

Until recently, Sharjah's main claim to fame (among the cognoscenti) was that it produced the red asphalt for the road outside Buckingham Palace. Its newest claim is that it's the youngest oil-producing sheikhdom. Half an oil-producing sheikhdom really. Its oil income is a secret; its only production so far is on that island it shares with Iran. But development is raging all over the country. It's even building a glossy new international airport, a short drive away from Dubai's glossy new international airport.

Joining the oil stakes (in 1974) is one thing. More significantly, His Highness Sheikh Sultan bin Muhammad al-Qasimi is the first university graduate to rule anywhere in the peninsula. It was another of those accidents, another of those families.

Sharjah's ruler, Saqr, was deposed in 1965 by the British for being as stingy as Ruler Shakhbut. A duly co-operative chap, Sheikh Khalid, was put in his place and all went well – until 72. Sheikh Saqr wanted his country back and shot Khalid dead in the attempt. Tricky business all round; the UAE President, Sheikh Zayid, decided a fair trial was called for. It was meant to be an open trial. It got tangled up in some unwelcome publicity and Sheikh Saqr now lives under 'house arrest' in Al-Ain, just round the corner from Sheikh Shakhbut.

Another new ruler was needed for Sharjah, but it would have been embarrassing to choose one of the assassin's powerful sheikhly brothers. In those days, Sheikh Sultan, Khalid's younger brother, was spending his time on his farm, trying out air-conditioning on his summer vegetable plants. Sheikh Sultan, a former technical college teacher, had recently come back from Cairo University. He went to do a degree in agriculture because it interested him.

Today, at thirty-eight, he's Ruler of Sharjah and a delightful man. He's resting outside in the dark in his palace garden when I arrive. He knows about my flu and sympathises. He's getting it too. We move inside but one of his tame gazelles tags along, spilling a vase of flowers and trampling the armchairs. Sheikh Sultan smiles and smiles.

Eventually the gazelle is shooed outside and the ruler explains that he wants his country to be different from certain others he's too tactful to name.

Bart Paff, an American economics technocrat from Washington, sits in, hands folded over his briefcase. He came here to do a short feasibility study and is now the ruler's permanent adviser. (How do they plan? 'We play it by the seat of our pants'.) Mr Paff has a touch of the Steve McQueen about him, especially when I ask if he's Sharjah's answer to Mehdi al-Tajir.

Sheikh Sultan and Paff know what they want: no middle-men, no percentage cuts, no ban on foreign Arabs owning property, no obligatory local partners, no everything that makes buildings fall down in Abu Dhabi and doing business complicated in Dubai.

Sheikh Sultan is bright. It's not just his university education, or his fluent English, Urdu, Farsi. 'He has his head screwed on right,' as Paff puts it. Except for his national dress, Sultan is light years away from the old-fashioned, Bedu-style sheikhs down the road. He doesn't take months off from running his country to go hunting; he takes two weeks' holiday each summer. He's the way they may all be in a few years' time. The rulers I've seen are already moving into history. Sheikh Sultan doesn't drink. He's careful not to offend conservatives by being seen publicly with his delectable young wife, Mosa. But that doesn't stop him inviting an English ballet dancer home to give Mosa conversation classes and private tutors from Cairo to coach her for a degree.

They live together in this house with their new daughter, the gazelles and soldiers on the gate. Without the soldiers I wouldn't know it was a palace. And Sultan isn't unadorned by cufflinks to make the right impression. He's past the stage of gew-gaws.

He's almost embarrassed at the white clinker-built yacht he inherited from his dead brother Khalid. He could moor it anywhere; the Sharjah coastline is his. He chooses to leave it on the quay opposite the camel slaughterhouse.

I must tell you about the slaughterhouse; there's a queue of patient camels waiting their turn and the stench is hellish. It's almost as if Sheikh Sultan wants to remind himself of the inevitable human condition.

His flu is getting worse. His almond-shaped eyes are turning pink. 'I want you to see Sharjah and I want you to be happy here. My cousin, Sheikh Ahmad, brought you to me and he will look after you.'

How I met Sheikh Ahmad is another of those tales.

Something borrowed, something blue

I'm in the lobby trying to escape the phone calls from Dubai's attentive director of information. I've never felt so blue. Which of us is delirious – me or Dubai? A young American and an even younger, owlish Arab peer at me anxiously: 'Are you all right?'

Since I'm obviously far from all right, they gingerly escort me to the coffee shop. Barry Qulick is a movie producer (of *Sitting Target* etc.). Sheikh Ahmad bin Muhammad al-Qasimi is from Sharjah.

Sheikh Ahmad quickly grasps the Dubai disaster. Five minutes later, he's arranged a visit to his cousin the ruler. Over the next three days, Barry Qulick is to wish he had ignored my plight. He doesn't get much done while Ahmad takes seriously the ruler's injunction that I'm in his care. He and Barry are going into partnership in an eight-lane bowling alley, cinema, snack bar and restaurant complex. That must wait.

Ahmad decides that a day in the country for me comes before a visit to the bank with Barry. He commandeers his Lebanese office manager (whom he met and hired in a furniture shop) with his Irish girl friend. I discover on the ride out that Lena, bouncy, rosy cheeked, sells encyclopaedia sets to Arab businessmen around the Gulf.

'Of course they always ask me for dinner but I say "I'll ring you tomorrow." They sign, I never ring and someone else goes to deliver the sets and collect the money. They never go back on a deal once they've given their word. That's what's so nice about them.' It's still crazy but I feel better already.

We drive to the famous Dhaid oasis. So this is an oasis: a

shrivelled collection of shops, donkeys, a few wilting trees and a farm belonging to Ahmad's father. Nothing much grows. I suppose it's all comparative. We drag a couple of armchairs out of the sitting room (Ahmad's father has installed air-conditioning, to the son's disgust) and sit on the verandah. The others fiddle with the barbecue and knock back beer.

Ahmad's twenty-one. Father Muhammad didn't get on with his brother, Ruler Saqr, so he took the family to Saudi Arabia and worked as a clerk for Aramco. Later he came back to Dubai, went into business and packed Ahmad off to college in London. 'I lived in a raincoat in one room in the Edgware Road. I was cold, wet and lonely.'

His father swiftly became the richest, most powerful sheikh in Sharjah apart from the ruler. The ruler is grooming Ahmad as a symbol of al-Qasimi reconciliation.

'My father will never get over the fact that his brother murdered the ruler's brother. Sheikh Sultan wants it all to be forgotten. He's given me land and told me what to build on it, apprenticed me to Bart Paff so I can learn. It's a strain, frankly. I've no money of my own, only land. I have to borrow capital from the bank like everyone else and I don't think I'm that clever.'

Ahmad is engaged to his cousin, Aisha, daughter of the man his uncle killed. That's another reason he's so important. This marriage will help to darn the past. We don't talk about that; we just watch the sunset in Dhaid and drive back to Dubai.

Next day. Ahmad comes to take me to the beach. I don't recognise him. He's wearing jeans. Al-Qasimis don't walk into the Intercontinental in jeans; there's got to be a reason.

We're sitting cross-legged on the sand throwing pebbles into the sea at Hamriyah. It's a beautiful fishing village. Where else would Prince Alfonso Hohenlohe be building a new Marbella Club but in Sharjah? It's better than beaten-up Spain any day and there's oil money on tap. In jeans and short-sleeved shirt, Ahmad still looks owlish behind those gold-rimmed spectacles. But he looks more vulnerable without his head-dress; he's also handsome, which hadn't occurred to me before.

'Wouldn't it be marvellous if Aisha could be with us? I talked to her on the phone for hours this morning. Although we're engaged I can't see her alone or take her out like this. My family say "What are you waiting for? Get married now." But I don't want to be married their way, living in a huge house with soldiers at the gate.

'I want the ruler to give us a small house, somewhere quiet, but Aisha's mother insists that the daughter of a former ruler must live in a certain way. I don't mind taking the house from the ruler, he gives one to every al-Qasimi, but I want to earn the money to furnish it myself and to furnish it our way. No one understands that.'

He'd like Aisha to go abroad to study for a while. 'Her mother won't hear of it. But I want Aisha to be the kind of wife who comes out, goes to dinner parties, does things with me. As long as she's only known her mother's old fashioned ways, she'll always think it's wrong for a wife to do anything like that.

'The jeans have made a difference haven't they?' I click. 'I couldn't have talked to you like this in formal dress. It doesn't matter to me, but it puts up a barrier for you.' He's right; even now those white robes still make me think of the men wearing them as set apart from my world. Some are; some of the younger generation, like Ahmad, aren't.

On the road back to Dubai, a 'Cadi-Rolls' zooms past with a young tiger at the wheel. Ahmad looks sad. It's his sixteen-year-old brother, Salim. 'He goes to London in the summer and stays in the Britannia Hotel alone and my family encourage him; they say he's sixteen and a man. He drinks whisky, chases girls and he's still at school. When I was his age, no one had even heard of Sharjah; we didn't have the money to live like that. Now I'm an oil sheikh and wherever I go it's "Sheikh Ahmad this" and "Sheikh Ahmad that". I can't stand it.'

We walk into the hotel. Barry Qulick is waiting, a picture of triumph. 'Ahmad, I've got it. We're going to have a special section in our snack bar serving Sheikh Ahmad's Milk Shakes.' The new oil sheikh from Sharjah goes dead quiet.

Epilogue

Epilogue

Stepping back through the mirror is disorientating. It takes a long time to feel at home again in London. I've clambered into those walled gardens of the oil sheikhs and I'm not certain what I feel about it. I had a clearer image of the oil Arabs before I got to know any. Being Jewish helped me to understand some things about the Arab way of life that many Christian Western Europeans might not: the close family feeling, for example, It also exorcised a fear that I didn't know I had until I went to Arabia.

Back home, at first I can't see the British in the streets for the Arabs. I realise I've got over that obsession the day a sports car rams my taxi. While the driver fights it out with a Saudi road-hog, I nip into another cab. It doesn't occur to me to ask the Saudi's name.

Other incidents mark the miles I've travelled. There's an invitation to dinner to talk business with an Arab diplomat. It ends as drinks with a madame from Surrey, a few of her girls and visiting dignitaries.

'Doesn't he have everything? Look at his eyes, look at his lashes curl,' enthuses the madame, one hand on an old friend's knee. 'I've loved this man so much that I would never let him pay. Isn't that true, sweetie?'

Sweetie is here tonight for the puppy-fatted body of sixteen-year-old Julie. He'll certainly pay for that amusement.

What would have outraged me before doesn't surprise now. It's almost what I expect. What I don't expect is the phone call from a Saudi host who had become a friend. He's in London with his family; he's curt, embarrassed, but asks me over. I don't believe the conversation:

'I'm sorry, Linda, I can't see you and I can't allow any of my family to. I'm only seeing you now because it's my way; I must tell you this face to face.'

'But why? What have I done?'

'You know what they're saying about you in Riyadh?'

'How can I? I'm in London.'

'They say you're a spy.'

'You're joking.' I laugh; he doesn't. 'Who on earth am I supposed to be spying for and what was I supposed to be finding out? You know what I talked about when I stayed with you. Did I ever once ask you about your job?'

'No, but "they" have departments that study us psychologically.'

His family don't see me. I'm hurt, but I don't take it seriously until a strange collection of visitors pitch up at home. The Saudi who doesn't believe I'm writing a book at all. Another Saudi believes I'm writing it – for a Zionist organisation. Taking courage in both hands, I tell him I'm Jewish but that I don't work for a Zionist organisation.

'Why didn't you tell us?'

'I wouldn't have got a visa.'

'I wish you hadn't lied about it. My government won't like it. Didn't you think that we'd suspect you of spying?'

'That, no. But does my being Jewish make a difference to you personally?'

'To me? Of course not, Linda.' I believe him; a good moment after all.

Then I see Dubai's Oscar Mandody in a roomful of people at the Hilton. He says he wants to talk. He comes for a brandy and orders a taxi ten minutes after he arrives. While he's waiting, his carefully-measured voice cuts into me.

'I've spent the day with the ambassador and we were talking about you. I think it would be a good idea if you gave up any thought of writing this book. You know what happened to the CIA man in Athens at Christmas?'

'Yes, Oscar, he ran into a bullet.'

'Do you know who killed him?'

'No.'

'Exactly. You don't know very much. You'd do a lot better to listen to what I say. I admire you, Linda, and it would be a pity if anything were to happen to you.'

For one night I'm terrified again. Then it passes; it's a catharsis.

Oscar wasn't threatening me; it was genuine concern for my welfare. How could I have misunderstood him? Now I know what I feel about the countries I've visited and the people. Do I like Arabs? Love some, hate others. They're just people.

I do know that they all hate the way the West laughs at their bad taste and over-spending. But that will pass.

The best comparison I can offer is with how Europeans felt after World War II. We seemed to be over-run by vulgar Americans in loud shirts and too-short trousers showing white socks. Europeans shuddered at the abrasive American greetings, the vice-like handshake. But Americans were the only ones with money in an impoverished, vulnerable continent. They were resented and laughed at then in the same way as Westerners now resent and laugh at oil-rich Arabs.

The oil Arabs want us to take the heat off them. They don't want our fascination with their wealth. They have enough problems and insecurities of their own, without running into the taunts of their friends. From underdogs to supermen in one hop is hard to take.

And they are our friends; we need those oil autocracies as much as they need us. Our governments help to prop up theirs. You may not approve of their autocratic set-ups, I don't. But how would you like Qadhafi in Saudi Arabia? Castro in Kuwait? If you would, fine. But remember that we need that oil sitting under Arabia. And as for the people I went to meet, I caught them during a period of change that is perhaps the greatest to hit their private world since the birth of the Prophet. I have no idea how they're going to cope; I admire them for trying. I know only that it was *the* place to be at this particular moment. Whatever changes take place in the next few years the summer and autumn of 1975 belonged to Arabia. The names that matter may change. Policies, even people, may change. But everyone will have to look back to that moment in 1975 to understand the evolution.

I do want to go back. That surprises me. But I'd rather not wait too long.

'I'm not sure that I'll want to come back here in ten years' time,' I said to one Saudi cabinet minister. 'I'm not sure that I'll want to live here in ten years' time,' he replied.

Index

Abdul Aziz, Prince, 243
Abdul Aziz bin Nasir, Prince, 67
Abdullah bin Faisal al-Saud, Prince, 24, 25, 64–7
Abdullah bin Nasir, Prince, 67–9, 70
Abu Dhabi, 2, 251–60
Abu Ghazaleh, Talal, 226
Abu Saud, Khalid, 184–7
Aden, 6, 150–1; *see also* Yemen
Adham, Kamal, 13, 125–9, 130–1, 234
Adham, Nadia, 131
Ahmad, Emir of Qatar, 242
Ahmad bin Muhammad al-Qasimi, 272–4
Ajman, 270
Al-Ain (Buraimi), 252–3
Alfonso Hohenlohe, Prince, 273
Algeria, 6
Alireza family (of Bahrein), 161, 163
Alireza family (of Saudi Arabia), 101, 119, 121, 139–43, 161
Alireza, Abdullah, 161, 162
Alireza, Abdullah Ali, 100, 121, 140, 141
Alireza, Sheikh Ahmad, 140–1
Alireza, Fahd, 140
Alireza, Hamsa, 142–3
Alireza, Hayyat, 140, 142–3
Alireza, Jugette, 121
Alireza, Muhammad (of Bahrein), 161
Alireza, Muhammad (of Saudi Arabia), 140, 142–3
Al Salam, 211
Al Yamaha Hotel, Riyadh, 45
Amin, Idi, 141
Amneaf Stable, 211
Annabel's, 36, 38, 226
Aramco, 83, 101, 115, 164, 234–5
Arbuthnot Latham, 122

al-Ared, Dr Medhat, 92, 93–5
Arnander, Christopher, 231
Arnander, Primrose, 231
Ashmawi, Ahmad, 132
Ashmawi, Elfrida, 132, 133
Ashmawi, Muhammad, 130, 131–4, 135
Ashmawi, Naveen, 132
al-Askari, Gida, 29
Asprey, Captain Algernon 'Algy', 169, 171, 173, 174
Asprey, John, 27–8
Asprey's, 27–8, 263
Aswan Dam, 217

Bahrain, 2, 147–77, 244–5, 251
Bandar bin Faisal, Prince, 70–3, 226
Bandri, Princess, 76
Bapco (Bahrain Oil Company), 172–3
Barnes, James T. Senior, 97
Behbehani, Mustata, 230
Benn, Anthony Wedgwood, 41
bin Ladin, Sheikh Salim, 137–9
Blatt, Henry B., 187–9
Blouet, Max, 15
Bolshoi Ballet Company, 191
The Boltons, London, 11
Bonsack, Godfrey, 27
Boustead, Colonel Sir Hugh, 259
British Aircraft Corporation, 41
British Airports Authority, 30
British and Commonwealth Group, 20
British Army, 151
British Bank of the Middle East, 172
British Leyland, 61
British Museum, 29
Brompton Bureau, 37
Buckingham Palace, 270

Cadogan Place, London, 13
Cairo, 5, 215–20
Caldwell, Vickie, 75–6
Callaghan, Audrey, 220
Callaghan, James, 41, 220
Carlton Tower Hotel, London, 35, 67–8
Carrington, Rupert, 116
Chase Manhattan Bank, 115; Manama branch, 152–3
Chicago Seven, 244
CIA, 129
Claridge's Hotel, London, 39, 120
Clermont Club, 23
Colchester, Charlie, 165–6
Collingwood's, 166
Concorde, 155
Connally, John, 97
Constantinople, 5
Cornfeld, Bernie, 14
Craig, Harry, 97
Cullinan, Mr, 231–2
Cullinan, Mrs, 231
Cummings, Bruce, 188

Damascus, 6
Davies, Myra, 212
Davies, Myra, 212
Delmon Hotel, Manama, 172
Dhahran, 48, 164
Dhaid oasis, 272–3
Dhofari rebels, 163
Doha, 243, 245–6, 247
Dorchester Hotel, London, 15, 58, 120
Douglas-Home, David, 115–16
Dubai, 2, 260–71

East India Company, 5
Eaton Square, London, 13
Egypt, 6
Elizabeth II, Queen of England, 40, 71
English Electric, 159
Evening Standard, 151

Fahd, Crown Prince, 23, 38–41, 56, 58, 83, 108, 125, 140

Faisal, King of Iraq, 6
Faisal, King of Saudi Arabia, 7, 54–6, 70, 71, 74, 82–3, 97, 101, 121, 123, 125–6, 129–30, 135, 138, 181, 187–188, 234–5
Faisal bin Fahd, Prince, 45, 47
Fakhroo family, 163
Fakhroo, Abdul Rahman, 163
Fakhroo, Ahmad Yusuf, 163
Faraun, Ghazzam, 102–3
Faraun, Jamida, 95–6
Faraun, Raith, 96–9, 102–3
Faraun, Dr Rashad, 92–6
Farouk, King of Egypt, 6
Fatima, Sheikha, 256, 258
Faulds, Walter, 45, 47, 50
Fawaz, Prince, 77–8
Fawzia, Princess, 77–9
First National Bank of San Jose, 98
First National City Bank, 115
Fortnum & Mason, 21
France, 5, 6
Fraser, Ian, 47
Frayer, Jack F., 45
Fu Tong, David, 31, 32–3
Fu Tong, Marion, 32, 33
Fujirah, 269

Gainsborough, Thomas, 189–90
General Motors, 65, 159
Genghis Khan, 5
Getty, Paul, 129
Ghaffar, Dr Hasham Abdul, 86
al-Ghanim family, 191, 225
al-Ghanim, Abdullah, 225–7, 229
al-Ghanim, Dirar, 225–9, 230
al-Ghanim, Lulua, 225–7, 229, 231
Giscard d'Estaing, Valéry, 241
Gloucester, Duke of, 39
Gloucester Hotel, London, 15
Goodyear, 159
Graff, Lawrence, 23–5
Graham, Billy, 60
Gray, Mackenzie, 165
Greene, Major, 177
Greer, Germaine, 206
Grosvenor House, London, 15, 120, 258

Guinness, Jonathan, 11
Guinness, Mrs, 11–12
Gulf Air, 152, 174
Gulf Hotel, Qatar, 247
Gulf International, 211, 215, 217

Haifa, Princess, 76
Hamad, Crown Prince, 173, 175
Hamad, Ruler of Bahrein, 171
al-Hamad, Abdalatif, 228–9
al-Hamad, Abdullah, 228
al-Hamad, Fattda, 228–9
Hamptons, 12
Hamriyah, 270, 273
Harley Street, London, 21–2
Harris, Lindsay, 21
Harrods, 27, 84
Hasa, Princess, 220
Hasa, Sheikha, 160, 169–70, 175
Hasana, Sheikha, 268
Hashimites, 5–6
Hassan, King of Morocco, 6
Hayya, Queen, 71
Healey, Dennis, 41
Heath, Edward, 211
Heffner, 22
Henderson, Ian Stewart MacWalter, 153
Hicks, David, 243
Hilal, 68–9
Hilton Hotel, Al Ain, 253; Kuwait, 152; London, 14, 15
Hockney, David, 28
Hunt, H. L., 129
Hunting and Equestrian Club, Kuwait, 229–32
Hussain, King of Jordan, 6

Ibn Saud, King of Saudi Arabia, 6, 7, 30, 54–8, 65, 73, 86, 92, 94–6, 108, 113–14, 121, 122, 125, 126, 187–8, 234, 237
Idris, King of Libya, 6
Iffat, Queen, 71, 75, 125, 130, 189
India, 5, 27, 261, 269
Intercontinental Hotel, Dubai, 261–263; London, 15
Iran, 154, 161, 182, 242, 269

Iraq, 6, 7, 182
al-Isa, Harla, 248
al-Isa, Johaina, 248
al-Isa, Johara, 248–9
al-Isa, Muhammad, 249, 250
al-Isa, Sharifa, 247–50
al-Isa, Sultan Saif, 247–50
al-Isa, Wafika, 249
Isa bin Muhammad, Sheikh, 147–50, 151
Isa bin Salman, Emir of Bahrain, 151, 157, 169–72, 175–7
ITT, 141

Jiddah, 113–23, 133, 135
Jordan, 6
Jourdan, Charles, 194, 195
Juffali, family, 236

Kandara Hotel, 115
Kanoo family, 159, 163
Kanoo, Maryam, 159–60
Kanoo Travel, 170
Kealey, Robin, 39
Keith's, 165
Kelvine Marine, 159
Kennedy, Caroline, 97
Kennedy, Edward, 37, 86
Kennedy, Joan, 93
Kensington Court, London, 30
Khalid, King of Saudi Arabia, 21, 54, 56, 64, 71, 76, 92, 123, 125, 235
Khalid, Prince, 76
Khalid, Sheikh, of Abu Dhabi, 259
Khalid, Sheikh, of Kuwait, 232
Khalid, Sheikh, of Sharjah, 270, 271
Khalifa, Crown Prince, 258
Khalifa, Emir, 249
al-Khalifa family, 147–9, 151, 153, 159–60, 162, 181
al-Khalifa, Sheikh Abdul Aziz, 167
al-Khalifa, Sheikha Dana, 155–8
al-Khalifa, Sheikha Hayya, 244–5
al-Khalifa, Sheikh Isa bin Abdullah, 155–8
al-Khalifa, Sheikha Maryam, 147–50, 151
al-Khalifa, Sheikh Muhammad, 172

Khalifa bin Hamad al-Thani, Emir of Qatar, 241–3, 245–6, 247
Khalthoum, Princess, 32, 33–4
Khalthoum, Umm, 66
Khashoggi, Adnan, 13, 58, 61, 96–8
al-Khatib, Kanaan, 128–9, 130
Kiawah Island, 185–6, 187
King Faisal Medical City, Riyadh, 45, 94
Kleinwort Benson, 172
Kutchinsky, 24
Kuwait, 2, 7, 181–237
Kuwait Fund for Arab Economic Development, 228

Las Vegas, 23
Latifa, Princess, 74–5
Lawrence, T. E., 5–6
Lear, Bill, 45
Lebanon, 6
Levin, Dr Arthur, 21
Libya, 6
Lloyds Bank, 115
London, 11–41
London Clinic, 19–20
Londonderry House, London, 15
Lonrho, 211
Lownes, Victor, 22–4
Lulua, Princess, 74–5
Lulua, Sheikha, 170

Maghrabi, Madame, 162
Maghrabi, Nevine, 161–2, 164
Maharishi Mahesh Yogi, 45
Makhtoum, Crown Prince, 269
Manama, 148, 151–2, 164
Mandili, Sharifa Fatma, 86
Mandody, Oscar, 261–2, 266–8, 269, 279
Marbella Club, 30, 34
Marks & Spencer, 18
Mason, Roy, 41
Masri, Abdullah Hassan, 243–4
Mecca, 4, 5, 6, 114,
Mecca (oil tanker), 65–6
Mereworth Castle, Kent, 13
Meridian Hotel, Cairo, 216

Metropolitan Police Dog Training Centre, 29
Middle East Airlines, 61
Miles, Roy, 190
Mobil, 133
Mobilia House, Kuwait, 194
Mongols, 5
Monte Carlo, 23
Morgan Guaranty Bank, 115
Morocco, 6
Muammar, Abdul Aziz, 123–4
Mubarak, Emir, 209, 221
Mubarak, Sheikh, 254
Muhammad, Sheikh, of Abu Dhabi, 258
Muhammad, Sheikh, of Sharjah, 273
Mulhurne, Bernie, 23–4
Mullah, Badr, 226
Musad, Prince, 56

al-Naqib, Hind, 200–1
Nasir, Prince, 68
al-Nasiriyyah Palace, 55
Nasser, Gamal Abdel, 6, 126
National Bank of Bahrein, 172
National Guard, Saudi Arabia, 56–7, 59
National Westminster Bank, 115
Nazer, Almira, 86–7, 88–9
Nazer, Hisham, 87–9
New York, 13
Nixon, Richard, 60
Northrop, 86

Obaid, Ibrahim, 35–8, 81–2, 91
Obaid, Mrs, 36, 37, 38
Obaid, Souad, 35–8, 81
'The Oil of Arabs', 235
Oman, 269
Onassis, Aristotle, 129
Onassis, Christina, 188
Onassis, Jackie, 188
OPEC, 35–6, 83, 128, 233
Oryz, 122
Osheh, Sheikha, 254–6
Ottoman Empire, 5

Paff, Bart, 271, 273
Pakistan, 260, 261
'The Palazzo', 38-9
Palestine, Palestinians, 6, 182-4
Park Lane, London, 15
Park Tower Hotel, London, 15
Philby, Dora, 95
Philby, H. St John, 95, 237
Philby, Kim, 95
Playboy Club, 22-4
Portman Square, London, 250
Presley, Elvis, 130

Qaboos, Sultan of Oman, 29, 61
al-Qadhafi, Muammar, 6
Qatar, 2, 7, 241-3, 245-50, 251
Qatar Flour Mills, 242
Qatar National Museum, 245
Qulick, Barry, 272, 274

Rahman, Abdul, 200-1
Rashid, Sheikh, 26, 69
Rashid bin Sayid al-Makhtum, Ruler
   of Dubai, 261, 262, 266, 268-9
Rice, Michael, 245-6
Richard I, King of England, 5
Richardson, Sir Gordon, 40, 186
Rifaa, 147-8
Riyadh, 45-55, 75
Rizk, Fuad, 130
al-Rodan, Khalid, 230
Rover, 61
Rowlands, 'Tiny', 214
Royal Garden Hotel, London, 15-16
Rutland Gate, London, 13-14

al-Sabah family, 181, 182, 208-12,
   218-19
al-Sabah, Ahmad, 212
al-Sabah, Amina, 223-4
al-Sabah, Awatif, 210, 218-19
al-Sabah, Sheikha Badria, 188, 189,
   220-5
al-Sabah, Sheikh Fahd, 209, 221-2
al-Sabah, Fatma, 223-4
al-Sabah, Hamid, 218
al-Sabah, Hasa, 212-13, 216-17, 218-
   219

al-Sabah, Khalid, 211, 212, 213
al-Sabah, Lulua, 222
al-Sabah, Mariam, 210
al-Sabah, Misha'al, 212, 213
al-Sabah, Sheikh Nasir bin Sabah,
   211-20
al-Sabah, Sheikh Saad, 210
al-Sabah, Sheikh Salim, 209
al-Sabah, Sheikh Saud, 209, 210,
   219
Sadat, Mrs, 256
Sadat, President, 101, 126
Safwa, Princess, 66-7
St Paul's Cathedral, 29
Saladin, 5, 21
Salamiyya, 194, 195, 230
Salman, Ruler of Bahrain, 156, 157,
   171
Sapiqi, Princess, 173
Saqr, Ruler of Sharjah, 270, 273
Sara, Princess, 75
Sassoon, Lady, 190
Saud bin Faisal, Prince, 41, 61, 76,
   112, 128-9
al-Saud family, 6, 30, 54-5, 159
Saudi Arabia, 2, 6, 7-8, 45-143, 154,
   243-4
Saudi Arabian Monetary Authority
   (SAMA), 115, 118
Saudi Press Agency, 41
Saudi Progress Society, 75
Sayid, Sheikh, 257-60
Sellers, John, 191-4
Senghor, Léopold, 241
Shakhbut, Sheikh, 251, 252, 254,
   258, 259, 270
Shakir, Ghassan, 58-61
Shammo, Ali, 269
Sharjah, 2, 266-8, 269-74
al-Sheikh family, 79-80
Sheikha, Sheikha, 149
Shell, 133
Sheraton Hotel, Kuwait, 187, 188
Shirawi, May, 168
Shirawi, Yusuf, 167-8
Sleter, Francesco, 269
Smith, George, 67-9
Sony, 65

Sotheby's, 29
Sportsman, Salamiyya, 230
Stark, Fortney H., 98
Stevens, Mrs, 223
Stirling, Colonel 'Bill', 257
Stutz cars, 130
al-Sudairy, Hassa, 108
Sulaiman, Abdul Aziz, 122-3
Sultan, Najat, 203-6
Sultan, Prince, 58
Sultan, Ruler of Abu Dhabi, 251
Sultan bin Muhammad al-Qasimi,
     Ruler of Sharjah, 266, 268, 270-71,
     273
Syria, 6

Taif, 93
al-Tajir, Mehdi, 13, 15, 262, 269, 271
Tamer, Lita, 119, 121
Tamer, Ma'amun, 119
al-Tariki, Abdullah, 233-7, 241
al-Tariki, Zakhr, 235-6
Taylor, Elizabeth, 19
al-Thani family, 247, 249
al-Thaunayan, Abdul Aziz, 74
Thompson's Beach, 176
al-Thuwaini, Major General Abdul
     Latif, 213
Tiffany, Charles L., 187
Tiffany's, 187-9
Times, 124
Toyota, 159
Tunisia, 6
Turkey, 5
Turqi, Prince, 30-4
Turqi bin Faisal, Prince, 226

Union Bank of Switzerland, 172

United Arab Emirates (UAE), 7,
     251-5
United Fisheries, 211
United Nations, 129
United Trading Company, 221, 223

Vinnell Corporation, 59-60
Volochine, Marina, 160-1

al-Wahhab, 6, 79-80
Wahhabi, 79-80, 124
Wahhabism, 6, 80, 246
Ward, Christine, 36-8
Waring & Gillow, 247, 250
Weathermen, 244
Wellington Hospital, 20-1, 258
West Bay Land Reclamation Project,
     242
Wilson, Harold, 39, 40
Wimpey, 159
Winston, Harry, 100, 119, 141, 189
Women's Club, Abu Dhabi, 256
World of Islam Festival, 29
World War I, 5-6

Yamani, Sheikh Ahmad Zaki, 13,
     35-6, 40, 80-4, 86-7, 89-92, 122,
     128, 234
Yamani, Tammam, 84, 86, 89-92
Yatim family, 159, 162
Yemen, 6, 163; *see also* Aden

Zarach brothers, 28, 31
Zayid Bejaseem, Muhammad, 261,
     264-7
Zayid bin Sultan al-Nahiyan, Ruler
     of Abu Dhabi, 11, 12, 251-3, 256,
     257-9, 270
Zuhair, General, 86

0352 Star

General (all are illustrated)

396865	Margaret Duchess of Argyll **FORGET NOT**	70p
398078	The Duchess of Bedford **NICOLE NOBODY**	75p
300485	Helen Cathcart **ANNE AND THE PRINCESSES ROYAL**	75p
397004	Tommy Cooper **JUST LIKE THAT!**	50p
39854X	Paul Dunn **THE OSMONDS**	80p*
397071	Margot Fonteyn **MARGOT FONTEYN**	75p
396601	Gerold Frank **JUDY (Large Format)**	£1.95p
300299	Noele Gordon **MY LIFE AT CROSSROADS**	50p
398108	Brian Johnston **IT'S BEEN A LOT OF FUN**	60p
396873	Renee Jordan **STREISAND**	75p
39644X	Hildegarde Knef **THE VERDICT**	95p
398841	Vera Lynn **VOCAL REFRAIN**	60p
300973	Ralph Martin **THE STORY OF THE DUKE AND DUCHESS OF WINDSOR.** **THE WOMAN HE LOVED.**	95p*
397039	Jessie Matthews **OVER MY SHOULDER**	60p
398396	Pat Phoenix **ALL MY BURNING BRIDGES**	60p
397578	Raymond **RAYMOND**	75p
396806	Brian Rix **MY FARCE FROM MY ELBOW**	75p
397497	John Stonehouse **JOHN STONEHOUSE — MY TRIAL**	95p
398876	Charles Thompson **BING**	70p
398264	Peter Underwood **DANNY LA RUE: LIFE'S A DRAG**	55p
397268	Mike and Bernie Winters **SHAKE A PAGODA TREE**	60p
398302	Mike Yarwood **AND THIS IS ME!**	50p
300000	**ERIC AND ERNIE:** **THE AUTOBIOGRAPHY OF** **MORECAMBE & WISE**	50p

*Not for sale in Canada.

COSMOLOGY

0352   Star

	Adi-Kent Thomas Jeffrey	
398820	**THEY DARED THE DEVIL'S TRIANGLE**	50p*
	Patrick Moore	
397764	**CAN YOU SPEAK VENUSIAN?**	50p
	Jack Stoneley & A. T. Lawton	
397810	**C.E.T.I. (COMMUNICATION WITH EXTRA TERRESTRIAL INTELLIGENCE)**	60p*
300604	**IS ANYONE OUT THERE?**	55p*
396199	**TUNGASKA: CAULDRON OF HELL**	75p

0426   Tandem

	Patrick Moore & Iain Nicolson	
088387	**BLACK HOLES IN SPACE**	40p
	Arthur Shuttlewood	
169263	**THE WARMINSTER MYSTERY**	50p
	Brad Steiger and Joan Whritenour	
163291	**FLYING SAUCERS ARE HOSTILE**	40p*
134427	**THE NEW U.F.O. BREAKTHROUGH**	35p*
163362	**STRANGERS FROM THE SKIES**	40p
	Paul Thomas	
127226	**FLYING SAUCERS THROUGH THE AGES**	35p*
	B. Le Poer Trench	
134508	**OPERATION EARTH**	35p
	Jacques Vallée	
130715	**ANATOMY OF A PHENOMENON**	35p*
157397	**PASSPORT TO MAGONIA**	45p*

SOCIOLOGY

0352   Star

	Derek Bowskill	
398310	**SWINGERS AND SWAPPERS**	60p
	G. L. Simons	
300302	**THE SIMONS BOOK OF SEXUAL RECORDS**	75p

0426   Tandem

	Lynn Barber	
086511	**HOW TO IMPROVE YOUR MAN IN BED**	60p
	Robert Chartham	
163958	**MAINLY FOR WOMEN**	45p
	Ian Stewart & Brian Downes	
085043	**THE GOOD SEX GUIDE**	45p
	Erna Wright	
141970	**THE NEW CHILDBIRTH**	50p*

0446   Warner

	Dr. I. C. Kassorla	
599859	**PUTTING IT ALL TOGETHER**	70p†

† For sale in Britain and Ireland only.
* Not for sale in Canada.

GENERAL NON-FICTION

0352   Star

396431	Frederick Anderson **ENGLAND BY BICYCLE**	95p
398914	J. Paul Getty **HOW TO BE RICH**	60p*
397829	**HOW TO BE A SUCCESSFUL EXECUTIVE**	60p*
397152	Nick Logan & Bob Woffinden **THE NME BOOK OF ROCK 2**	95p
398566	Harry Lorayne & Jerry Lucas **THE MEMORY BOOK**	60p*
39692X	Henry Miller **THE WORLD OF SEX**	60p
396407	Milligan & Hobbs **MILLIGAN'S BOOK OF RECORDS**	75p
396733	Sally O'Sullivan **THINGS MY MOTHER NEVER TOLD ME**	85p
397640	David Reuben **HOW TO GET MORE OUT OF SEX**	85p*
398779	Fiona Richmond **FIONA**	50p
300213	Ernest Tidyman **DUMMY**	45p*

0426   Tandem

181123	Eppstein (Editor) **THE BOOK OF THE WORLD**	£1.75*
08571X	Hyam Maccoby **REVOLUTION IN JUDAEA**	75p
163877	James Hewitt **ISOMETRICS AND YOU**	40p
168623	Xaviera Hollander **THE HAPPY HOOKER**	60p*
163443	**LETTERS TO THE HAPPY HOOKER**	60p*
168038	**XAVIERA GOES WILD**	75p
166787	**XAVIERA, ON THE BEST PART OF A MAN**	60p*
17996X	Xaviera Hollander & Marilyn Chambers **XAVIERA MEETS MARILYN CHAMBERS**	60p*
124820	Charles Lindbergh **THE SPIRIT OF ST. LOUIS**	95p
124901	Fridtjof Nansen **FARTHEST NORTH**	£1.00
175158	Sakuzawa Nyoiti **MACROBIOTICS**	50p*
181204	L. Sprague De Camp **ANCIENT ENGINEERS (large format)**	£1.95*
134931	**THE WOMANLY ART OF BREAST FEEDING**	60p

*Not for sale in Canada.

GENERAL NON-FICTION

0426   Tandem

	Gerty Agoston	
162580	**MY BED IS NOT FOR SLEEPING**	50p*
162841	**MY CARNAL CONFESSION**	50p*

	Nigel Balchin	
175824	**THE BORGIA TESTAMENT**	60p
175905	**THE SMALL BACK ROOM**	60p
176030	**MINE OWN EXECUTIONER**	60p
176111	**A SORT OF TRAITORS**	60p

	Bill Bavin	
180593	**THE DESTRUCTIVE VICE**	75p

	Aubrey Burgoyne	
152026	**THE AMAZONS**	45p

	Catherine Cookson	
163796	**THE GARMENT**	60p
163524	**HANNAH MASSEY**	60p
163605	**SLINKY JANE**	60p

	Jean Francis	
162803	**COMING AGAIN**	45p*

	Joe Green	
151496	**HOUSE OF PLEASURE**	50p*

	Brian Hayles	
165209	**SPRING AT BROOKFIELD**	50p

	Harrison James	
172167	**ABDUCTION**	50p*
135148	**COMING MY WAY?**	45p
150937	**HAVE IT YOUR WAY**	45p

	Olle Lansberg	
045386	**DEAR JOHN**	40p

	Julie Lawrence	
151577	**BLONDES DON'T HAVE ALL THE FUN!**	50p

	Keith Miles	
16539X	**AMBRIDGE SUMMER**	50p

	Jack Millmay	
171446	**REVELATIONS OF AN ART MASTER**	50p

	Ingeborg Pertwee	
16248X	**TOGETHER**	50p

	Betty Smith	
178815	**JOY IN THE MORNING**	70p*
179455	**MAGGIE: NOW**	75p*
178734	**TOMORROW WILL BE BETTER**	70p*

	Joannie Winters	
151224	**HOUSE OF DESIRE**	50p*

0446   Warner/Wyndham

	Alex Cord	
597724	**SANDSONG**	60p†

	Annabel Erwin	
799416	**LILIANE**	95p

*Not for sale in Canada.

GENERAL FICTION

0352   Star

396423	Mary Ann Ashe **RING OF ROSES**	60p
396938	Andre P. Brink **LOOKING ON DARKNESS**	95p
398663	Jackie Collins **THE WORLD IS FULL OF DIVORCED WOMEN**	50p
398752	**THE WORLD IS FULL OF MARRIED MEN**	50p
300671	Eric Corder **HELLBOTTOM**	75p
300086	**THE LONG TATTOO**	40p
398515	**RUNNING DOGS**	60p*
396857	Terry Fisher **IF YOU'VE GOT THE MONEY**	70p
39840X	Knight Isaacson **THE STORE**	60p
398981	Jeffrey Konvitz **THE SENTINEL**	70p*
396334	Gavin Lambert **THE SLIDE AREA**	75p
398299	Robin Maugham **THE SIGN**	55p*
397594	Clayton Moore **END OF RECKONING**	60p*
397608	**141 TERRACE DRIVE**	60p*
397543	**RIVER FALLS**	60p*
397667	**SECRET FIRE**	60p*
397659	**THE CORRUPTERS**	60p*
397551	**WESLEY SHERIDAN**	60p*
300809	Molly Parkin **LOVE ALL**	50p
397179	**UP TIGHT**	60p
396946	Judith Rossner **TO THE PRECIPICE**	85p*
397144	Alan Sillitoe **THE FLAME OF LIFE**	70p
398892	**THE GENERAL**	50p
300965	**THE LONELINESS OF THE LONG DISTANCE RUNNER**	50p
300949	**MEN, WOMEN AND CHILDREN**	50p
398809	**THE RAGMAN'S DAUGHTER**	50p
300981	**SATURDAY NIGHT AND SUNDAY MORNING**	50p
396415	Hubert Selby Jr. **THE ROOM**	75p
398884	Ernest Tidyman **STARSTRUCK**	60p*

*Not for sale in Canada.

Wyndham Books are obtainable from many booksellers and newsagents. If you have any difficulty please send purchase price plus postage on the scale below to:

**Wyndham Cash Sales,
44 Hill Street
London W1X 8LB**

OR

**Star Book Service,
G.P.O. Box 29,
Douglas,
Isle of Man,
British Isles**

While every effort is made to keep prices low, it is sometimes necessary to increase prices at short notice. Wyndham Books reserve the right to show new retail prices on covers which may differ from those advertised in the text or elsewhere.

**Postage and Packing Rate
U.K. & Eire**
One book 15p plus 7p per copy for each additional book ordered to a maximum charge of 57p.

These charges are subject to Post Office charge fluctuations.